Montana's Benton Road

By
Leland J. Hanchett, Jr.

Pine Rim Publishing

Wolf Creek, Montana

Cover

   We are privileged to have a copy of Peter Toftt's 1866 watercolor on paper painting of Prickly Pear Canyon, King and Gillette Toll Road-No. 2, on the cover of this book. The original is held by the Montana Historical Society Museum. Toftt, a disabled veteran of the earlier Indian Wars of Montana Territory, apparently sold copies of this painting as well as his work on Gillette Point (see front of Chapter Eight) to both King and Gillette as well as Mr. Comstock. Shortly thereafter he traveled to England to further his studies of art. In due course he became a well known landscape painter in California.

Typeset in Cheltenham by Barbara Rodriguez

Photo color correction by Kraig Bancroft of Craig, MT

Printed and Bound by Walsworth Publishing Company

ISBN No. 978-0-9637785-9-8

Library of Congress Catalog Card No. 20077939043

PRINTED AND BOUND IN THE UNITED STATES OF AMERICA

This book is dedicated to Marine Corporal Phillip E. Baucus, a young man to whom we all owe so much. He gave his life to protect our freedom and by his heroic deeds earned the respect and admiration of his community, his state and his nation.

Contents

Introduction v

I. The Mullan Military Road 3

II. Travelers on the Mullan Road 15

III. Building the Toll Roads and Bridges 33

IV. Supplying the Mines 53

V. The Indian Menace 77

VI. Operating the Stage Lines 95

VII. Traveling by Stage Coach 117

VIII. Perils on the Road 151

IX. Impressions Along the Road 165

X. Mr. Hill's Railroad 181

Chronology 197

Art and Photo Credits 199

Acknowledgments 203

Bibliography 205

Index 209

About the Author and Researchers 217

Introduction

It's a day in late September and Montana "shines." The deep blue sky kisses the snow covered mountain tops. Busy creeks rush past the brightest of autumn hues. A well rutted dirt road winds in and out of hills and gullies, going nowhere in particular, or so it seems. On this day we are thankful that the Lord has given us a chance to live in this beautiful place called Montana.

A second look at the wandering trail catches our attention as we see the remains of an old clapboard barn not far from the base of the butte known as Bird Tail. The question begs an answer. Who would build a barn out in the middle of nowhere? What useful purpose could it possibly serve? On asking descendents of those who settled this place nearly 150 years ago we learn that we are on the Benton Road, and back then it was the only way to get wherever you were going.

The research starts, but at first the story comes slowly. Soon the facts are moving with lightning speed, faster than anyone could assemble or record them. One particular quote emerges from the stacks of data for it sums up the story of this road in just a few sentences.

Mr. Fisk Ellis in the 1950s stated that: "No older, no more picturesque trail exists than the old Helena-Fort Benton stage road. Laid out in 1860 by Lt. Mullan, connecting Fort Benton, head of navigation on the Missouri river, with the Dalles or Walla Walla, the head of navigation on the Columbia, it is now ninety years old, alive with human interest, romance and pictures of by-gone days. Over it, supplies landed from steamboats at Fort Benton were hauled by wagons, pulled by oxen or mules to Helena, Bozeman, Deer Lodge, and other cities. From the whistle of the first steamboat at Fort Benton till the last big outfit toiled back and forth over many streams, over miles of hot dust or floundered through flooded streams, across stretches of bottomless mud, in Territorial days the history of this road was practically the history of north and central Montana."

The road carried stage coaches as well with drivers and passengers who were willing to risk it all to get wherever they were going. The road might have been choked with dust or flooded from rain, or even worse, buried in snow. It didn't matter, if you were without horse or carriage, a stagecoach was the only way to get to your destination.

Of course, it was folks from Helena who gave the road its name. If you lived in Fort Benton you would refer to the road as the Fort Benton to Helena road. In the beginning Fort Benton was the most important spot on the map. By the time citizens of the territory were thinking about railroads, Helena had gained the prominence by becoming the capital and the hub of mining activities.

Years later, well known television anchor, Chet Huntley, described his trip by rail along the most scenic part of the road in his book *The Generous Years*:

> At last the train moved out of the station [at Great Falls], swung around the falls of the river and raced across the plateau. To the east I caught glimpses of a mountain range, and to the southwest there was another, their peaks snow-splotched and shining in the morning sun. Then we descended into a gorge, twisting past outcroppings of rock, the flanges of the wheels screaming against the rails. A stream appeared

on the right, and through the fresh spring foliage I could see it dancing over its stony bed, collecting itself in dappled pools, resting a moment, then furiously boiling over its obstacle and resuming its chase.

Halfway through the canyon the train made its stop at Wolf Creek. On either side the mountain walls rose upward and disappeared in a wilderness of fir and spruce. The rush of the stream could be heard up and down the gorge. The aspen, mountain ash, chokecherries and willows sported their new June growth, and the air was carbonated with vitality.

Wolf Creek shall forever be special in my memory. It was my personal "Gates to the Mountains."

We probably will never know how many men, women or children traversed the Benton Road, but we can take a brief look at the impressions left by a few of those who traveled down that dusty path or resided in its beautiful setting. Only their own words could adequately convey their feelings about this very special corner of the world.

The Medicine Rock

Approximate Route of Mullan Road North from Medicine Rock Mountain

Chapter I

The Mullan Military Road

Ostensibly searching for a rail route across the Continental Divide in 1853–54, Lieutenant John Mullan was additionally looking for a possible wagon route to join the Missouri River, in what would become Montana, to the Columbia River, in Washington. After much lobbying, and several assignments away from his pet project, Mullan finally got the green light in the form of sufficient congressional funding, in May of 1859, to start his now famous military road. Actual construction, beginning at Fort Walla Walla commenced on June 25, 1859.

For at least 100 miles the band of road builders ripped their way through a dense forest. They built bridges and graded banks in hundreds of places. By December 4, they had established winter quarters at the St. Regis River. From there Mullan sent out his topographer, P. M. Engel to explore the balance of the route to Fort Benton.

On January 8, 1860, Engel, made his report to Mullan from Fort Owen describing his findings during an exploration of the final portion of the proposed wagon road. The reconnaissance, stretching from St. Regis Borgia River to Fort Benton, was conducted during the late fall and early winter of 1859. It was an incredible journey fighting the harsh winter weather. The route over Medicine Rock Mountain, north of the Sieben Ranch was covered with two feet of snow. Engel never let Mullan forget the difficulty of this assignment and the determination needed to complete it.

This same Medicine Rock was described in the February 8, 1882, issue of the *Helena Independent* newspaper.

Medicine Rock Pass is where the old Mullan road crosses the ridge a couple of miles beyond Fergus's ranch on the Little Prickly Pear, at the head of the canyon. The Medicine Rock being a ledge of white quartz, which projects some 10 or 12 feet above the ground and on which the Indians, up to 1865, deposited arrows, beads, paint, tobacco, etc., as they passed that place.

The ledge is about two miles north of the Sieben ranch near the crest of Medicine Rock Mountain. Today the ledge is only about four or five feet in height, appearing like a dorsal fin for some sea going monster.

Excerpts from Engel's Report, as contained in the book *Report on the Construction of a Military Road from Fort Walla Walla to Fort Benton*, follow. The National Archives owns the original handwritten letter from Engel.

At the foot of the divide [below what became Mullan Pass], a quarter mile from the top, I struck the waters of Big Prickly Pear Creek. ...

Today, this is Austin Creek up to the confluence with Greenhorn Creek which emerges from the Greenhorn Mountains to the northwest of Mullan's Pass. Engle then followed what he called Stormy, now Greenhorn Creek, until he reached the location of today's town of Austin.

Starting at the Austin location Engel noted:

The wagon road leaves the Indian trail, which leads along the Big Prickly Pear and takes to the north, over a small side hill covered with large pedrigal rock and in a half mile crosses a dry water run. In one-eighth mile further a second one is crossed; then a half mile, over a gently-sloping hill covered with pedrigal rock, a third water run is crossed. Ascending now a gentle hill covered with a few red cedars, I gained, in a half mile from the last dry water run, the narrow valley of Fir Creek [now Park Creek], a tributary to the Big Prickly Pear Creek. A few steep places in the descent will offer no difficulty for wagons. The ascent on the other side of Fir Creek is very steep; but a ravine running to the right of the trail will facilitate the location of the wagon road. One-eighth mile is the distance from the creek to the top of the hill, which slopes very gently. We then travel for a quarter mile towards a dry pond, which extends to the next hill, of easy ascent and descent, the latter terminated by a dry water run; distance from the dry pond to the dry water run is three-quarters of a mile.

The next prairie hill is tolerably high, and the grade so steep that doubling teams will be necessary for heavily laden wagons. ... Ascending a hill a quarter mile long, from the top of which we enjoyed a fine view of the Upper Missouri Valley, the gate of mountains [Lewis and Clark discovery], and a small portion of the Rocky Mountains, Heart Mountain can be distinctly seen, and also the direction of the wagon road for 10 or 11 miles, to a point where it crosses Soft Bed Creek [now Willow Creek]. After crossing a dry waterway, we passed over some rolling ground and descended to Silver Creek, one of the tributaries of the Big Prickly Pear creek, thence to camp. ... Our animals getting weak; the want of sufficient nourishment commences to tell on them.

November 29. Started 9:05 a. m. Our horses had wandered far off during night in search of grass. Mild, cloudy morning. For five miles and three-quarters we passed over undulating, firm prairie ground, to a small creek with miry shores, bordered by small willows, whence its name, "Willow Creek" [?] then two and a quarter miles over a very gently downward-sloping prairie, part of which is covered with brushwood, to Soft Bed Creek [today's Willow Creek], a branch of Small Prickly [Pear] Creek, ...

At this point the account gets very confusing. Somehow both Engel and Mullan inserted another creek between Silver Creek and today's Willow Creek. Possibly, their original Silver Creek was really Three Mile Creek. Silver Creek before it merges with Three Mile Creek was then called Willow Creek.

Engel then traveled East and eventually North on today's Willow Creek ultimately intercepting Clark Creek, which flows northward to the Sieben Ranch and the opening to the Little Prickly Pear Canyon.

At this place the valley widens considerably, and a good camping place can be found for a large train. I suppose, though, that the valley must be wet, as the trail keeps on the westerly side hills, and re-crosses the creek[today's Willow Creek] only three-fourths of a mile below, where the valley bends to the north. In 50 yards the trail re-crossed and continued the west side of the creek [today's Clark Creek] all the way to the Little Prickly Pear Creek. In two and a half miles more it passes along an easy slope, which is occasionally cut up by small ravines, but offering no difficulty to the location of the wagon road. Little Prickly Pear Creek, which runs, at the place where I struck it [Sieben], is twelve feet wide and one and a half feet deep, the banks of which, in this plain, are lined with willows, but higher up and lower down larger trees will be found.

The creek, coming from the Rocky Mountain chain, cuts through a narrow canyon [Upper Little Prickly Pear Canyon] to gain the broad bottom [now Sieben], and in three miles forces its way through a Rocky Mountain range, forming a narrow gorge [Lower Little Prickly Pear Canyon, now Wolf Creek Canyon]. After crossing the creek, we proceeded in a northerly direction towards Medicine Rock. The day had become very warm, and we had hoped to have been able to reach "Mullan's Creek" [now Lyons Creek] before dark; but after riding for one mile a sudden northeasterly gale forced us to seek shelter in the willows of the creek just crossed. In less than one-half minute our horses were covered with white frost, and the air was filled with an icy, foggy substance which, after some time, gave way to a heavy snowfall. Re-crossing the Little Prickly Pear we found a tolerably good camp in the willows, having made fourteen miles headway [this camp was at Sieben Ranch].

November 30. Remained in camp. The gale has not abated in the least, and the snow still falls heavily.

December 1. The night was cold and stormy. At 9 a. m. the sun broke through the clouds, and I started at 11 a. m. It was very cold, and the snow five inches deep. The road leading to Medicine Rock strikes, in three-fourths of a mile, a little creek, and following it up for one-half mile strikes the foot of the hill range, where the trail takes a very steep ascent, which the wagon road can make more gradually by keeping to a ravine running to the left of the trail, when reaching the top of the first hill a good road with easy grade leads towards Medicine Rock, and in two miles from there descends to a small creek, called Medicine Rock Creek, the descent to which will require some side-hill work in places where the slope is too steep. In three miles we reached Mullan's Creek [now Lyons Creek], where work will be required in different places, as the trail keeps along the side hills. Two hollows, the first one pretty deep, will have to be passed, and a few trees to be cut to bring wagons through with four or five yoke of oxen. The ascent on the east side of the creek [North Lyons Creek road] is steep but short, and then the character of the ground for two miles further remains the same as described. At the end of that distance the road leads towards Prickly Pear Valley, [now Wolf Creek] thence over a bare hill the descent of which in itself will offer no difficulty except at one point, which, for the present, is made passable by a couple of logs stretched from side to side of a low, rocky precipice, to give, in that narrow passage, the required breadth to the road. Reaching the valley, I crossed a creek coming from the west, [probably Little Creek] one-half mile distant from the bending point of the trail on the top of the hill; then one-half mile through the bottom of the valley, keeping close to the hill-side, through which, in connection with the vegetation of the valley, makes me believe that it is of a miry character. Taking again to the side hills, I reached, in two miles, the head of what is called Prickly Pear Canyon [at the present town of Wolf Creek], and went to camp. The last portion of the road will also require some side-hill work, which, in places, may prove more difficult as the ground is rocky. We made today 15 miles.

December 2. The wind blew a perfect gale during the night. The morning is very cold and our animals appear much reduced. The snow in the valley is four inches deep and covered with a hard crust, which makes pawing the grass for the animals difficult. At the head of the canyon, through which the road passes, a small creek [Wolf Creek] coming from the north empties into Prickly Pear Creek, and I was told that by following up this creek a good road can be obtained, avoiding, thereby, all the crossings, which are inevitable by following the Little Prickly Pear. In taking this direction a little detour might be made but it is said that no obstacle of any moment would be in the way.

Started at 9:25 a. m. At the entrance of the canyon [State Route 434], where the first crossing will have to be made, after having crossed the creek alluded to at its mouth, we found that the usually traveled road had been made impracticable by beavers. Finding a good place to cross, we followed the canyon for eight and a half miles, making seven crossings of the creek, all which were greatly obstructed by ice. The intermediate ground is partly covered with pine timber and partly with brushwood of different heights. After the seventh crossing the canyon becomes wider and forms a valley, affording ample space for camping places, with good grass on the low side hills for the animals. For one-half mile from the seventh crossing I reached the eighth, which is situated at the foot of the northerly bluff. All the crossings are shallow, with firm gravelly bottoms, and the banks offer no difficulty. After ascending the low bluff, which will be easily rendered practicable for wagons, the road leads over prairie ridges, with easy slopes, to a small creek [Rock Creek] two and a half miles distant, which empties into the Missouri a few hundred yards below the Little Prickly Pear Creek. From the crossing point the road follows the creek for three miles, for which distance no work will be necessary, except at one point where the side-hills close in narrowly. At the end of this distance a low but steep ridge is ascended, before reaching, which the wagon road must cross the creek and follow it for three-eighths of a mile, then re-cross and surmount the ridge, which is of easy grade and offering no difficulty by its slope. The descent, which terminates at a dry creek, one and three-fourths mile distant, is in some places steep but not sideling. The next ridge, measuring from base to base three-fourths of a mile, is not so high as the previous one, nor is it as steep. After crossing a dry branch I reached in two and three-fourths miles, traveling over undulating ground, which would require no work, another dry water run. At this point the above mentioned road, which leaves the one here described at the head of the canyon, would again unite with the present wagon road. In three miles further I struck the Dearborn River Valley, the ground being undulating prairie, and in one-half mile a small creek will be crossed; no characteristic can be mentioned regarding it. A high and well-timbered ridge to the eastward indicates the Missouri River Valley, and a curiously formed hill range, lying to the north of the Dearborn, are good landmarks for the traveler who cannot form his course by the uniformly undulating plateau. The road will have to keep up the Dearborn River for half a mile, in order to reach the best crossing. Its valley is richly timbered, but cut up by a great many sloughs and ditches, which run in every direction, The river is a shallow stream of from 50 to 60 feet in width, with a gravelly bottom and swift current. The wind has been blowing hard and cold all day from the southwest. Made 17 miles. Snow five inches deep.

December 3. It has been a windy night. Our tent was blown down, and we were fearful that some of the shallow-rooted trees, would be blown upon us. This morning it is quite mild. Started at 7:45 a.m. to make Sun River in good time. The ground is gently undulating from the north bank of the valley to the crossing of Beaver Creek [probably Flat Creek], which is five miles distant. The road first follows a dry creek, crossing and re-crossing it several times, and then leads over a wave-formed plain, which now and then is cut up by long, dry hollows. After crossing Beaver Creek the trail commences the ascent of the divide between the Dearborn and Sun Rivers [Bird Tail Divide], and, if I understood aright, the present wagon road keeps to the left, making a detour of four and a half miles, avoiding thereby the steepest portion of this rocky divide. Just as we commenced the ascent an icy northwest gale sprang up, driving before it a storm of small crystals, which made it almost impossible to keep the eyes open; and the wind continually increasing in force, we became doubtful whether our animals would be able to carry us

to Sun river, and were obliged, after having made two and a half miles more, and nearly gained the summit of the divide, to turn back and seek refuge in a small ravine, where we found just wood enough to build a fire, and stow away our baggage. Made seven and a half miles. The storm continued with fearful severity; it was extremely cold, and the snow fell heavily. We had an idea that we might be caught here by a long, lasting snow-storm, which was anything but pleasant, as wood was scarce, provisions nearly exhausted, our animals in a distressed state.

December 4. The weather had not moderated in the least, and I judged that the thermometer must have been at about forty degrees below zero. It still snowed but not so heavily as yesterday. We were undecided whether to push on to Sun River or go back to the Dearborn. To retrace our steps seemed the most sensible in our present condition, as we would have the wind in our backs, in a short ride could reach shelter and food in a large Pend d'Oreille camp, which we left at the Dearborn River; but then the snow might fall to such a depth that we would be cut off from Fort Benton. At 10 a.m. we decided try to reach Sun River Farm, and at 11 a.m. started for that point. It was terrible weather, and we could distinguish nothing at a distance of 100 yards. After a ride of three and a half hours we reached Sun River Farm, which was twenty-three and seven-tenths miles distant from our last night's camp. We were all more or less frost-bitten, and had suffered extremely. Colonel Vaughan, Indian Agent for the Blackfoot Nation, received us very kindly, and with his well-known hospitality, offered us accommodations at the agency for any length of time that we might wish. The weather continuing very cold, and our animals requiring some rest after our last march, we remained at the farm during the fifth and sixth, and left on the seventh, of December. The cold being too severe to take notes on our march, I did so (for this portion of the road) on my return; but will give the description of it here, in order to keep the same traveling direction in mentioning the different objects of the road. From the crossing of Beaver Creek to the top of the divide, which forms a narrow rocky gap, the distance is three and one-fourth miles. It is not one gradual slope, but the ascent is formed by a succession of hills of different grades and heights, which will occasion some work in a few places if the road should be located in that direction. Hitherto it has been thought a matter of impossibility to follow with vehicles of any description the Indian trail; but in coming back from Fort Benton I brought over it a two-wheel cart, and found but little difficulty. The descent on the other side is gradual, and is practicable for wagons in its present state. Bird Tail Rock Creek, a little stream, which bends near the divide, is followed down by the trail for one and one-fourth mile, and then, at a point where it turns short to the west, the trail takes for two and a half miles over prairie hills, until it strikes the creek again, and also the present wagon road, which gains the creek about one and a half mile below the above mentioned turning point, and follows its valley downwards, crossing and re-crossing the creek, which is made necessary by the closing in of the small side-hills. In three miles the trail comes opposite to Bird Tail Rock, a prominent peak of a mountain chain running between the trail and the Missouri River. Following the valley of the creek for three miles, I reached a low, rocky bluff, through which the creek has forced its way. Here a little side-hill work will be necessary, as also at some places above. In three and one-fourth miles, over an almost level plain, the road crosses Crown Butte Creek, about two miles below the mouth of Bird Tail Rock Creek, and gains in one and three-fourths mile a small rock ridge, which is easy in its ascent; the descent is sideling, and encumbered by big boulders, which will have to be removed. The Big Knee, Crown, and Square Buttes [the latter made famous by the Charley Russel painting of that name], which have been in sight for some miles back, are now fully exposed to view. A kind of prairie saddle ridge, which connects the Big Knee and Crown Buttes with a gentle slope, will have to be ascended. The road passing midway between these two prominent points, begins the descent, which is very gradual. The direction, which I followed brought me opposite to the agency, but I think the wagon road must keep closer to the Big Knee, and strike Sun River about three miles below the farm, in order to gain a point where the crossing towards Teton River can be accomplished without distressing the teams. Sun River, which I crossed at a point where it forms an island, was frozen over. A luxuriant growth of cottonwood lines both sides of the

stream at this place, and extends up it for some distance. Distance between the last-mentioned little ridge and Sun River Farm is eight miles. By information I learned at Sun River, that the distance to Fort Benton by the shortest route was estimated at 55 miles. At 19 miles from the farm, the road reaches a shallow lake [Benton Lake], and seven miles further is a small spring [Twenty-eight mile spring], both of which are destitute of timber. In summer the lake often dries entirely up, and at all events becomes unfit for drinking or cooking purposes, besides that in both places it is strongly mixed with alkali. On the strength of those statements, I resolved to try to find a wagon road leading to camping places where wood and good water could be found, and concluded to strike the Missouri River somewhere below the Great Falls. The interpreter of Mr. Dawson being at the time at the farm, I accepted his offer to guide us to the fort.

December 7. Started at 10.15 a.m. Mild weather. Followed down the Sun River Valley for about 12 miles and then struck across an insignificant prairie ridge towards the Missouri River. Before I left the valley, which we did at point about three miles above the mouth of Sun River, I crossed a deep ravine with running water 10 miles from the farm. After 18 miles we arrived at the edge of the prairie plateau, and had to accomplish the descent towards the Missouri River by following the winding of a coulee ridge, gaining the coulee bottom itself, which quickly enlarges to a narrow valley with a few cottonwoods. We reached in one mile the river itself. We intended to follow down the Missouri for 1 1/4 mile farther and camp on a small prairie opposite the mouth of Highwood Creek, but the river ice had blocked up the trail, and we were forced to remain where we were, having made 31 miles. The Missouri River is so poorly timbered between the mouth of Sun River and Fort Benton, that if a road could even be found in that direction, the greatest inconvenience for want of wood would ensue for small or large parties. During the night a furious gale forced us to secure our blankets and baggage with logs and rocks, and even those precautions proved to be insufficient.

December 8. Started 9 a.m. Our guide advised us to head to the coulees, and therefore started back to gain a ridge about five miles to the northwest. The day was clear and

Captain John Mullan

warm. After a ride of 28 miles, during which we crossed the Grand Eight-Mile coulee, [Eight-Mile Spring] and descending near Discovery Butte into the Missouri River Valley, we arrived at Fort Benton, and were most kindly received. There was scarcely any snow here, but the river was frozen solid, which was a fortunate circumstance, as we could drive across our animals, that would have starved on this side. The necessity to give rest to my animals and some delay in my preparations for the return trip, induced me to remain seven days at Fort Benton, during which time I received from M[alcolm] Clark, esq., of Fort Campbell, a howitzer belonging to the government, which I intended to bring over the mountain, and, with an odometer on the wheel, measure the road.

It is fascinating to note how often Engel refers to the existing wagon road and Indian trail. The Indian trail is not surprising, but who made a wagon road through this region prior to 1859?

Engel and his party didn't get back to Fort Owen until January 6, 1860. It was near the end of June before Mullan's full force was engaged once again in road building

On February 14, 1663, Captain John Mullan sent his final report on the construction of the military road to Major J. C. Woodruff, Chief of Topographical Engineers. We pick up his narrative, from the same book containing Engel's report, as he proceeded down the eastern face of the Continental Divide. At that point he was moving west to east with a destination of Fort Benton and a rendezvous with Major Blake. Blake was leading 300 recruits from St. Louis to Fort Walla Walla, Washington. They would follow Mullan's road as a consequence of Mullan's suggestion to the War Department.

The first stream touched upon the eastern slope is the Big Prickly Pear Creek. It rises at the foot of the pass, and, draining a region twenty miles in width, empties into the Missouri. Its valley for two miles partakes of a canyon-like character, where, however, with moderate work, we secured a good location; at the end of this the valley widens, until, near its junction with the Missouri, it has become a prairie ten by fifteen miles in extent [this is now the Helena Valley]. Many fine, though small tracts of tillable land are found within it, and, at present, game abounds. Once in the valley of the Big Prickly Pear we had made our extreme point of southing, and were enabled to turn all the eastern spurs and take a direct line for Fort Benton.

Our location involved three crossings of the Big Prickly Pear, making which, on the morning of the 18th of July, we left its valley and moved northeasterly over rolling hills until we reached and encamped upon Fir Creek [Park Creek], distance four miles. In this stretch only light work was required.

The plateau of the Fir Creek is about forty feet above its bed, to descend into which required a side cut of sixty feet, and a bridge of thirty feet; making these, on the morning of the 19th of July, we again moved over a rolling prairie region, and in five miles reached and encamped upon the Silver Creek [Three Mile Creek?]. We had now left the more difficult sections of the mountains, and skirted along their eastern bases over the long lateral spurs making out from the main range; these spurs were untimbered, and here became reduced to easy rolling hills; only light work was needed in this last section, so that, on the 20th of July, we again moved forward, and in five miles reached the Soft Bed Creek, [Willow Creek] crossing in the interval the Willow Creek [Silver Creek] before it joins with Three

Mile Creek]; this last unites with the Silver Creek, which, with the Fir Creek, become tributaries of the Big Prickly Pear. None of these streams interpose obstacles to travel, except during the higher freshets, and then only for a few days. The Soft Bed creek is a stream of inconsiderable extent, and flowing into the Little Prickly Pear. This last rising in the prairie hills, rises in the main chain of the Rocky Mountains, and flows through a canyon [Upper Little Prickly Pear Canyon], with intervals of bottoms, until within three miles of the Missouri, when the hills that bound it recede, giving its valley a width of three miles. It drains a considerable extent of country, and in this vicinity is one of the larger tributaries of the Missouri.

Along the Soft Bed Creek but slight work was required to secure a good road; so that, on the morning of the 31st of July, following up this creek to the hills in which it rises, we crossed these hills with moderate work, and at once fell upon another tributary of the Small Prickly Pear, which we called Hard Bed Creek [Clark Creek], which only flows for a portion of the year; its valley is from a fourth to a half mile in width, bounded. by low timbered spurs, and is about eight miles long. We now entered upon the red sandstone and slate formation, the country generally giving every indication of the presence of gold; we followed this stream to its junction with the Small Prickly Pear, which last we crossed, and now entered upon the last point of material difficulty before reaching Fort Benton. The junction of the Hard Bed Creek with the Little Prickly Pear affords one of those prairie intervals before referred to, which, at this point, is one by three miles in extent [Sieben Ranch]; at the eastern limit of this prairie the Little Prickly Pear again enters a deep rocky canyon [Lower Little Prickly Pear Canyon], a perfect defile, leaving no berme on its either side. This difficulty drove us over a broken section, which we termed Medicine Rock Mountain, and where we worked the road for four days. Its peculiar features of difficulty, and the short time allowed us in which to reach Fort Benton, where Major Blake awaited us with much impatience, all determined me to secure the cheapest and most rapid location; and, for this reason, after descending once more into the valley of this stream I made eighteen crossings, and again reached

its more open valley within three miles of the Missouri River. This last was the nearest point of our road to the Missouri, until we reached it at Fort Benton.

On the Medicine Rock Mountains we found traces of quartz, and continual indications of gold; one of my men found ten cent prospects in the Big Prickly Pear at the point where it enters the rocky defile referred to, and the Indians gave me to understand that two miles higher up the stream, in another canyon, gold had been found by them. The Medicine Rock section was by far the most difficult of any point along the entire line, from Hell's Gate to Fort Benton, and to it attention will again be given.

Completing this work by the 22d of July, we again moved forward over prairie hills for nineteen miles, when we reached the Dearborn River. We now left both the mountains and their spurs behind us, and emerged upon the broad, swelling prairies of the upper Missouri.

Mullan not only hurried along without making much of a road building effort from Wolf Creek to Dearborn Crossing, but also forgot to tell us what route he took.

The Dearborn River rises in the main chain of the Rocky Mountains, and for six or eight miles winds through a deep sandstone gorge, when its hills gradually recede, giving place to prairie bottoms covered with cottonwood. Its stream is two hundred feet broad, and fordable, except during the freshet, at which period it is subject to rises that flood its banks and sweep everything before it. The party under Mr. Kolecki, sent to explore the valley of the Big Blackfoot, rejoined us here.

While encamped upon the banks of the Dearborn we were overtaken by Mr. W. W. Johnson, direct from Washington, with dispatches, setting forth a continuation of our appropriation, and orders countermanding instructions that had been issued relative to my command, and the action taken by Major Blake in regard to the same.

From the Dearborn, on the morning of the 27th of July, we traveled over an easy prairie, region to a camp at the Bird Tail Rock, passing along the Beaver Creek [Flat Creek] for three miles, and finding during this length an excellent location, requiring but little work. From thence, on the 28th, we proceeded to Sun River, crossing the same at a ford where is situated the Indian agency of the Blackfeet, then in charge of Colonel A. J. Vaughn.

At this point our work proper ceased, for the remaining distance of fifty-five miles to Fort Benton was over an easy and almost level prairie road, with no running streams. The prairie is thirteen hundred feet above the Missouri at the Fort, and broken at its southern edge by deep coulees and ravines making into the river, and on its northern edge by similar formations making into the Teton River. A knowledge of the topographical face of this country would therefore show that a feasible line would lie over the high table land and between the beads of the coulees, on its either side, provided water was supplied. This is afforded by a lake [Benton Lake] sixteen miles to the eastward of the Sun River, and by springs seven miles to the east of the lake [Twenty-eight Mile Springs]. These points subdivided the distance of fifty-five miles from the Sun River to Fort Benton into convenient day's marches. It will be readily seen that the character of the region immediately bordering the Missouri and Teton Rivers precludes the possibility of carrying a road by either of these sections.

On the morning of the 29th of July, leaving a portion of my escort in camp on the Sun River to await my return, I divided the remainder of my party into four portions, each to proceed to Fort Benton by different routes; one to camp at the lake, one at the spring, the third to proceed to the Teton direct, and the last to move up the Sun River to the Old Blackfoot mission, striking thence across to the Teton, and down it to Fort Benton. This was done for the purpose of examining the country, as well as to bring in a report of each route, which would enable me to judge which was the proper location for a permanent line. When the different reports were presented, I found that the one via the lake, the spring, and thence to the Fort, possessed advantages over all the rest, and was consequently the one chosen for the permanent road.

The Sun River rises in the main chain of the Rocky Mountains, in latitude 48 degrees, and empties into the Missouri about nine miles above the falls. Its border is fringed with cottonwood, and its valley is from one to three miles broad, possessing many tracts of arable land. The Blackfoot agency has large fields under cultivation, where wheat, oats, and every character of vegetable is raised. There are many beautiful agricultural tracts to the south of the Bird Tail Rock, along the many little creeks that rise in the broken section lying between it and. the Missouri. Fuel is abundant, though timber for building purposes is scarce. Our different parties that left the Sun River on the 29th of July all reached Fort Benton by the 1st of August. Here we found Major Blake encamped, with three hundred recruits, awaiting our arrival. We remained here until the 5th of August. A Mackinaw boat was built for a party to descend the Missouri to St. Louis, composed of discharged civilians and such soldiers as were near the expiration of their term of service, all under charge of Lieutenant J. L. White. This party made the trip without accident, and for a portion of the distance in company with one of the boats of Captain Raynolds, of the topographical engineers, who for three years had been exploring the country from Fort Laramie to the head waters of the Yellowstone and Missouri, and who had reached Fort Benton only two weeks in advance of our own party. The arrival of Captain Raynolds was of advantage to ourselves, as he was enabled to add to our transportation a large number of pack animals.

Every available means of transportation being turned over to Major Blake for the use of his command, and having completed all the arrangements that our mission called for, we left Fort Benton on the morning of the 5th of August, on our return to Fort Walla-Walla.

At Fort Benton, Mr. Sohon [the artist] was transferred to Major Blake as a guide and interpreter to his command; Mr. Creighton, one of our wagon-masters, was also transferred, and to their joint good services Major Blake was largely indebted for the success of his march. Such other of my men as could be spared were also turned over to him, so that, so far as our means could supply him, he had nothing of which to complain.

My plan in returning was to pass rapidly over the line, keeping always in advance of the major, and making such repairs as the condition of the road called for and as time allowed. Having turned over to Major Blake's command every wagon taken by us to Fort

Benton, and using pack animals ourselves, we were enabled to make excellent time till reaching the Hell's Gate Valley, where, having left a few wagons, we were enabled to put our pack animals into harness and used wagon transportation for the remainder of the distance. Our work in returning was limited to repairing the road, excepting at points more especially referred to hereafter. We made no radical change in the location, except in passing from Belknap's camp to the Deer Lodge Valley.

Mullan was finished with the road at this point, or at least he felt that with minor improvements it would be adequate for Blake's purpose of moving 300 soldiers to Walla Walla, Washington.

Nearly two years later Mullan finally declared that the road was really completed. By then emigrants were beginning to make use of the road to travel to the mines of Montana and Idaho or to establish new homes on the Pacific Coast.

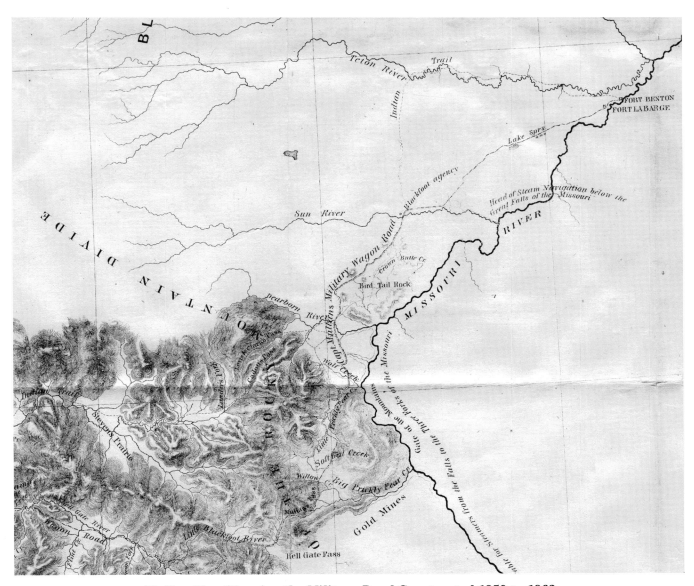

Mullan Map Showing the Military Road Constructed 1859 to 1862

Benton Lake on Mullan Road

Mullan Road Cut on Lyons Hill

Lyons Hill near J. P. Lyons Gravesite

Tough Grade North from Medicine Rock Mountain

Chapter II

Travelers on the Mullan Road

Three separate accounts of travel on the newly completed Mullan Road give a first hand look at the quality of the construction and other frustrations experienced on the road in the first two years of its use.

First Lieutenant, August V. Kautz accompanied Major George A. H. Blake of the First Dragoons and about 300 recruits from St. Louis to Fort Benton and across the almost completed Mullan Road. Kautz kept a daily log of his experiences along the route, which was published in the *Pacific Northwest Quarterly* for June, 1946. During the months of May and June, 1860 they were traveling up the Missouri River on the steamers Spread Eagle, Chippewa, and Key West. By July they had arrived at Fort Benton. We pick up his narrative on the second of July.

July 2, 1860. We all remained on board the boat, as we arrived too late to go on shore and camp.

July 3. We were quite busy moving into camp today, and the boats were very busy discharging. We located Camp Chutaux [Chouteau] a few hundred yards above Fort Benton on the plain, and pitched our tents and in a short time we had a very pretty encampment made of Sibby [Sibly] tents, new and clean. We find Lt. Lyon [Hylan B. Lyon, Second Lieutenant, Third Artillery] of Mullan's escort here. He has brought over some beef cattle for us. Mullan cannot furnish more than about twenty five wagons. He has wagons, but no oxen or horses for them, and they were not to be had in the country. Reynolds has not been heard from. Mr. Pierce, who was officer of the day, was very drunk, and absent from camp. The Maj. sent Mr. Livingston and I to look for him, and we found him in a room in

the Fort among some Indians, lying on the floor, drunk, and very sound asleep. We brought him up, and he was confined to his tent in arrest, and relieved from the duties of officer of the day. He will probably not escape the penalty this time.

July 4. This day passed off without any demonstration of patriotism, as everybody was busy with their own affairs, writing letters, and arranging things to send back with the steamer in view of the limited amount of transportation. I wrote a letter to father. I have nothing to send back. My luggage is very small. We all went down to the boat and took a farewell drink on the boat from a few bottles of champagne. Mr. Chutaux has been very kind to us, and has presented us with champagne and other liquors and done us many other favors. He has a remarkable temper for business, never goes to extremes, and always ready to accommodate. Mr. Pierce called me in to ask my advice as to what he had better do. I advised him to tender his resignation and return on the steam boats, a proposition that he does not seem to relish, and he hoped to be relieved from arrest under another promise to abstain. He will probably go over with us in the hope that something may turn up to help him out of it. I told him candidly that I did not think that he could remain in the service under any circumstances. A man who will violate one promise only requires time to violate any amount of them. He has been advised by others in the same way, and I think he is a little surly now, and keeps very quiet.

July 5. This morning after sunrise the steamers took their departure with all the pomp and ostentation that swivels [a mountain howitzer] could give. The day was devoted to the duties of camp. There are no mosquitoes in our camp, but it is exceedingly dusty and unpleasant on account of the high winds that seem to prevail every afternoon.

July 6. Mr. [Malcolm] Clark sent his wagon down from Fort Campbell and Capt. Jones, Livingston and I rode over to the Teton. We found the river very muddy, and in no stage for fishing. I caught a catfish. We returned in time for dinner. No news as yet from Mullan, although the express should have returned before this. Lyon will leave tomorrow for Mullan's camp.

July 7. Marched on officer of the day and remained in camp all day. I spent my leisure time fixing up the tent. The Major received a letter from the Spread Eagle. One of Capt. Jones men, a man named Irwin was drowned swimming the river below the fort. Last night was quite cold, and the weather today was cool and pleasant. I am suffering from a cold in the head that makes me very uncomfortable. There was an extensive arrival of Indians on the other side of the river, and they were crossing in great numbers. About sundown an exciting scene occurred. One of the rafts, which the Indians were ferrying across broke up, and some women and children had a narrow escape from drowning.

July 8. Sunday. I went fishing this morning, and lost both my lines before I had caught any fish. We had Mr. Dawson and Col. Vaughan over to dinner. The afternoon was spent in camp.

July 9. Commenced drills this morning. Afternoon I went up the river fishing. A heavy rain came up, and I got quite wet. The afternoon became quite cold. The morning was spent visiting Mr. Dawson and Col. Vaughan at the fort.

July 10. Spent the day in camp. Nothing transpired. About six in the evening the Indians produced a war dance on horseback. They were very gaily decked out with feathers and paint and skins. It was a very interesting sight. They rode round our camp in single file, and then assembled at their lodges, where some Indians kept time with drums and sang a monotonous song. The Indians here are not prepossessing in feature, nor so remarkable for their size as the Sioux or Mandans. But they seem to have acquired less of the conveniences of the whites, and to have been less under their influence. One of the chiefs gave the Maj. a horse, as did also another

Indian, presents that rather embarrass the Maj. than flatter him.

July 11. The day was spent in garrison. Compared to yesterday it was exceedingly warm. Hardin and I took a bath in the river that was very refreshing. Capt. Jones went out to look at the road a little in order to find a convenient camp with wood and water. He reports that ten miles distant we can camp on the Missouri by working the road a little on the hill.

July 12. A fishing excursion having been arranged for today, Dr. Head, Livingston and myself crossed over the river, where a civilized Indian called "Blackfoot" had a wagon, and in four hours drove us over the prairie to Highwood Creek, where we arrived about three o'clock. We immediately commenced fishing, and in two hours I had captured eighteen small trout with flies. I think, however, that grasshoppers are better, as I found upon examination that that is their principle food. I had an unpleasant colic, having had no dinner, although it did not prevent me from eating a hearty supper of fish. Livingston caught ten, and the Dr. fourteen. Quite a thunderstorm threatened us going over, but it passed off with very little rain. We passed through several villages of prairie dogs, the first I have ever seen. They look more like a squirrel than a dog, and should more properly be called ground squirrels.

July 13. Livingston and I slept under the same mosquitoes bar last night, and he reproached me this morning for allowing the mosquitoes to enter on my side through an aperture that I had overlooked. We all set out fishing this morning, and I did not return until noon, when I found Capt. Raynolds, Lt. Mullins [not Mullans], and Mr. Stewart in camp. They arrived and camped on the creek on their way to Fort Benton. They have had a rough trip through the mountains, and a long one. I was quite successful fishing. I caught forty-five, the Dr. and Livingston together caught forty-five, also, making ninety that we took home with us to supper. We left the creek and reached camp in time for supper with our news of Raynolds' arrival, which was not credited at first. We found that a Mr. Irvin formerly of the Rifles, came over from the Bitter Root, and reports Mullan getting along very well.

July 14. Spent this day in camp. Nothing transpired worthy of note except Capt. Reynolds' arrival. I was occupied fixing up my tent, which Upham has permitted to get into considerable disorder in my absence. He is exceedingly careless. Capt. Reynolds and Mullins spent the afternoon in camp. Col. Vaughan delivered the annuities to the Indians today. There were fifteen hundred to two thousand men, women and children present.

July 15. Sunday. The young gentlemen are all investing in horses, and embarrassing themselves with taking care of them. Marched on officer of the day, and remained in camp all day. Nothing of note transpired.

July 16. Spent this day in garrison. Nothing of note transpired. We are visited by the gentlemen from Mr. Mullins' camp. They assembled in the evening at Fort Campbell for a game of cards. I went up there and had a long talk with Mr. Irvin about the country and its resources.

July 17. Capt. Jones and his company went out on the road about ten miles to do some work. I am to meet him out there tomorrow and go with him to the Great Falls of the Missouri. Spent the day in camp without any event of note.

July 18. The morning was spent in camp, loafing. In the afternoon I got ready, and went out to Jones' camp accompanied by Hardin and a guide named Antoine furnished by Mr. Clark. I found that the Capt. had nearly finished his road working. Dr. Cooper, who intended to go with us to the Falls has become disgusted, and will not go. Mosquitoes are very troublesome at this camp, as at all camps on the Missouri at this season.

July 19. We started the men back to Fort Benton, and about eight o'clock started for the Falls. We kept along the river nearly all the way, leaving it only at short distances. We reached the Falls about two o'clock, and were fortunate enough to get our horses down to the (indifferent success) river, where we camped, just below the Great Falls. The place is very interesting. We spent the afternoon fishing, and were very successful in catching trout and catfish in abundance. The mosquitoes proved very troublesome. Antoine says we are the first party that ever took horses down to the Fall. I think the height of the Fall has been, overestimated. It looks to be about sixty feet high.

July 20. I took a hasty sketch of the Falls this morning before leaving, We left the Fall about seven, and reached Fort Benton about four. The distance is at least thirty-five miles by the river. The morning was cloudy and pleasant, but the afternoon exceedingly hot and uncomfortable. I killed a rattlesnake with nine rattles. We saw many antelope. We met quite a train of half-breeds and Indians and voyageurs with their women on a hunting excursion, some of them are perhaps moving over into the Bitter Root Valley. We heard considerable news by the arrival of Father Cargiatti [Congiato]. There is another Indian war in Utah Territory with Utahs. Mullan has crossed the divide of the Rocky Mountains, and will be here in ten or twelve days. An express arrived from Mullan also this evening in which it appears that Mullan is very short of transportation, and his long communication to the Major is prolific of suggestions. The Maj. is very much irritated at Mullan's reproaches for having discharged his astronomers, which I thought very wrong on the Major's part at the time. The Maj., however, thinks himself authorized by his instructions from the Secretary of War in so doing. He does not, however, defend his position well, and I am inclined to think that he feels himself in the wrong. I felt quite tired, not having ridden on horseback for a year, and went to bed early.

July 21. Spent this day in camp without any incident of importance. Another express arrived from Lt. Mullan to Mr. Dawson, asking for advice where to locate the road from here to Sun River. I was down at the Fort this evening, and had a long talk with Father Cargiatti and Houken. They are very pleasant. I picked up some news about Washington Territory.

July 22. Sunday. Marched on officer of the day and spent the time in camp. I also closed up my Ordnance and Company papers to send with Capt. Raynolds, who leaves tomorrow in a Mackinaw boat to survey the river.

July 23. Capt. Raynolds left today about ten o'clock. Maj. Blake also left on a visit to the Falls, taking with him Livingston, Dr. Head, Smith and Upham. Mr. Clark goes with them also, in a wagon. Smith has left me to look after the Quarter Master Dept. I went up the river and took a sketch of Fort Benton and the camp. Capt. Jones dispensed with the evening drill, and substituted dress parade. Father Cargiatti and Col. Vaughan left for Sun River.

July 24. I took a sketch from down the river of Fort Benton. The afternoon I spent in camp, reading and sleeping. The days are intensely warm, and mosquitoes sometimes troublesome in the evening.

July 25. I remained in camp all day copying a map of our route. The weather was very warm. Nothing transpired of note.

July 26. I spent the forenoon mapping. In the afternoon I went up the river fishing, but returned unsuccessful. The Maj. and party returned from the Great Falls, having visited all the Falls, and they express themselves highly pleased with their trip. They caught a great many trout, but they were not so successful as we were. They seem very well used up.

July 27. An exceedingly disagreeable day, heavy winds and dust all day. I tried fishing, but was unsuccessful. Could not do anything in camp.

July 28. Spent this day in camp. Nothing occurred except an express from Mullan informing the Maj. of the revocation of the order relieving Lt. Mullan from the wagon road, and that he is to continue on the work. His assistant, Mr. Johnston has arrived with the intelligence of an increased appropriation. He sent me a paper and a speech, neither of which have any news in them. He will be here on Tuesday or Wednesday, as he expected to be at Sun River tonight. I was officer of the day.

July 29. Sunday. This day was spent in camp without any incident. The weather continues warm, notwithstanding the rain we had two days since. We are becoming very impatient for Lt. Mullan's arrival, as we are anxious to be on the move. It is impossible to do anything and the time is mostly spent in lounging and gossiping about camp. Some of the gentlemen manage to kill a great deal of time sleeping. I find it unpleasant to sleep in the daytime.

July 30. No event worthy of record. We begin to count the hours now to the arrival of Lt. Mullan. We learned that a portion of their train camps this evening a few miles above on the Missouri. Mullan seems to have divided his party into two or three divisions, coming by different routes.

July 31. The advance of Lt. Mullan's party arrived this afternoon. Mr. Williamson with his train arrived this afternoon about four by the direct route from Sun River. Capt. DeLacy is with it. I went down and had a talk with him about the road. He has no news from the States or from the Territory. He left Puget Sound about the same time I did. Genl. Harney has left the Dept. of Oregon, and Col. Wright is in command. Lt. Mullan has another appropriation of one-hundred thousand dollars for the Road, and will continue upon the Road for another year. Lt. White and Lt. Lyon arrived this morning. They came by the Missouri route.

Aug. 1. Lt. Mullan arrived in the afternoon by the Teton route. A heavy rainstorm prevailed this afternoon. It rained very hard, and the wind blew with great violence. I had a long talk with Mullan about his road and his troubles. He is decidedly more monomaniacal in his demonstrations than I ever knew him. He imagines everybody who is not in favor of his road to be against it. He has no doubt been very badly treated by Genl. Harney and by the Secretary of War. White and Lyon came up, and spent the evening in camp, but Mullan did not come up, much to the Major's disgust. I heard a remarkable sound in the air as of somebody passing through the air from northwest to southeast, making a noise like that of a cannon ball. It preceded the storm about ten minutes. The gentlemen all collected at Fort Campbell for a game of cards. I went up and staid until after twelve, and came home in the rain, which continued all evening.

Aug. 2. A very cool day. I went down at Mullan's request, and came up with him to see the Maj. Their interview proved more amicable than I anticipated. The day was spent in camp reading the *Pioneer and Democrat* of the latest date, which I borrowed in Mullan's camp. Lt. Mullan has turned over all the wagons he has in possession, and takes our pack train in exchange. The Major intimidated Mullan into letting him have all the wagons by telling him that he would not move without them. Mullan is quite a monomaniac about his road.

Aug. 3. There seems to be some prospect of starting soon. Lt. Lyon has dispatched his supplies in advance. Col. Vaughan distributed some annuities to the Piegan Indians today. About two-hundred warriors with their families arrived on the other side yesterday. The weather has improved very much, it is much cooler and more agreeable. We are all preparing for our departure. Our sick and disabled go down with Lt. White to Fort Leavenworth.

Aug. 4. Marched on officer of the day. Spent the day in camp writing and attending to papers. No event of importance, except the dissolution of our mess. We have divided up into company messes. I commenced a letter to Father, and mailed a letter to Capt. Maloney, which I wrote yesterday. We will not get off before day after tomorrow.

Aug. 5. Sunday. Lt. Mullan left today on his return to Walla Walla. He goes in advance of the command to prepare the road as much as possible. I finished my letter to Father. The day was spent in camp. DeLacy has gone back with Mullan.

Aug. 6. White set out this morning. I mailed a letter to Mendall, and forwarded one to Carr. We sent back about twenty sick to Fort Randall. He went off in good style about one o'clock down the river with a well loaded boat. We are all ready to depart ourselves, and the order has been issued to start in the morning. We are all ready and anxious to leave this camp.

Aug. 7. We broke up our camp this morning. A heavy rain fell in the morning that made it quite unpleasant, but it cleared up, and the tents became almost dry before the oxen could be yoked. There was much delay about getting off, and we did not get started until about ten o'clock, and went into camp on the bluff at the Grand Coulee before descending. The Maj. had intended to camp on the bluff on the other side, and the wagons were to be sent round the Coulee in preference to descending, by which we maintained that he would double the today march for the wagons and save very little for tomorrow. But he was obstinate even after seeing Lt. Mullan's maps. But he avoided the responsibility of carrying out his idea, and remained behind under the expressed idea of seeing Mr. Dawson off with our provisions, and Capt. Jones took the responsibility of camping according to his own notion. I went fishing, and caught a few fish, and Upham shot some little birds. I went to bed with a headache, and

about ten o'clock awoke with such a violent headache that I went to the Doctor, and he prescribed a dose of oil which I took. I bathed my head with cold water, and was soon enabled to go to sleep. I marched with the men today, but the fatigue was nothing, and I account for the derangement of my stomach by the change in time of eating, and being so long during the day without anything to eat.

Aug. 8. We had a long and fatiguing march without any water by the way. We carried water with us, and the men suffered very much. We marched twenty-five miles, and were overtaken by Dawson's train. The Maj., Dawson and Col. Vaughan came up, and we camped at the lake [Benton Lake]. They are all quite merry. McCullaugh is with them, and we shall no doubt be compelled to take care of him. He is quite tight, also. We have very good water, but no wood except what we have hauled with us from last night. Smith has furnished me a mule to ride, but I do not expect to ride much, and only take [it] along in the event that I might wish to ride sometime. I like to have it along, as some of my men may give out. I turned it over to Sgt. Hanley this afternoon, who seems to have failed today. There have been some appointments in my company. Sgt. Law has returned, and Sgt. Bailey has resigned to drive the ambulance. Sgt. Taylor thus has charge of the Company as lst Sgt. Chancelor and Haley are made Sgts., and Pvt. Horgan and Emmet Corporals. It was half past five before we got into camp, but we brought wood with us, and are therefore quite comfortable, and the men have less to do than yesterday.

Aug. 9. I slept soundly this morning, and felt quite well this morning. We did not get off until half past seven, and reached Sun River at two. I marched at the head of the Battalion as D Company was in advance. I did not feel much fatigued. I spent the evening writing up my notes, and itinerary, after which I took a bath. We had an excellent camp, except that we were not very close to wood and water. Mr. Dawson's train passed us today on toward the Bitter Root.

Aug. 10. We camped at the Indian agency about ten, having had an early start, and made the crossing of the Sun River. In the afternoon we went over on an invitation from Col. Vaughan to partake of what he calls a Rocky Mountain vegetable dinner, which was as amusing as it was primitive in the style, in which it was served. To its good qualities, however, no exception can be made. Col. Vaughan, Dawson and McCullaugh came over, and the latter got so drunk that he could not return. Col. Vaughan was extremely kind, and gave us an abundance of ice and vegetables, and presented me with a very nice Indian pony. Mullan is only one day in advance of us, and is quite sick, so we heard from Mr. Mark.

Aug. 11. We got off at twenty minutes after six, and by one o'clock we reached Bird Tail Rock, where we camped, 76 miles from Fort Benton. Our camp last night was good, but wood and water are not abundant for large commands like ours at our camp today. We entered a more broken country, almost destitute of timber, but grass good. Veins of basalt appear above the surface, forming singular hills, like the Knee and Crown Buttes.

Aug. 12. Sunday. We made an early start, and by one p.m. we reached the Dearborn, a clear, beautiful trout stream. We did intend to lay over a day here, but on account of the cattle the Maj. determined to go one day more, as the day after tomorrow will be very hard on the oxen. I spent the afternoon trout fishing. I caught quite enough for supper. We made sixteen miles. The afternoon was varied with some heavy thunderclouds, but not much rain. The country has become quite mountainous.

Aug. 13. We made an eighteen mile march, and camped at the Little Prickly Pear Creek, about three miles from where it runs into the Missouri. From here to the last crossing of the Prickly Pear we expect a bad road, and shall lie over tomorrow. I went fishing this evening, and caught quite enough for supper and breakfast. We killed some rattlesnakes, which are quite common. Many of the gentlemen are quite as successful fishing. Mullan's party is five miles above.

Aug. 14. We did not move camp today, and the gentlemen spent the day hunting and fishing. Hardin and I went to the Missouri, and I caught a few of a new species of fish. We then went to the mouth of the Prickly Pear, and waded up, and by two o'clock I returned to camp with quite a large string of fish. The evening was spent in camp. It is quite windy in our camp, and sometimes very unpleasant. The scenery has become quite wild. Pine has

become abundant, high mountains surround us. I took a nap in the evening.

Aug. 15. Upham, who is on guard today, had us turned out at two o'clock this morning instead of three, and we got off at half past five, but did not get into camp until after seven in the evening, at the last crossing of the Prickly Pear, and made only fourteen miles. The road was very hilly where it was compelled to leave the river, and on the river there were a great many crossings to make. On two big, steep hills we had to double teams. We met Lt. Howard of the 3rd Art., and Mr. Irvin and a Mr. Davis. They brought some letters for the gentlemen of the party, but none for me. They bring us the news of Genl. Jessup's death, the arrival of the Great Eastern in New York, and the nominations of the Democratic party for president. The two sections have nominated Douglass and Johnson and Crittenden and Lane. There are thus four candidates in the field, and the election will probably go to the House. Mr. Irvin went on to Fort Benton, Mr. Howard and Mr. Davis returned to Mullan's camp.

Aug. 16. We crossed over to the Softbed Creek, a distance of nine miles, where we encamped. We made a short march on account of the fatigue of yesterday to the cattle. The country is very beautiful, though sparsely wooded, and not very fertile. The men succeeded in marching very well, and we would average twenty miles per day if the oxen could make it.

Aug. 17. We passed over a rolling country to the head of the Big Prickly Pear, where we camp, having made fourteen miles. The hills kept the animals back, and we did not get into camp until near three o'clock. Lyon and Mr. Johnson were in camp during the afternoon, and brought us over a couple of papers that Mr. Davis brought up. Mullan is encamped about five miles ahead of us, across the Divide. Spent the evening in camp. Nothing of note transpired. The weather continues fine.

Aug. 18. We got an early start, and after assisting the wagons up the hill to the Divide, we pushed on. I conducted the Battalion, and in order to pass the wagons we marched very rapidly. For some reason, either a rivalry among the companies or a disposition to tire me out, the men toward the latter part of the march increased their gait so much and showed such a spirit for marching that I let them go into camp, without the usual rest. The rate was about five miles per hour towards the latter part. Some of the men with longer legs could walk faster than I, but I think that if we had gone about six miles farther they would have yielded. They were already flagging when the sight of camp revived them. We marched seventeen miles through a beautiful country and a good road. The divide is the most practical pass I ever saw in any mountainous country. Lt. Mullan spent the afternoon in camp, and took dinner with me. He is quite well again. We went out fishing this afternoon, and I caught two messes of very fine trout. The weather continues very fine. Tomorrow being Sunday, and a good camp, we remain in camp.

Aug. 19. Sunday. We remained in camp all day today, and gave the animals a rest. I went fishing in the morning, and caught over twenty excellent trout. The afternoon I spent in camp. The weather continues fine and pleasant. The gentlemen went fishing, though one or two went hunting. There does not seem to be much game in the country, and fishing is better rewarded than hunting.

Aug. 20. We were disgusted at only marching eight miles. We went into camp about nine o'clock by a small creek about four miles from Buffalo Creek, which we passed also. The guide said it was twelve miles to wood, water and grass, and the Maj. feared a twenty mile march was too long. Livingston and the Dr. went fishing. I went out after them. They caught one, and I caught half dozen, which rather disgusted them. The evening was spent in camp.

Aug. 21. We crossed over to Deer Lodge Creek, which unites a few miles further down with the Little Blackfoot, and forms Hell Gate River. We found it nine miles, and were again disgusted that we did not make it our camp last night. We went eight miles farther, and camped on Rock Creek, a branch of Hell Gate River. It is a very rocky, rapid stream. I went fishing, caught half dozen, which was quite sufficient, and returned to camp where I spent the afternoon.

Major Blake reported from Hell Gate River on August 23, 1860, that he found Mullan's Military Road to be "very practicable" and that it was "well worked." Blake and his recruits reached Fort Walla Walla in early October having been on the march for nearly two months, covering some 600 miles

from Fort Benton. This was the only significant movement of military forces over the road.

Mullan returned to Fort Benton on June 8, 1862, having at last completed his work on the road. In his final report, Mullan reveals some interesting prospects for the portion from Deer Lodge to Fort Benton. Keep in mind that Helena and the rich diggings at Last Chance Gulch would not be established for another two years. His further comments also shed some light on the origins of young Mr. Lyons (See Chapter 2, Warren C. Gillette autobiography) after whom Lyons Hill and Creek would be named.

On our trip from Deer Lodge to Fort Benton we performed no work beyond what our immediate wants demanded; but I was enabled to mark in detail the points where additional repairs were yet required. The chief point was over the Medicine Rock Mountain. It is barely possible that the Medicine Rock Mountain might be avoided by following down the Big Prickly Pear, immediately on crossing the Rocky Mountains to the Missouri, and working a road along that river to near the mouth of the Little Prickly Pear. I am not positive whether this can be done. I examined this section in 1854, and my recollection of the region was against its feasibility. In case the road should be reworked it is worthy [of] a special examination. There is no other way of avoiding this mountain, and should this prove impracticable nothing is left except to work the high water trail throughout over the Medicine Rock Mountain; this, in many places, will be through rock, but with time and means a good road can be made. After this a good bridge should be built over Willow Creek; the two crossings of the Big Prickly Pear should be avoided by work over the hills and the entire section along the north fork of the Little Blackfoot should be worked by excavating a road along the northern side hills, wherever the ground is wet and marshy. Two crossings of the main Little Blackfoot should be avoided, and a bridge built over its third and last crossing. With these improvements, and such other slight work as the nature of the repairs may demand, the road from Deer Lodge to Fort Benton will be an excellent one at all times, and upon which, in time, there will be much travel. I returned to the Deer Lodge Valley, at the American Fork, by the 24th of June, meeting several wagon trains en route for Fort Benton, to freight out supplies for the Bitter Root and Deer Lodge Valleys. At the American Fork I was overtaken by Mr. Steele, from Fort Benton, with the intelligence that four steamers had arrived at that point since the date of my departure, [the steamers Emile, Shreveport, Key West and Spread Eagle arrived in June 1862] with three hundred and sixty-four emigrants from St. Louis, for Walla Walla and other points en route; that they were provided with saw and grist mills, and that there were among them many miners who intended prospecting the country en route; also, that another trading house, under the auspices of La Barges, Harkness & Co., of St. Louis, was to be established near Fort Benton. This cheering intelligence was very gratifying to me, seeing in it the commencement of a long line of emigrant travel, which in years to come must course along these rivers in search of new homes towards the Pacific slope.

Emigrants were the next heavy users of the Mullan Road, just as Mullan had predicted. In June of 1862, four steamers arrived at Fort Benton loaded with miners, merchants, tradesmen and wealthy lookers on. John O'Fallon Delany was one of those aristocrats who just wanted to see what it was like to travel to the frontier and watch men scrambling to make their fortunes. Fortunately, he kept a detailed diary of his journey, which was published in the Missouri Historical Societies publication, *The Bulletin* for October 1962, and January 1963.

Sunday, June 15

Was up early. Assisted at Mass. Stopped to wood twice. I cut down two trees. The tiller rope broke in going over a very rapid place. We laid up early waiting for the small boat to get over. A mackinaw boat came down from Ft. Benton with some of Mullan's men & stopped to give us very favorable news from the mines. Weather damp, raining & disagreeable.

Monday, June 16

A very cloudy & damp day. The freight was all taken off the Key West & put on this boat as it is the Captain's intention to try to go to Ft. Benton right straight in this boat.

Tuesday, June 17

Rained nearly all day & was very disagreeable. The scenery becoming very fine. Two buffalo were killed.

Wednesday, June 18

Fine pleasant day. We reached several rapids & had to all go out & cordell the boat over three of them. The river is remarkably high. More so than it has been in the remembrance of the oldest traders. Went to bed early.

Thursday, June 19

Very fine day. Passed the most picturesque part of the river. The sandstone is seen in all the shapes possible, like tombstones, castles, forts, etc. The most remarkable we saw was Hole in the Wall. Stopped to wood & went ashore on some high hills, which commanded an extensive view over the surrounding country & Bear Claw Mts. I went in bathing in a delightful place. The Emilie passed us about noon on her way back to St. Louis. Our military Co. was drilled for the last time & disbanded.

Friday, June 20

Got up late. A very fine day. Called a meeting of the passengers. Mr. Manderville was called to the chair & myself. Mr. Risely & Shipman appointed a committee of three to wait on the Captain to whom an address of thanks was presented & a few bottles drunk to his health. Just in sight of Ft. Benton we were stopped by a rapid. The yawl was sent out with a rope & in returning it was dashed by the current against the steam boat & capsized. Four out of seven men were drowned. Jake was rescued just in time to save his life. Sadness prevailed all over the boat. We reached Ft. Benton about four o'clock & visited the Fort & the encampment of the Emilie passengers.

Saturday, June 21

Went ashore. Had Father De Smet's tents pitched & took possession of them & joined Mr. Campbell's party, composed of Lyle H. Boyle. Went in partnership with J. P. Lyons.

I was on the go all day going from one place to another until I was worn out at night & retired early on the boat in Mr. Risely's room. Smith's party came very near breaking up during the day but concluded affairs before night. The [steamer] Key West started back. Weather very fine but warm.

Sunday, June 22

I got up in time for breakfast. After attending Mass said by Father De Smet in the of the Fort at which Father De S. preached. The sale of horses commenced during which a good deal of excitement reigned.

We succeeded after some trouble in getting ten horses for our party. The Spread Eagle took her departure & it was with a sad heart that I saw her disappear in the distance. Mr. Smith returned in her. I took a ride on horse back.

Monday, June 23

We began making our preparation for departure.

Tuesday, June 24

The day relied upon for our departure was a wet & gloomy one so we did not get off.

Wednesday, June 25

Dr. McKellops party got off. A terrible storm of hail & rain perfectly inundated our tents. We were prevented from starting by the walking off of a couple of Mr. Campbell's horses. Mr. Valle [?] & party were obliged to return. We moved up to the upper fort & slept in the priest's house.

Thursday, June 26

We called up all our accounts with Mr. Dawson & made our final arrangements for departure tomorrow.

Friday, June 27

The horses were sent out to graze until mid-day. Soon after dinner we put everything in the wagons, bid our last adieus to all our friends & started. We were detained some time getting up a very steep hill [Helena Hill] . [I] drove one of the four horse teams. Went about three miles & encamped. Slept in the open air. Weather cloudy & cool.

Saturday, June 28

We were up at 4. Started without breakfast. Found we had got on the wrong road & spent a couple of hours before we found the right one. Buda [?] met us after a drive of about 8 or 10 miles over the undulating prairie. We pitched our tent at the Coulee [eight mile] a point where the Missouri River. is accessible from off the high prairie. Took breakfast at 1 p.m. We did not go any further but allowed our horses to graze at their ease. Anderson joined us. I went in bathing. We kept regular watches at night as there is some danger of the Indians stealing our horses.

Sunday, June 29

Very fine & warm day. After watering our horses & getting breakfast we set out on our journey. From the prairie, on which we traveled all day yesterday & a few miles today we ascended to one some 100 or 200 feet higher by a very steep ascent. We met some three or four men with a drove of horses on their way to Fort Benton. I wrote a few words to Father De Smet. We did not succeed in reaching the Lake [Benton] we were steering for although we traveled from 10 1/2 a.m. till 9 1/2 p.m. without even stopping to eat. We camped on a hill & retired to our hardy couches tired & hungry having only some crackers & cheese to break our long fasting of some fourteen hours. The mosquitoes were in schools & of a prodigious size & remarkably voracious.

Monday, June 30

We were on the move at 8 1/2 a.m. after a restless & sleepless night. Some travelers were seen, who when they approached, we recognized Mr. Worden who told us we were only four miles from the Lake & gave us other valuable information. We therefore got ready & pushed forward weak & dispirited [?] by hunger & thirst & reached the long wished for Lake about 9 a.m. A good hearty breakfast quite set us up & our poor thirsty horses quenched their thirst for water, of which they had been deprived for more than 24 hours. We hurried on again as soon as possible for the mosquitoes & horse flies were in a great number and rendered the horses backs perfectly raw & in a bleeding condition. Mr. Sutton & Tacket were of our party. Our road lay over a gradually ascending plain for several miles & went down very abruptly into a narrow valley, which had the resemblance [?] of having once been the bed of a river. In crossing a small rivulet Mr. Campbell's wagon bogged in a hole of alkaline mud which is perfectly white. Alkaline water is practically considered unhealthy & is said to have the effect of increasing thirst instead of alleviating it. Some four or five teams with some of the finest oxen I ever saw came along & pulled his wagon out of the mud. We met several families of Indian travelers with all their household property. We encamped on a hill just at the crossing of Little Muddy. A fine view is obtained over Sun River Valley & the stream of the same name as it pursues its course in graceful curves. We were here obliged to hoist our mosquito bars for the first time, the mosquitoes being in schools. Weather fine but very warm.

Tuesday, July 1

We got up a little later than usual. After a hearty breakfast on prairie dogs we went to work & made a crossing for the oxen. The river, which together with getting the wagons over took us some four hours. Two men with wagons & a great many horses came to our camp to borrow a knife & wrench. We started again & had to travel for some distance over a very marshy flat plain, which was very hard on the horses & thence to climbing over slightly elevated hills owing to the frequent rains & high water. Mullan's road is quite impassable at this point. We reached Sun River about 5 p.m. & encamped on its banks in a beautiful grazing plain. This river is quite wide owing to the high water. In its ordinary stage it is fordable. We feasted on a hind quarter of antelope killed this morning by some travelers who have been stopping here since several days. Weather fine & warm.

Wednesday, July 2

We laid over all today to rest our horses & ourselves. Dave Risley having parted from his party at Bird Tail Rock started on his way back with Dr. Atchison. One wagon also returned belonging to other partners in despair of getting along. I washed some clothes for the first time, found it a tough job. Wrote a letter to Father De Smet & one home to send by Dave Risley. What is called the farm is here. The Indian Agent has his quarter near here. Weather fine & warm.

Thursday, July 3

It took us several hours to pack up & cross the river on the ferry at mid-day. The road is very good the whole way to Bird Tail Rock

with the exception of the crossings of several small rivulets which are rather steep & sometimes boggy. We encamped for the night near Bird Tail Rock. Weather rather windy & cool & turned really cold in the night.

Friday, July 4

We were under way about 8 o'clock. Our road lay over some very steep & stony hills. I did not feel very well & begin to wish I was back at my comfortable home. In driving up a very steep hill our axel tree gave way & of course we had to come to a halt. We encamped therefore about 4 o'clock in a beautiful valley shut in on all sides by very high mountains. Two of the party immediately set out with axes to cut a pine to make another axel. We slept out in the open as we generally did except when it rained.

Saturday, July 5

All day was taken up in working at the axel tree. I remained up at the top of a high hill watching our wagon. Mr. Valle & several other parties came by with their pack horses. Anderson encamped all night with us. Weather excessively warm.

Sunday, July 6

Half the day was spent finishing off & getting the axel tree. We got started again about 3 in the evening & went over some very steep hills indeed. Came very near being upset. We reached Dearborn River about dark & crossed & camped about a mile from the crossing.

Monday, July 7

We traveled all day over a fine road one hill only gave us some trouble & camped for a few hours on the top. We reached the 1st crossing of the Prickly Pear about dark. We found Valle, Sullivan, Shipman, Anderson & several others encamped here & quite a shower came up & we all got soaked.

Tuesday, July 8

Soon after starting we were detained a couple of hours at a crossing which the horses could scarcely pull over. Steep hills & bad crossings be-set our road all day. One hill particularly was very rocky & long & almost perpendicular. We had to go down to ford [?] the Prickly Pear a second time. We stopped & took a lunch & proceeded to the 3rd crossing where we found ourselves stopped by the most steep hill we have come across on [?] the crossing of a deep [?] stream 13 times. We decided to stop & pack over & therefore camped here. We had a glorious supper on baker's bread & stewed apples prepared by our excellent cook Marsh Pyle. Our watches were changed from 2 1/2 hours for each two, to 1 hour for each one. Weather fine & warm during the day & a light shower of rain towards dark.

Wednesday, July 9

We were up early & proceeded to unload our wagons & make the different things into packs, which were transported a mile & a half on the other side of the hill. It was the hardest days work we have had & many times did I wish myself home. When the last load had started I consoled myself in thinking of home. Mr. Worden rode up about mid-day & took dinner with us. Major Graham & two other gentlemen came by in the morning. Lyle Boyle & myself remained in the camp all night. The rest slept over at the other camp. Weather excessively warm. Swarms of mosquitoes. We are now becoming accustomed to those troublesome insects.

Thursday, July 10

We were up late. Campbell & the rest came over with the horses about 10 o'clock & took his wagon over. We hitched up & I drove over one of the most dangerous & worst roads I ever saw or wish to see. Lyons & myself had very hard work gathering up our small things & making them into packs to carry over on horses in a most boiling sun. We succeeded at length in getting all in the wagon & driving over to join Campbell. The Mining & Exploring Co. with one wagon. They were obliged to do as we did, pack. We at length got underway again but did not go very far as another very steep hill stopped us before we had gone two miles. We doubled teams & with great difficulty. After setting things to right we started once more a little after dark. We got to a very bad descent & an ascent not much [better]. I could scarcely see to drive the horses & succeeded in getting down safely but the horses could not pull up so we left the wagon & went & encamped on the hill on the opposite side of the road from where the Exploring & Mining party & several other parties were encamped. Weather changeable.

Friday, July 11

We were up early notwithstanding it was past midnight when we lay down. Lyons had some hard words with Campbell & Lyle before I was awake & the latter refused to cook him any breakfast. We took down four extra horses & brought our wagon. We [were] fixing everything to start. Lyons & myself were standing by [?] our wagon putting things in order. I was standing on the back wheel & he on the front when he—attempted to pull out my gun, which was wedged in between the side of the wagon & the different articles, in doing so the hammer of the left hand barrel caught in something & the piece went off, lodging six buck shot in the right lung of poor Lyons. His only exclamation was, "Oh!" & he fell to the ground lifeless. The horror of all present was indescribable but the accident had happened & nothing was to be done for the poor fellow. We immediately proceeded to examine his wound & wash the blood away & wrapping him up in some canvas we dug him a grave near the road side in which sad Mr. Lynch, Mud & several gentlemen of the Exploring party had the kindness to assist us. We engraved his name on several trees & pieces of wood & deposited his body in the grave, & performed the last duties towards him in reading the prayer for the dead. We constructed a kind of pen with logs around his grave so as to prevent the wild beasts from scratching up his remains. Soon after this duty done we packed up & proceeded on our way & bid an everlasting adieu to poor Lyons. After going down a very steep & rocky hill where we had to let down the wagons with ropes & tie a tree to them to prevent their running down too fast, we reached a creek which we crossed several times. At the last crossing Mr. Campbell's wheel dashed in the [?] & we were obliged to stop to fix it. Johnny Grant, the great man of Deer Lodge Valley passed us with several others. We went half way up Medicine Rock Mountain in doubling harness & camped. This Mountain is the highest we have to cross & is very steep both in ascent & descent. Weather is quite cold.

Saturday, July 12

We continued up the Mountain after breakfast & then descended to a fine valley on the banks of the Little Prickly Pear. Mr. Campbell's wheel came very near giving way

& became so insecure that when we [?] reached the further end of the valley it was decided that it would not be safe to continue any further with that wheel & that it would be more advisable to pack as much of the stuff as possible over to Deer Lodge on horses. Weather warm but pleasant.

Sunday, July 13

Spent the morning packing & making our last preparation & started at 3 p.m. Tacket, Campbell, Boyle & myself. We drove eight pack horses. I rode & the rest walked. We reached Silver Creek just about dark having gone 16 miles. Weather fine & pleasant.

Monday, July 14

It was nine o'clock before we got every thing ready to start. We traveled over some pretty rugged roads & gradually wound our way around mountains until we reached the summit of the Rocky Mountains. It was quite pleasant there although there was still quite a large patch of snow still remaining unmelted. From the summit we descended into the valley of the Little Blackfoot, a stream which takes its source just near this pass & which we crossed seventeen times in a distance of 20 miles. We met some men prospecting & fishing & a luscious mess of trout they had. We encamped for the night some ten miles from the summit. The pass is now called Mullan's Pass but used to be called Hell Gate Pass. We made a very good supper off of flap jacks. Its the first time we have had any.

One of the earliest merchant explorers, James Harkness, of the firm La Barge, Harkness and Company, kept a diary of his trip from Fort Benton to Deer Lodge. The year was 1862 and the trip was fascinating especially since his travelling partners included his wife, son, and daughter. This account was published in the Montana Historical Society's publication, *Montana Contributions*, Volume II, 1896.

Sunday, June 15. Did not start as early as usual owing to the rain. Made Dauphan's Rapids early in the morning and got over without much trouble. Passed Judith River and overtook the Shreveport just below "Drowned Men's Rapids" where she was "wooding." Procured some dry wood and passed the rapids without much delay. Dropped a line to

the Shreveport and helped her over. The rain fell in torrents, but the passengers walked over with cheers; quite a number were acquainted with each other on the boats. We had a very agreeable time, and I found my son and daughter in good health. Laid up for the night at 8:30 p.m. Invited all the passengers of the Shreveport over to listen to a discourse by Rev. J. F. Bartlett. Night cold and rainy.

Monday, 16. Started at 4 a.m. and "wooded" at eight, getting the wood from the side of a mountain by a difficult road. The bluffs are grand beyond description. The sandstone is washed into every conceivable shape imaginable. Animals and birds are very scarce. Went on board of the Shreveport and staid all day; she is in tow of the Emile and runs very well in slack water. Bob La Barge killed an antelope at long range. The storm is over and the afternoon beautiful. The country is changing to prairie, and the peaks of the Little Rocky Mountains are in view to the northwest and the Judith Mountains to the southeast. At 7 p.m. passed the Marias River. Took on wood and staid all night just above. The river is now higher than ever known at this time of the year and still rising, and the mosquitoes are more plenty than agreeable. The trip is now drawing to a close and I will have a new field of operations to work in. I found flax in full bloom at our "wooding" place, and the sight brought to mind my native island home; I gathered a few flowers for my daughter.

Tuesday, 17. Was late in starting owing to difficulty in "wooding." Morning cool and clear. All is bustle and activity on board at the prospect of a speedy end to our long journey. Men on horseback are to be seen on the hills, quite a novelty to us. We came close to the Fort and found a very short turn and rapid current; we tried it for half an hour, but could not pass, then dropped the Shreveport and passed up, and then dropped a hawser to her and she passed up with the use of the "nigger." Landed at Fort Benton at noon on a prairie devoid of timber. Some of the attaches are glad to see us, and have offered their services. Little Dog, the chief of all the Blackfeet, has pledged his friendship to us in all things and sent out runners for his people to come in. He is of low stature, well built, and has an intelligent countenance. Both boats are discharging freight as fast as they can, with nothing but the prairie for a store-house. There is no use for a saw mill at this point, there being no timber. Traded for a few robes in the evening. River four feet higher than ever before known; it is a torrent from here to Fort Union. We were thirty-four days making the trip from port to port; the passengers are well pleased and give great credit for success. Had a business meeting of all the partners and decided to build our post a mile and a half above Fort Benton, naming it Fort La Barge.

Wednesday, 18. Discharged the Emilie, putting the freight on the prairie. Horses scarce, owing to the absence of Indians. Began the erection of a canvas store, and goods are selling fast. Very warm, one hundred degrees in the shade.

Thursday, 19. The Emilie left for St. Louis at 6 a.m. Goods all in confusion and no help to pile them. Mr. Clark arrived and stopped the sale of horses. Galpin helped all afternoon to arrange our goods.

Friday, 20. The Spread Eagle came into view early; she had four men drowned while getting over the rapids, and it was late in the day before she made port. Beat the Spread Eagle by seven days. The Key West is also in port. Goods are meeting with a ready sale.

Saturday, 21. A pleasant day. A number of men started for the mines. Key West started for St. Louis. Indians drunk, in consequence of which our trade was spoiled for the day.

Sunday, June 22. Spread Eagle left at 3 p.m. Rained all the afternoon.

Monday, 23. Trading and arranging the goods as well as circumstances will permit. Very warm.

Tuesday, 24. Business good. Mr. Filley went to the government farm with Mr. Reed and some of his people. Some persons washed a color of gold from the black sand above the Fort.

Wednesday, 25. Very warm this afternoon, one hundred and four degrees in the store, but it rained and turned so cold that we made a fire in the cabin of the Shreveport. Galpin and party arrived from their trip up the Milk River; had a rough time.

Thursday, 26. Trade good until stopped by one of the most terrible hail storms I ever saw. The ground was covered to the depth of

several inches. The roof of the boat was cut so that she leaked in many places.

Friday, 27. Cold and cloudy. Filley returned; the farm is under water, and there is no crop of much consequence; house not fit to live in. Indians drunk and in consequence trade spoiled.

Saturday, 28. Laid out Fort La Barge, three hundred by two hundred feet. Madam La Barge drove the first stake and my daughter, Margaret, the second. Eugene Jaccard and all of the officers of the Shreveport were present. The pack horses came in with the robes that Galpin bought on the Milk River. Trade dull.

Sunday, June 29. A beautiful day. A number of us went out on the hills for a walk.

Monday, 30. A party was made up to visit the Great Falls of the Missouri. It consisted of Eugene Jaccard, Father De Smet, Giles Filley and son Frank, Madam La Barge, Margaret Harkness, Mrs. Culbertson and son Jack, W. G. Harkness, Tom La Barge and Cadotte, the guide, the last three being on horseback, and the others in an ambulance drawn by four mules. They started at 4 a.m., and in the afternoon met some Blood Indians, relatives of Mrs. Culbertson, who were friendly under the influence of Father DeSmet and Mrs. C. An antelope was killed and cooked for supper, and the party camped for the night. They started next morning about 4 a.m. and reached the Falls about 9 or 10 a.m. Madam La Barge and Margaret Harkness, leaving the ambulance, ran to the point from which the first glimpse could be had, and are the first white women to have seen the Great Falls of the Missouri. They found the way down to the river with difficulty, and looking up saw the Falls in all their beauty and grandeur. They started on their return trip Tuesday afternoon, and reached the boat Wednesday at 10 p.m., having had a pleasant time.

Tuesday, July 1. Discharged the Shreveport. Sold a large quantity of goods. Put up a lot for I. Chambers to trade at Milk River. Very hot, one hundred and five in the shade. Good reports from the mines.

Wednesday, 2. Wm. Terry brought in $1,400 in gold dust from the mines. Frank Worden's train came for freight. Weather fine. Doing a fair business.

Thursday, 3. John Williams, Graham, and others from Deer Lodge, are here to buy goods. Started the men to cut logs; three deserted this morning. Emigrants nearly all gone. Got 12.50 (dollars or ounces) in gold dust from Graham.

Friday, 4. Thermometer fell to fifty-two degrees this morning; a change that would try the constitution of any one.

Saturday, 5. Bought oxen and horses today, and am packing up for the mines. The Shreveport is preparing to leave for St. Louis. Business good.

Sunday, July 6. Boat left at noon. Felt a little low-spirited bidding them all good bye. Nearly all of the people who came with us are gone.

Monday, 7. Selected goods for the west. A violent storm arose this evening, and a loaded wagon was blown into the river. Had great difficulty in saving goods on the bank, and got very wet.

Tuesday, 8. Selected cattle and loaded. Got everything arranged as well as I could, which was not very well.

Wednesday, 9. Started the ox teams early. Got four mules and an old white horse. Mules so small that I had all of the harnesses fit to them. One of them kicked the harness off on the prairie. Have had no meat for two days.

Thursday, 10. Reached Sun River at 5:30 p.m., opened pack, and got some supper.

Friday, 11. Spent a very unpleasant night; the mosquitoes were intolerable. Had to hobble the oxen and mules and watch them all night. Left at 4 a.m., crossed Sun River at ten and camped a few miles above. While coffee was preparing I caught a pan of fine fish. Camped at a spring at 5 p.m.

Saturday, 12. Started at 5:30 a.m. The mountain road begins at this camp. Camped at Bird Tail Rock. The day is fine and Cadotte's Pass is in view; some snow on the peaks. Have only seen one antelope since leaving the Fort. Camped at 5:30 p.m.: two miles to wood.

Sunday, July 13. Took a cut-off and saved in distance and hills. Reached Dearborn at noon and camped one mile below crossing. Lost best mule owing to flies and wild disposition. Caught ten trout. Hobbled oxen. Very warm and grass good.

Monday, 14. Started at 5:30 a.m. Oxen better for the rest. Crossed the Little Prickly Pear this afternoon at four o'clock without accident.

Tuesday, 15. Had a fine camp last night. Started at five this morning and commenced to ascend the Prickly Pear. At the foot of the mountain found four trains trying to cut a road: helped them till noon. It is about one and one-half miles in a direct line to where we had dinner yesterday. The work done in the creek by Mullan all lost—washed away by the torrent in the rainy season. If he had made the road on the hills it might have been permanent. They had twenty yoke of oxen to one wagon and could not take it up. They have cut logs all day to place across the gullies, putting on cross-pieces to make a road. It is now evening and they are going to try the new road. I hope there will be no accidents. A miss of six inches would have sent them five hundred feet into the creek bottom. At 4 p.m. all hands began the ascent. The trains put on from eight to ten yoke. We put on five and went up with as much ease as they. Hauled up the ambulance with oxen and camped at the top at 7 p.m., making two miles in two days. The guide says Sun River and the divide can be seen from the peaks above. Completely tired out with hard work which, however, must be done.

Wednesday, 16. Up at 4 a.m. and started at 5:30 and at eight reached a creek one and one-half miles distant. Wagon broke down and it was ten before it could be repaired and reloaded. The road is bad beyond description. The wagons had to be slid down the mountain. It is now noon and we have made but two miles this morning. The road is filled with other trains, and we have concluded to stay here the rest of the day as we cannot get ahead of them. Caught plenty of trout to eat. Vreeland passed us on his way to the Fort for the balance of his goods. He does not speak encouragingly of the mines. No game of any kind. I eat all kinds of berries and drink at every brook. I want to leave the dyspepsia in these mountains if I can. The hills are covered with pitch pine. Walked over a rattlesnake today. Both scared.

Thursday, 17. Up at 4 a.m. and off at six. Went up the hill without accident. Overtook the trains at 10 a.m. Caught trout for dinner. Came to the big hill where Clark's teams were stalled, helped them up and camped on Silver

Creek. Crossed the Prickly Pear five times today. There is no change in the character of the mountains except the rock is a deeper red in color. Isadore, a half-breed, made us a present of a quarter of a big-horn (mountain sheep). Game very scarce owing to the emigrants. The sun sets at about 8 p.m. Found a few small strawberries. Passed the grave of a miner, who, in taking his gun from his wagon, accidentally shot himself [J. P. Lyons].

Friday, 18. Up at four o'clock, but did not start until six. The hill we helped Clark up is known as Medicine Rock Hill. The rock is a ledge of syenite and projects out of the ridge at one place about five feet. The hill is one mile in length (up and down) and is a severe tax on teams, the west side being the worst. It is two, long, weary months since I left home, and I have done a great deal of hard work and yet have accomplished but little. Will I live to reap the benefit or not?

Saturday, 19. The night was cold and a little rain fell. The men were up at the usual hour, but I was not able to rise before breakfast. We followed the other trains, the road being much better today. We ascended one hill fully a mile and a half and the descent was about a mile. The wind blows fresh and cool, and snow banks are only a few miles distant. The south side of most of the hills is timbered. Red currants are to be found along the water courses, the bushes growing from three to seven feet high. I found a few fine gooseberries today. Flowers are scarce, principally Bachelor-Buttons in all colors. Nooned at 11 a.m. Met three different parties returning from the mines, who say they are all humbug. Met Dr. McKellops, Jones, Chapman and others going back to the Fort for the balance of their goods. They intend going to the Salmon River mines.

For the military and the emigrants the Mullan Road worked, but just barely. Something better was needed, especially over the steep grades and wide fords. Private enterprise was the answer. Hard working, creative pioneers succeeded where government money failed.

Steamer 'Far West' at Cow Island, 1880

Fort Benton 1860

Mackinaw Way Home to the States

Upper Little Prickly Pear Canyon

Entering the Sieben Ranch

The Pillars on Little Prickly Pear Canyon

The Old Road in Little Prickly Pear Canyon

Chapter III

Building the Toll Roads and Bridges

Two amazing entrepreneurs undertook a task that apparently was unthinkable to Lieutenant Mullan. The construction of a road within the nearly perpendicular walls of Little Prickly Pear Canyon was very doable to the likes of Warren C. Gillette and James King. These lifelong friends did not know the meaning of the word failure.

King and Gillette were not the first to envision such a project. Malcolm Clark and Edward A. Lewis, one of the earliest settlers of northern Montana, were granted a charter by the First Territorial Legislative Assembly, in the year 1864, to create the Little Prickly Pear Wagon Road Company.

AN ACT to incorporate the Little Prickly Pear Wagon Road Company.

Be it enacted by the Legislative Assembly of the Territory of Montana:

Sec. 1. That Malcolm Clark and E. Lewis, their legal associates and successors, are hereby constituted and declared a body politic and corporate, under the name and style of the Little Prickly Pear Wagon Road Company, and by that name may sue and be sued, plead and be impleaded, and may have a common seal which may be altered at pleasure.

Sec. 2. The line of said road shall commence at the Little Prickly Pear, running thence down said stream, avoiding the hills on what is known as the "Mullan Road," through Medicine Rock Canyon, and through the canyon below Lyon's Hill {Lyons Creek} on the said "Mullan Road."

Sec. 3. It shall be lawful for said corporation to acquire and hold all real estate necessary for the use of toll keepers, on line of said road, and for no other purpose whatsoever, and dispose

of and convey by deed, any real estate so used and occupied for the use of toll keepers on said road, whenever they shall deem it for the interest of said company to do so.

Sec. 4. Said corporation shall have power to make and afterwards to alter and change all needful rules and regulations government and management of said road; and shall elect a president, secretary and treasurer, at such time and place as the said corporation may agree upon; and annually thereafter to elect president, secretary and treasurer, who shall be shareholders in said company. Provided, however, that the said secretary treasurer may be united in one person, if deemed advisable by said corporation.

Sec. 5. Said corporation, by their agents, shall have power and authority for a term of ten years to collect toll, as hereinafter mentioned, from all persons traveling upon and over said road, wagons or vehicles of any sort, with horses, mules, asses, cattle, sheep or swine; and any person who shall pass any toll gate upon said road authorized to be erected and, established by said corporation, without first having paid toll, as required by this act, shall forfeit and pay for each and every offense the sum of twenty-five dollars, to be recovered by an action of debt by said corporation.

Sec. 6. In all recoveries had by said corporation, as provided in the last preceding section, one half of the sum so recovered shall be for the use of the informant, and the other half for the use of the county in which said toll gate may be situated; and it shall not be necessary to be stated, in the demand of the plaintiff, that the sum sued for as provided in the last preceding section, shall be stated for the use of the informant and said county, nor shall the interest of the informant in the recovery of the said one half of sum preclude him from testifying in the case, nor shall it preclude any citizen of the territory from so testifying on the part of plaintiff.

Sec. 7. There may be erected upon said road toll gates to the amount of two, and no more, at which gates respectively there may be collected, upon all wagons, vehicles, horses, mules, asses, cattle, sheep and swine, passing over said road, the following tolls and no more, viz: Upon each wagon or vehicle drawn by one span of horses, mules, or yoke of cattle, the sum of one dollar and fifty cents; upon each additional span of horses, mules, or cattle, the sum of twenty-five cents; upon each riding horse or mule the sum of fifteen cents; upon horses, mules, asses, and cattle driven loose, sum per head of twenty-five cents; upon pack animals, per head, the sum of fifteen cents; upon all sheep and swine driven over said road, the sum per head of three cents.

Sec. 8. Upon complaint being made to any justice of the peace in any county through which said road extends, that any portion of the road is not in reasonably good condition for the passage of wagons or vehicles, the said justice shall summon the gate keeper nearest the place on said road complained of, to appear before him a day certain, not more than five days from the day of complaint, a certain hour of the day to be by the justice fixed, and if it shall appear to the justice that the complaint is true, judgment shall be rendered against the said corporation, as defendant, for the date of the proceedings, and thereupon no tolls shall be collected by said gate keeper, so summoned, until the said road shall be put in good repair for the passage of wagons and vehicles.

Sec. 9. If any gate keeper shall demand and collect any tolls before the said road shall be repaired and made passable as provided in the section above recited, he shall forfeit and pay the sum of twenty-five dollars, which may be sued for by any person, for the use of the informant, before any justice of the county in which said gate keeper may reside. Provided however, that if by reason of high water or snow, it shall be impossible for any person with reasonable expense to repair said road, a reasonable time shall be allowed for repairing the same, before any judgment for costs shall be rendered against said corporation or said

Warren C. Gillette

gate keeper shall be restrained from collecting tolls, as provided in section eight of this act.

Sec. 10. This act shall take effect and be in force from and after its passage.

[Approved January 19, 1865.]

By summer of the year 1866, Clark and Lewis had sold their charter to King and Gillette who promptly went to work building the toll road.

Warren C. Gillette was born in Orleans County, New York, in 1832. He was described as a "Man of medium height, slender, light complexioned, and of quick, alert manner." Coming from a refined background, Gillette exhibited speech and bearing uncommon to the frontier west. Gillette died in Helena in 1912.

Fortunately, Gillette took the time in his later years to record some of his early Montana experiences. A portion of that autobiography as printed in the *Valley Tribune* newspaper of August 18, 1927, follows:

I was living in New York City in the spring of 1862, when I received a letter from James King of Galena, Ill, stating that a number of our friends had gone to Salmon River mines, Washington territory, by steamboat from St. Louis to Fort Benton, and thence overland to the diggings. He asked me if I would be willing to join him and go by the next boat, which would leave about the 1st of July. I immediately replied that I would be glad to go, and would meet him in St. Louis in time to make arrangements for the trip.

On my arrival in St. Louis, we proceeded to buy a span of mules, wagons, and provisions enough to last us a year. We did not get away until about the 12th of July. Joseph La Barge was the Captain until we arrived at St. Joseph, where we met the Boat Emile, returning from Fort Benton, where his brother, John La Barge, took his place. We learned from the passengers who came from up the river that mines had been discovered near Cottonwood, which is now called Deer Lodge, Montana, and on account of this news we added to our stock, more miners' supplies. At Sioux City, La Barge, Harkness & Co., who owned our boat, the "Shreveport" (and the Emile), had purchased horses to be taken on the boat, to be used in freighting goods to their destination, should they be unable to reach that point by water. These horses were to be loaded at Yankton that was several miles up the river. Captain La Barge kindly gave me permission to put my mules with them and to help drive the animals from Sioux City to that place.

In making this trip we crossed the Vermillion River and I was then deeply impressed with its beauty and the great fertility of its valley. At Yankton we put the stock, on board the steamer. The man who helped me drive the horses was a French half breed by the name of Juneau, a thorough frontiersman. At Fort Pierre we tied up for several hours. Major Vaughn was one of the passenger. He was formerly an Indian agent under President Buchanan, and had with him his Indian wife and child. Her relatives lived in the vicinity of Fort Pierre. It appears that the Major had purchased, at St. Joseph, for his wife an elegant silk, gown, brocaded with satin figures. She went on shore for a visit with her relatives, and with them went on a burying expedition attired in this gown. When she returned this garment was a sight to behold, and the Major, using language more forcible than polite, declared that hereafter she should be clad only in the regulation Indian blanket.

Excitement in Sioux Country

It being rather late in the season of navigation, we made slow progress, with frequent delays on sand bars and frequent stops for wood, at which times passengers readily assisted the roustabouts in gathering and loading; nevertheless, I remember that we enjoyed the trip. A day or two before we reached the mouth of the Yellowstone, we came upon an immense herd of buffalo. They approached the river from our right in one vast army, reaching far as we could see, and going out on the other side after swimming across. Our boat pressed through this living mass, which quickly closed behind us. The passengers shot down into this huddling herd until the river was red with blood. Three were secured and landed on board by the crew. We had some Indians on board, who, when the buffaloes were being dressed for the boat's use, procuring the offal, emptied the grass from the first stomach and ate the warm, raw tripe with evident relish.

Nothing of more than ordinary interest occurred until after we passed Fort Union, near the mouth of the Yellowstone River, for up to this time we had seen only friendly Indians, but now the Captain said we were in the Sioux country, and a stricter watch was kept when we tied to the bank at night. One morning, before we had left the bank, we were aroused by the cry of Indians. They were seen in a bend in the river a couple of miles below. The Captain had a barricade of boxes made upon the shore and sent a runner up the river to a camp of friendly Indians for assistance. The Sioux made signals by flashing the sunlight from their mirrors from the opposite cliffs. When the friendly Indians came, they were mounted on slick ponies; the men had on their war paint and war bonnets, and after a harangue from the chiefs, dashed off to where the hostile Indians had been seen. It was a fine sight, and looked much like war but two or three hours later they returned without any scalps, after driving the Sioux into the hills. In recognition of their valor, the Captain gave them a great feast, consisting of hard bread, coffee and sugar, with buffalo meat ad libitum.

We were unable to proceed above this place but a few miles, for the water seemed to lessen every day. Finally the Captain gave orders to pull ashore where there was an old stockade fort, and we were put ashore. Here the cargo was discharged and moved to the abandoned stockade. As soon as the Captain ascertained that we could proceed no further by water he dispatched an Indian runner to Fort Benton with an order for teams to help transport the Shreveport's cargo and passengers. Some of the passengers returned with him, having had enough of upper Missouri life. We met many mackinaw boats coming down from Fort Benton, carrying from three to five men each. These men had come from the Pacific coast, and they told us of the rich diggings there, and also of the prospecting on the Prickly Pear (near where Helena is now situated), which made us anxious to get along; so, after remaining at the old stockade about a week, we got Mr. Picotte, in whose charge the Captain had left the passengers and cargo, to take what teams we had and move on up the river, and not wait for the outfit from Fort Benton. One time, after several days travel, we made a camp near the mouth of Milk River, in a very level country, and nearby there was the largest aggregation of Indian lodges I had ever seen. There were several thousand Indians of different tribes. I remember the names of three only: Crows, Gros Ventres, and Assiniboine. I have forgotten what the object of this great council was. Femmisee (Sitting Woman), who was the head chief of the Gros Ventres, was there. He was very friendly to us. Here we had our first actual trouble.

Chief Femmisee Friendly

Some Indians came into our camp and tried to take our guns away from us and acted in an ugly manner. It appeared that the Indians were divided as to whether we should be permitted to go any farther through their country or not. The Chief, Femmisee, said that we could go through, but was opposed by the younger Indians. That evening our party took a vote as to whether we should move on next day or turn back. A majority voting to return, in the morning we headed for the old stockade, but after we had gone only a short distance several warriors rode up to our leading team with drawn guns and arrows strung, and compelled us to turn again in the direction of Fort Benton.

Mr. Picotte informed us afterwards that the Indians also had a council, and it had been decided that we were to go through, and that Chief Femmisee, in enforcing his authority, had shot and wounded one of the opposition. Mr. Picotte made many presents to the head men, and from this time on we had no more trouble, though we met many Indians. There were 15 white men in our party and several half-breeds. We took turns standing guard at night, making two watches: one from dark till midnight, the other from midnight till morning. After several days travel we met the company's teams from Fort Benton on their way to the stockade; they were in charge of Robert Lemon.

We reached Fort Benton without other important incident and made our headquarters at what was then styled Fort La Barge; an aggregation of log houses situated about three-fourths of a mile above the old Fort Benton, which was occupied by the American Fur Company and about a quarter of a mile above Fort Campbell, whose only occupants were Malcolm Clark and family.

Malcolm Clark and family would later play an important role in the development and history of the Benton Road.

A day or two after our arrival we awoke one morning to the sound of alarm, and saw a war party of Indians circling about in the bluffs to the west. At Fort La Barge all was excitement, a canon was brought and preparations for defense quickly made. This post was unfortified, while Fort Campbell and Fort Benton had walls of adobe with bastions and heavy gates. Clark sent up for someone to come to Fort Campbell to help him hold the Fort, and I was deputized for that duty; I got my gun and marched down. The heavy gate was opened and Mr. Clark welcomed me to his little garrison. The Indians, for most of the day, could be seen among the bluffs, but finally a parley was secured, presents were given and the war was over.

Christopher L. Payne, who was one of our party and had some goods to go over the mountains, bought some ponies and I broke them to harness and we waited a few days for him, as we wished to go together. During this time we heard that good diggings had been found on the Big Prickly Pear, and we left for that point, following the Capt. J. L. Fisk trail, whose expedition had preceded us about a month. Near the last of October we arrived at where is now located East Helena. Here we found several families who had come through with the Fisk Expedition, among whom was E. M. Dunphy.

Indians Demand Whisky

We made arrangements with Dunphy to go to Benton with four wagons with oxen for our goods and bring them to the Prickly Pear camp where we expected to winter. I preceded him on horseback, and on reaching Fort Benton, learned that no tidings of Lemon's train had been received. I kept on down the river and fortunately met him below the mouth of the Marias River after one day's travel from Fort Benton. Mr. Lemon reported that after leaving Milk River he encountered a party of Indians who demanded whisky and were very troublesome, cutting his harness and making threats of murdering the whole outfit. To escape them he took the heroic measure of rolling out a barrel of whisky and setting it on end; he knocked in the head and they were soon all dead drunk. While they were in this condition he pulled out his train, and rushing on night and day, he saw them no more.

Dunphy's wagon being loaded, we started back, leading behind one of the wagons a little black mare. This mare had been purchased off a half-breed at the Fort by Mr. Tingley, and he wanted me to take her to the camp on the Prickly Pear. Reaching Sun River, we found, four lodges of Blackfeet.

Here was stationed a government farmer who was teaching the Blackfeet Indians how to cultivate the soil. His name was Vail, and he had an interpreter who informed me that the chief of the Blackfeet camp said that the mare, which I was leading belonged to his squaw and he wanted me to give her up. I told him it was not my mare, that it had been entrusted to me and I could not do it. The Indian said that so far as he was concerned he did not care, but that it was a pet of his wife's; that she was crying and nothing but the mare would console her. I finally settled the matter by his giving me another horse, and I turned over the animal and one plug of tobacco. In the meantime the wagons had gone on and I followed an hour or two later on horseback, leading the new horse.

About 12 miles beyond Sun River, as I was riding slowly up a rocky hill, I heard a sound and, looking back, I saw an Indian on horseback within 20 feet of me and he was warning me of some danger, so I hurried on and overtaking the wagons, I informed the men of the incident, and when we went into camp, which was opposite the Bird Tail Mountain we deemed it wise to place the wagons in a square and, putting the horses inside, we slept on our guns that night, but had no trouble. The next night we camped on the Dearborn River.

The days since leaving Fort Benton had been beautiful, and when we retired to our blankets that evening the weather was mild, but in the morning we awoke to find ourselves covered with a foot of snow and the Dearborn River frozen over. We laid two days and nights and on the third day traveled to Wolf Creek, about 17 miles, when we found that the snow had all disappeared. The next day we passed over the hill into Prickly Pear Canyon, where there was the grave of a young man named Lyon[s], who had accidentally shot himself but a few week's before. He was buried where he died and a rough headboard gave an account of his death. This point was called then and is still known as Lyon's [Lyons] Hill.

Speculation has persisted to this day that it was Lieutenant Harlan Lyon from Mullan's crew who had been the namesake for Lyons Creek and Hill and that he had died while building the Mullan road and been buried on North Lyons Creek road. Supposedly, a stone, inscribed with the name J. P. Lyons, had been found and kept hidden for many years. We know today that Harlan Lyon not only survived until the twentieth century, but played a major role in the Civil War, fighting on the Confederate side.

Mr. J. P. Lyons the young man who really was buried along the road arrived on the steamer Spread Eagle on June 17, 1862. By July 11, of that year his group of emigrants was rounding the east side of today's Lyons Hill when he accidentally discharged his firearm creating a fatal wound in his body. In the diary of his fellow traveler and wagon partner, John O'Fallon Delaney, Lyons was noted as a merchant from St Joseph, Missouri who boarded the steamer there for the trip to the mines of Montana.

Prickly Pear Abandoned

The third day from Wolf Creek at Three-Mile Creek, which is three miles south of Silver City, we met Mr. King, accompanied by "Gold Tom." It appears that the camp on the Prickly Pear had been broken up and nearly all had moved out to go to Gold Creek and Bannock; so Mr. King had come to tell us to keep our wagons moving and to go over the Mullan Pass.

About the last of November we rolled into Deer Lodge. Here we stored our goods in one end of a building owned by A. Fall. In the meantime we purchased an unfinished building owned by C. A. Broadwater, who was living there then. It was there I first saw Kohn Kohrs. He had come to Cottonwood to buy some cattle of John Grant to be butchered in Bannack. For want of funds he was unable to buy more than three head, while a few years later his herds were counted by thousands. Also Capt. Nick Wall came up from Gold Creek on his way to the states. He had with him Thomas Levatta, a mountaineer whom he had hired as a guide, and was going by the way of Bannack and Salt Lake. Mr. King was induced to join him and I was left to sell our goods and send the dust down the river the coming spring.

As trade was dull in Cottonwood, I hired Dunphy to haul my goods to Bannack and put me up a cabin. It took about a week to make the trip going over the mountains and down the Big Hole River. The weather was clear, but cold, with no snow except upon the divide. We reached Bannack about the 20th of December. At Bannack I saw a rustling mining camp, with many saloons and gambling houses. Goods commanded astonishing prices.

I here met the Minnesota contingent, some mining, others keeping boarding houses, and all seeming to prosper. It took but a short time to dispose of the major part of the goods at a sound profit in gold dust. Knowing that I could obtain goods at Fort Benton, which I could pack over the mountains and sell at Bannack at a good profit, I left my place in charge of Warren Whitcher and started about the middle of February, 1863, on horseback with James Gourley for Fort Benton. This distance from Bannack to Fort Benton is about 300 miles, and we made the trip in eight days. Major Dawson was the manager of the American Fur Company at Fort Benton and Matthew Carroll and George Steel were his head men and did the trading.

Good Profit in Merchandise

This company had a large herd of horses which were kept up the Missouri River about 50 miles. They bought many of these horses very cheap for when a man got ready to go down the river it was the company's price or nothing. I bought 15 of these horses at from $30 to $40 each, and enough of such goods as were in demand in Bannack to load them. A good horse would easily carry 200 pounds. I hired a cook, for his board and passage, and returned to Bannack without accident. Tobacco, for which I paid $2.50 per pound sold for $10 and $12. Seven by nine window glass brought $1 per pane; other articles in proportion. The venture having proved so profitable I was soon on my way back to Fort Benton.

Henry Plummer gave me a letter for Miss O'Brien, who was the sister of the wife of I. A. Vail, the government farmer who lived at the crossing of the Sun River, so that when the pack train reached the river my men camped across from his house, and I went over to deliver the letter and on invitation I remained all night at the farm. In the morning one of my men came over and told me all of the horses had been stolen, which proved to be true, and Mr. Vail had only one horse left. It was a sore-backed sorrel that had been left in the corral over night, which I bought for $30, and started for Fort Benton, 60 miles away, to buy more horses in order to move my packs. After traveling 12 miles I left the river and took a trail up the hill, now known as Frozen Hill, and in a little hollow, I took off the saddle and picketed the horse that had been all night without food. I laid down intending to rest about an hour. As I was very tired I went to sleep. I could not tell how long I had slept when an Indian aroused me and, as I looked back down the road, I saw quite a large party of Indians coming up the trail. I hurried to my horse, quickly put on the saddle and rode on. The Indians left the trail on the top of the hill and bore off to the northwest to my great relief. I did not get into Benton until after daylight. There they told me that, from my description, the Indians I met were Little Dog, a Blackfeet Chief, and his band, and that Little Dog was a friend to the white men.

I told Major Dawson my trouble and that I wanted to buy some horses: he gave me a good horse to ride and sent me with "Buffalo Bill," whose name was William Keyser, to the horse herd. We forded the Missouri River where the city of Great Falls in now located, then went over the hill to where Paris Gibson's stock farm was later situated, and found the horses in charge of herders. After the roundup of the band I selected the horses I wanted and drove them up to where my packs were, crossing the Missouri where we forded it the day before. My men had recovered some of the stolen horses that had given out and were abandoned. The Indians who stole the horses were Shoshones or Snakes and had followed me from Bannack. They had killed one man near Square Butte who was employed by Mr. Vail as a hunter and his widow, a Blackfeet squaw, had cut off one of her fingers as an evidence of sorrow and was bewailing his death with loud cries, sitting with other women on the side of a hill. Taking another start, I got to Fort Benton, bought more goods, and returned to Bannack.

When Plummer Killed Cleveland

While I was in Bannack this time occurred the shooting of Jack Cleveland by Henry Plummer. He was shot in a saloon, which was opposite my place. I heard the shots, and going to the door I saw Plummer come out of the place with a pistol in his hand and walk with a friend down the street. I immediately went across to the saloon and saw Cleveland lying on the floor with a bullet hole in his cheek and surrounded by a string of men. He would raise himself on his elbow and mutter some words and then fall back. Someone in the crowd asked him if he had any friends. He said "Old Jack has no friends," when one of the crowd replied, "Yes, you have; you bet your life." He was shortly removed to a butcher shop, which was nearby and he lingered for a day or so and died. Plummer was tried and acquitted, as it was proven that Cleveland had said that "Plummer was his meat."

There were frequent rumors of robberies by road agents, and among trusted friends, men would be pointed out as belonging to such organizations, and that Henry Plummer was their leader. James Gourley once informed me that he had good reason to know that I was once followed, when on a trip to Fort Benton to buy goods, by three of Plummer's band who intended to rob me in the Sun River country, but that they were delayed on account of

losing their horses and did not reach that place until I was well on my way to Benton.

The weather during the whole winter and spring had been wonderfully fine, with only one or two snow storms. On my last trip to Benton that spring I carried considerable dust and some mail; letters coming from the states by the way of Walla Walla often costing from $1 to $2 each. When Oliver's express was started, letters from Salt Lake cost $1 each and newspapers 50 cents. The gold dust I carried was not all my own. I put the purses (buckskin) in an old carpet bag, which was put on the top of the pack on the back of one of the pack horses and securely lashed it. We proceeded along without any trouble until one morning at a camp on Willow Creek the horse carrying the dust became fractious and tried to buck off his pack. The dust, being so heavy, burst through the lining of the carpet bag and scattered the sacks of gold. After some little search we found all the purses and, taking care that such an occurrence should not happen again, I finally landed the treasure safely in the American Fur Company's safe.

Virginia City Wonderful Camp

Owing to the light snows in the mountain, the Missouri River was low and the steamer Shreveport, which carried the goods that Mr. King had purchased in the east, did not reach Fort Benton, and had to unload her freight at Cow Island, where she arrived about the last of June, 1863. Capt. Nick Wall of I. I. Roe & Co. of St. Louis, also had merchandise on this boat. Cow Island was inaccessible to wagons on account of the high bluffs without the construction of a road. So after waiting some time for La Barge to get the freight up to Benton, we made a contract with Wall to haul his goods to Virginia City in Alder Gulch (a newly discovered mining camp) for 30 cents per pound. We did not get this freight to its destination until the middle of November, hauling our own goods at the same time. This proved to be a wonderful camp. The times were good. It was a question of how much you should ask for what you had to sell, for gold dust was plentiful.

The next spring, 1864, I opened a new road to go to Fort Benton by the way of the Jefferson River, White Tail Deer, Boulder and Big Prickly Pear. Heretofore, wagons had to cross the main

Billing Slip for Toll Road

divide twice. C. A. Broadwater was the wagon master. I had about 25 teams and hired a hunter who kept the train supplied with game, which was principally antelope and deer. It took about a month to make a passable road for freight teams.

In the fall of that year, 1864, gold was discovered in Last Chance Gulch, and the goods which we shipped the next spring, 1865, were taken to Helena and Last Chance Gulch. We put up a store house here, and the coming spring, 1866, we bought of Malcolm Clark and Edward A. Lewis their charter for a toll road through the Little Prickly Pear Canyon. This road was finished in time for the travel from Fort Benton that season. Owing to the high price of labor and the rocky character of the canyon this road cost about $40,000, but as tolls were high also, it took only about two years to get it back. The charter of this road expired in 1875, and it now belongs to Lewis and Clark County.

Sells His Freight Trains

In the summer of 1865, I sold to Mr. Copeland for the I. I. Roe & Co. two freight trains of 24 wagons each and 200 head of oxen. That year Copeland had much freight put off near the mouth of Milk River on account of low water. This was the commencement of the Diamond "R" Freight Company. Cattle in those days varied much in price. Then ox teams brought freight all the way from Leavenworth, Kan., and St. Joseph, Mo., and the cattle lean, and with tender feet, would be often sold for $30 or $40 per yoke. A few months of rest and

feeding in the native grass, and they would treble in value.

As far as possible, merchants held their dust until the spring of the year and sent it down river in preference to having it go by stage coach by way of Salt Lake. I remember (I think it was in 1865) leaving Helena with $8,000 in dust to take to Fort, Benton. I carried it in canteens on the horn of my saddle. When I got to the Dearborn crossing, I found among others camped there for the noon, Malcolm Clark. He was traveling with a light spring wagon and he kindly consented to carry my canteens and lighten my load as the gold alone weighed over 40 pounds. He said he wanted to give his horses rest and would not start till late in the afternoon. I saddled up and went on and had gone about 18 miles when I saw some person ahead coming toward me driving a packed mule. He was going as fast as possible, whipping the mule continually. When we met I saw it was a man by the name of Soppick, whom I had known in Virginia City. He was much excited and told me that a runner (Joseph Kipp) had come to Sun River in the night, and that he had been sent from Fort Benton to warn all the travelers that there had been an uprising of the Indians, and that they killed 10 white men on the Marias River and were murdering all the white people they could find. Coppick said he would rather take chances with the road agents than the Indians, and that he would go back to the states by the way of Salt Lake. I tried to persuade him to turn and go on to Sun River with me, that it was only 12 miles away, and as there were several outfits camped there, would stand the Indians off. He said he had on his mule about $30,000 in dust, and he believed it would be safer to go the other way.

Murder Story Was True

I went on to the crossing of the Sun River, but kept a sharp lookout for the redskins all the while. I found there quite a large party of freighters who by arranging their wagons, were prepared for any surprise the Indians might make. During the night who should come into the camp but Coppick. It appears that Mr. Clark had persuaded him to put his gold into his wagon, and that, as they would travel at night, they might get through safely. We lay at this place all the next day and at night started for Fort Benton, getting there in the morning. We found that the story was true; that Barris, Angevin, and eight others who had been camped at the mouth of the Marias, were waylaid and all killed.

Up river freights that had been from 10 to 18 cents per pound came down in a few years to three, and wagon freights from Benton to Helena from six cents to one cent. Business conditions changed as gold and greenbacks were approaching equality in value, and goods purchased in the east were sometimes sold at a loss. I virtually went out of merchandise in 1869.

James King, on the other hand left little information concerning his experiences as a Montana pioneer except for the footnotes in Miller's *Illustrated History of the State of Montana*. We do know that he was born in Morrisburg, Canada in 1835 and in 1851 moved to Chicago, Illinois. Up to 1858, he worked for the Illinois Central Railroad and then for the wholesale dry-goods firm of Mills and Company. The 1860 census shows him living there with wife Elizabeth (Lunn) and child Walter. King was, at that point, working as a shoe merchant. In 1862, King joined Gillette in the adventure of a lifetime. The two journeyed from St. Louis to Fort Benton on the steamer Shreveport and after wandering around the various mining districts over the next few years ended up in Helena, a partner in the well known King and Gillette Freighting and Mercantile Enterprise. King's most significant accomplishment, beyond the construction of the Little Prickly Pear Wagon Road, was probably his presidency of the Montana

National Bank, which opened in 1872. By 1877, their partnership was dissolved. In the year 1876, King lost his wife, Elizabeth, while she was visiting in the city of Chicago.

The *Helena Tri-Weekly Republican* of July 26, 1866, printed the following information concerning the King and Gillette toll road:

Little Prickly Pear Canyon - Twenty-three miles from here is to be found one of the most beautiful passages of mountain scenery on the continent. The Little Prickly Pear River, after winding about distractedly in a small valley, seemingly hesitating whether or not it will attempt to overcome the mountainous barriers it finds in its path and pursue its way to the Missouri, suddenly becomes determined, and rushing to the very heart of the range before it cuts its way in rocky gorges through all obstacles, and rippling and foaming in its crystal strength, flows onward to join the great river of the Northwest.

In 1853, when the Mullan expedition passed through this country, they found the defile in all its primitive beauty. Upon one side of the rapid stream rose towers and battlements of solid rock, some of them presenting a bold and connected front, with overhanging parapets, and others standing detached, like solitary watch-towers, now deserted by the ancient giants that we may imagine to have lived amid the grandeurs of the Rocky Mountains, fit inhabitants of a region where all nature is developed in its most colossal proportions. On the opposite bank of the mountain river, rising like giant steps, one above the other, were immense masses of rock, approximately cubical in shape, and in many cases presenting the appearance of moldering tombs, in which the feudal lords of the castles near at hand had been sepulchered.

Throughout this giant cemetery, were thickly set the pine and fir trees, while the immediate banks of the stream were lined with quaking aspens and beautiful groves of cottonwoods. The sole inhabitants of this sylvan retreat were antelope, deer, and the sure footed mountain sheep, disturbed only occasionally by the adventuresome hunter. No Indian trail passed through the mountain pass, for the thick growth of timber as well as the general ruggedness of the surroundings prevented a Little Prickly Pear Canyon passage. The men under Lieutenant Mullan, at the time mentioned, cut down a few trees as if about to attempt the passage of the canyon, but even with appropriations from Congress to the amount of about $300,000 at their backs, preferred to content themselves with saying that more work would be required than the time at their command would allow, and to follow the old trail across the mountains, and by the Medicine Rock, where beads, arrowheads and bits of old trinkets marked the place of the Indians superstitious devotions and the boundary of the territory of the Blackfeet Nation.

One year ago we passed over this same trail, and looking down over the cliffs, wondered as to the scenery and hidden mysteries of the unexplored depths below. Our curiosity has been satisfied. A few days since, we paid a second visit to the locality. The cemetery of the giants was defiled and the castle walls frowned upon the desecraters. A passage way was hewn through the rocks and trees and constructed across the ravines and bogs at the bottom of the defile, and man looked up triumphant where before he looked down and acknowledged his own impotence. Thanks to the energy of Messrs. King and Gillette of this town, a wagon road had been built through a place, which it was supposed by many would forever remain impassable, this road is some six miles long and has, without doubt had more work done on it than has been bestowed upon the entire length of traveled way between Helena and Salt Lake. By the first Legislature a charter was granted for construction of a toll road through the pass in question.

This charter passed into the hands of King and Gillette, and in February last, they commenced building the road, which is now so far completed that trains are constantly passing over it, gladly paying the toll for the sake of saving one day in time and avoiding the horrible passage of the Lyons and Medicine Rock Hills. Upon this six miles of road there are two miles of cribbing, four bridges already constructed and five others to be built, and cuts throughout nearly its whole extent. When fully completed all the fords upon the Prickly Pear will be avoided. When it is understood that there are twenty-seven of these upon the old road and that as first projected, there would have been forty-eight crossings upon the new road, the great amount of work done

can be appreciated. There is only one point upon the road where the grade is as heavy as that upon Bridge Street, and that is only for a short distance.

Those that have passed over the Lyons and Medicine Rock Hills; and during two days of vexations, and momentary fears of having their teams dashed to the bottom, have blocked wheels and cursed oxen, will appreciate the new enterprise. The new road, besides avoiding mountains, is several miles shorter than the old one, and we predict will soon become entirely deserted and that the traveler will soon look up with as much wonderment to the tops of the surrounding and unfrequented peaks as he formerly looked down into the depths of the defile.

Messrs. King and Gillette have forty men still at work upon the new road, daily improving it and expect to have it in complete shape within a month. A glance at the traffic between here and Benton will show the importance to be attached to the undertaking, and at the same time serve as an excuse for having devoted so much space to the subject. On our last visit we were not out of sight of a train between Helena and the canyon, and could easily believe the statement of one of our oldest freighters that on a recent flying trip to Benton, he counted 1,500 teams upon the road. It is estimated that during this summer, not less than 2,500 teams with 20,000 oxen and 3,000 men have been employed in the freighting business upon the Benton Road. This being the case, the enormous outlay made by the proprietors of the Benton Canyon Toll Road bids fair to prove a profitable investment.

Depending on which report you might believe, King and Gillette spent between $40,000 and $150,000 in building the Toll Road. They seemed to have recovered the sum expended within two years of the road's opening. Users were said to be happy to pay the toll in lieu of crossing the mountains.

King and Gillette certainly solved the problem of travel between Helena and Fort Benton. Being freighters themselves, they well understood the problems involved in crossing significant hills and the solution available by following the course of the Little Prickly Pear Creek. What they might have overlooked was the resulting increase in competition once a more viable road was completed. According to Gillette, the drop in price per pound for hauling freight between those two places led them to go out of the freighting business and eventually out of merchandising altogether.

Within a few years even their personal relationship was undergoing changes. Although they both resided under the same roof in 1870, by March 24, 1877, they dissolved their long standing partnership and within a few months were engrossed in a series of civil suits. Ultimately, Gillette dropped his case and paid all the costs for both sides.

Gillette then went into the sheep business at Dearborn. The *Helena Independent* newspaper of June 18, 1878, carried the following item of interest:

Indian Highwaymen

The report was brought here yesterday by passengers on the Benton coach that Mr. W. C. Gillette, while going to his sheep herd on the Dearborn, was overtaken by two Indians, who robbed him of a fine chronometer, valued at $400, a fine saddle and all the money in his pockets. The Indians said they were Sioux, and nothing further is known of them.

James King held interest in and became superintendent of a gold placer mine at Diamond City, Montana Territory. According to the 1880 census, King was a resident at the Diamond City Hotel. Diamond City was the mining camp for the mines at Confederate Gulch, fifteen miles from Townsend, Montana. The census of 1910 shows King as a resident of Los Angeles, living with his daughter Laura B. King, who was then forty-five years of age. King died in 1911 in that city.

By 1875, Lewis and Clark County had taken over the King and Gillette Toll Road and were searching for contractors to repair the bridges. As of April 2, 1875, they had rejected three bids offered for the repair work.

Upper Little Prickly Pear Canyon Toll Road

Another toll road through the Upper Little Prickly Pear Canyon, from just below Silver City to the Clark Ranch, was created by Nicholas Hilger, Billy Johns, and another man whose name we do not know.

The Board of Supervisors for Lewis and Clark County at their meeting of November 2, 1869, recorded the following.

Upon petition numerously signed by citizens of Lewis and Clark County, it was ordered that the Little Prickly Pear and Silver Creek Toll Road Co. be granted a permit to establish a toll road as follows: Commencing at a point known and designated as the outlet or mouth of the canyon on Silver Creek at the place where said Silver Creek enters into the Valley of the Big Prickly Pear, running thence up and through said canyon and along the said Silver Creek to a point about three-fourths of a mile below the Town of Silver City thence in a direct line or as near as is practical to the entrance of the canyon just below the Ranch known as "Buffalo Bill's Ranch" [now Chevaler Ranch]on the Little Prickly Pear Creek, running thence down said canyon to King and Gillette's Toll Road at the ranch known as "Clarks' Ranch" [now Sieben Ranch] on the Little Prickly Pear Creek.

Provided the establishment of such road shall in no manner conflict with any right heretofore acquired by any person or persons whomsoever and provided further that the Board shall have the right to establish the rates of toll on such road when completed.

At the meeting of the same Board on February 8, 1870, a report was read by the chairman of a committee, which had been assigned the task of inspecting the nearly completed toll road and recommending tolls for it.

On the fourth day of February, A.D. 1870, we passed over the line of the road from near Silver City to Clark's Ranch and after an examination of the bridges, road bed and grades made by said company all of which are completed, except the lower grade, which will be completed in a few days, and around which they have opened a road for the present use of the public, we would state that the road is in good condition and safe for all kinds of vehicles to pass over and that the said road was built where there was no natural road and does not interfere with any public road but avoids the heavy grades of the old Fort Benton Road.

This road the company states cost over six thousand dollars and from the amount of work done, we are satisfied that the above estimate is correct. We would further recommend that the said company be allowed to establish one toll gate at a convenient point on said road and collect the following rates of toll:

> For one span of horses, mules or oxen and one wagon....$1.00
>
> For each additional span or yoke over one.... .35
>
> Each trail wagon.... .30
>
> Each horse and rider.... .25
>
> Each head of lose work stock.... .10
>
> All other loose stock, each head.... .05
>
> All of which is respectfully submitted:
> >   H. W. English
> >   T. VanGosh
> >   W. S. Baker

According to the census of 1870, Billy Johns is listed as a "toll gate keeper."

Nicholas Hilger's daughter, Mary Hilger Dougherty, left an undated piece on her family entitled "In and Out of Montana." In it she discusses her father's construction of the toll road from the Fergus Ranch to Helena along with several other events of interest. Her narrative also covers some aspects of their trip from Minnesota to Montana Territory.

Their adventure began in the summer of 1867, at a point eighty miles northwest of Fort Wadsworth, North Dakota. The wagon train consisted of nearly 300 wagons conveying twenty-four families with thirty to forty children and 160 single men. Captain Davy was their leader.

We pick up her narrative as they neared Helena, Montana Territory, their final destination.

We were now nearing our destination, Helena. Most of the emigrants went on to Oregon over the Mullan Trail. Some of them were stranded in the Coeur d'Alens. Their cattle gave out, some of the people got sick and the government hearing of their plight sent relief. Instead of driving into Helena we stayed on a ranch in [Upper Little] Prickly Pear Canyon near, Silver [Silver City.] It was called "The Priests' Ranch" as it was owned by the Jesuit Priests of Helena and it was there that we lived our first year in Montana. Father Minetry often stopped there on his way to St. Peter's Mission. He brought us children a

lamb. Sheep were very scarce in Montana in those days. We were so delighted, he was such a frisky little play fellow having no toys and playthings like children of today we were easily satisfied. There was a little calf that my brother David trained to pull a large box. He was soon strong enough to draw us all and we soon had a trail to [a] knoll and made ourselves a fort to hide from Indians if they should appear. We were a happy bunch with the lamb frisking along. We spent our first Christmas there and we were wondering if Santa Claus would find us there. When our good friend Father Minetry came along a few days before we asked him about it and with a merry twinkle in his eye he said, if he didn't see old Santa himself he would leave word with the good Sisters at St. Peter's Mission so we wouldn't be forgotten. And he came along on Christmas Eve. Mother had trimmed a lovely tree for us and while it didn't have candles or glittering ornaments she made birds and animals and stars out of cookie dough and it looked beautiful to us, and there seemed to be a mysterious air about the place. Mother also prepared a cabin for a chapel where Father Minetry said Mass early the next morning at which we all attended and after that we got our gifts and were as happy as children could possibly be. In Father's package there was a prayer book for David and Rosary Beads for Susan. Because I had learned to sew there was a thimble and little scissors and the two smaller girls got dolls and a pretty dress for the baby. That Christmas stands out in my memory as the best of all.

The only neighbor my mother had was an Indian woman who was married to a white man, but she was a kind and thrifty woman and made a good wife, and she was so neighborly. She insisted on making moccasins for us children and some of them were ornamented with beads. Mother often sent her nice things she cooked and she helped mother when she or any of us were sick. We all liked her. Being an Indian didn't seem to make any difference. Mother said she was the best neighbor she ever had.

All our cooking was done in a big fireplace. Big kettles were hung on hooks directly over the fire but the baking was done on the hearth in Dutch ovens. Mother understood the method wonderfully. Live coals were heaped around the sides and on the top and replaced with a shovel as they cooled. She seemed to know just how long to gauge the baking. Bread took the longest to bake thoroughly and she also accomplished pies, cakes, biscuits, and cookies. I can still taste the delicious wild chicken or grouse, ducks and rabbits she roasted in those Dutch ovens. We had lots of milk, butter, and eggs. The vitamin lore wasn't in existence then, people naturally knew what food was good, and what was not. We all kept reasonably well and grew up strong and healthy. One commodity we did not have was lamps and kerosene. Our lights were home made candles. Not a bit of tallow was wasted. It was rendered and clarified and poured in frames for that purpose to harden. I used to watch mother thread the tubes, six in a bunch, with wick that was fastened across the open top of the tube and run through a tiny pointed opening at the bottom. It wasn't an even light but answered the purpose until we moved to Helena.

One day in spring us four older children decided to take a long walk and do a little exploring. Mother cautioned us about the creek that ran into Prickly Pear which was pretty swift and deep in places. We took a lunch. The time passed so quickly and we were so interested before we were aware of it the sun was getting low. David said we can't go back the way we came as it would be dark before we reached home and then we remembered about bears having been seen along the creek and as the stream made a big bend, by crossing it we would soon be home. We began to look for a crossing and found where a big tree had fallen across [the creek]. It was rather high at the opposite side, where we would have to make a jump to the bank. David climbed on to the log and took Louisa on his back and made it safely and Susan who was sure footed followed and when I got on the log I was afraid of the swift water running below and called out that I would fall as it made me dizzy. I was told to straddle the log, which I did, and slowly worked ahead. I was about half way when my skirt caught on a snag and I could not move and I cried out in terror. My guardian angel must have had a task keeping me from losing my hold. I don't know what might have happened if my father had not appeared on the scene and taken me across. We were so glad he found us but he did give us a lecture that we never forgot. As we realized how easily I might have drowned.

An Indian Scare

Father used to go to Helena occasionally for groceries and supplies and would be gone several days. One evening, while he was away, the Indians began riding up and down past the ranch just as fast as their ponies could run and occasionally let out a war whoop. Mother knew that something had happened to arouse them and she prepared to spend a night of terror. She and David barricaded the doors and windows. The rest of us children were put to bed and Mother prayed with us. The chasing kept up far into the night. I could not sleep as I heard my mother and brother whispering as they peeked out of the windows. The Indians left toward morning after they had stolen a couple of horses. I have often thought of the anguish my mother endured that night. The next day Father got back and he was mighty glad that the Indians were satisfied with their plunder and did not molest us or burn our cabins, but he decided then to move to Helena just as soon as he could make arrangements.

While we still lived at that ranch Father discovered a route to Helena which would make it much shorter as it cut out a long grade over a mountain. He kept it in mind and intended later, with help, to build a new road. And now we were ready to leave the Priests' Ranch. Us children were very sad about leaving our lamb, which had grown to full size, and our bully, grown big then too, and we never saw them again.

Helena

So it was in the fall of 1868, we first moved there and it was not much more than a mining camp then. The business part was on Main St. and part of Clore. There was a school house about where the present court house stands. It seemed to me that all ages and sizes went there. Four of us children started to school as soon as we were settled. Father became. interested in mines and mining but soon interested two men to go in with him to build the short cut from "Johns" [actually, all the way from Fergus' Ranch to just below Silver City] to Helena. He was out there most of the tine until it was finished. They built many bridges and did much grading along the [Little] Prickly Pear Creek, and as it was a private piece of construction it was a toll road. One of the partners whose name was Johns built a house at the gate and with his family kept the station, collected the fares and served meals to travelers. Later on the government bought the road and the station to this day it is called "Johns". After that Father resumed placer mining operations as he owned land east of Dry Gulch, which is now Davis Street, and from 5th to 7th Ave. inclusive. The ground was mined with hydraulics hose.

Helena had its first disastrous fire soon after we moved there which left the greater part of Main Street in ruins. It was in 1869, on Oct. 10, that the first Sisters of Charity from Leavenworth, Kansas arrived in Helena to open a school and later on a hospital. As soon as the building was completed we were among the first pupils of St. Vincent's Academy and I can safely say that in years to follow we helped wear down Catholic Hill going to and from school. We children had never seen Sisters before but we soon learned to love those pioneer Sisters and as we grew older we realized what hardships those fine women endured. But with toil, patience, and cheerfulness they won out. And beautiful St. Vincent's and Sisters of today may well be thankful for the courage of its founders. At that time Father VanCorp was in charge of the Catholic Congregation and Mission of Helena. We knew him well. He was such a gentlemanly scholar and wonderful speaker and had scores of friends among all denominations. Later on he exchanged places with Father Paladino of St. Ignatius near Missoula. He was in charge at Helena for many years.

It was in 1870, that my Father had some cabins moved from Montana City which had seen a mining boom before Last Chance but now it was deserted and most of the cabins moved to Helena. And our first home was built from some of them. Ours was the first dwelling east of Dry Gulch on ten lots facing north on 6th Avenue and as it was we were living in the suburbs. And we could and did keep cows and chickens and had a big garden. I don't know where the strawberry, gooseberry, and currant sets came from but everything thrived as there was an irrigating ditch near by. In 1870, Father was elected and served with credit for two terms as probate judge for Lewis and Clark County. He spoke and was conversant in several languages which was a valuable assistance in the discharge of his duties especially in probate handling of estates with

other countries. He gained the reputation of dealing out justice where it was due. In one case two hard characters were given a jail sentence. They declared they would get even and tried later on. During those times there were a number of lynching's that took place. The only one I saw one morning we were going to school and saw a crowd around Hangman's Tree and saw two bodies hanging from it. We had heard the story of how the night before two men had followed a rancher who had sold a load of products and he had treated the crowd and exhibited a purse of money at a saloon. The temptation was too great. They immediately rented two horses and followed the rancher and in a lonely place, where he was unaware, rose up on either side and slugged and robbed him and left him for dead. Soon after he was found and given medical aid and revived. He remembered seeing, a pinto horse that one man rode and by that they were caught and hanged on April 26, 1870. This hanging was done by the Vigilantes who were law abiding men forced to protect their lives and property from a number of ruffians and deep dyed criminals who entered Montana during the gold rush. Their greed for another's hard earnings was the cause of wholesale robberies and murder. And it was this state of affairs which brought about the forming of the Vigilantes, and those same gold and blood thirsty demons got their just dues. The names of those particular men I saw hanging were Mac Compton and Joe Wilson. The accompanying picture of Hangman's Tree was taken by Helena's first woman photographer. On that particular occasion she got my brother David to carry her tripod. There were no taxies those days. She promised David she would take his picture, which she did, and he is the lone boy in the foreground. This hanging made a lasting impression on us children, more so because we used to see those men in their blacksmith shop on our way to school every morning. That tree was not so far from our house, three blocks south on the same side of the gulch. It was cut down later and we were glad to lose sight of it.

About this time one day, when I came home from school and stepped in, I saw my father and a man whom I recognized as Henry Brooks, a miner, and friend of our family each carrying an armful of baking powder cans. They just smiled and proceeded down a trap door going to the cellar. I looked surprised and Mother put her finger to her lips and said "sh..." and then told me Mr. Brooks brought his gold dust from his placer diggings near Marysville and was storing it in our cellar until he could ship it out of the country safely and Mother made me promise not to say a word to anyone as some robbers might break in and steal the gold. I was afraid and uneasy until it was removed. I imagined every noise or creak I heard at night might be robbers. Men who owned or worked placer ground had to be on the watch, especially when they made a clean up of their sluices. Road agents were continually watching to make a haul. Mr. Brooks and Brother later located in Fergus County and were some of the pioneers there.

In 1872, I recall very clearly Helena's first earthquake. In our early geographies the pictures of earthquakes were very crudely demonstrated with big openings in the earth and houses and people tumbling in. Just to look at it made me shudder, however, I reasoned childlike that those things happened in far distant lands and not in Montana and so this quake was our first experience in that line and I will write what I remember about it. My sisters and I were attending school at St. Vincent's Academy. One class was being dismissed from an upstairs recreation room. We were going downstairs in double file when we felt the building tremble. The Sister in charge realized immediately what it was. She raised her hand for attention and said "Stand still, there is an earthquake let us pray." She made the sign of the cross and said a short prayer and it was all over before we had time to cry or become frightened. The original St. Vincent's was frame and as far as I know no damage was done. When we got home mother was outside talking to some neighbors. We told her that we had felt an earthquake and she told us of her experience. She was sitting at her sewing machine and the younger children were playing around her. At first when the sewing machine moved away she thought it was from a jolt from one of the children. She moved her chair closer and it kept moving, which frightened her and she took the children and ran outside and that was all we or my sisters knew about it. This quake took place in 1872 and it left no impression of fear. In the years to follow we never dreamed that an earthquake calamity could befall Helena. In

1873, Father bought the famous Hilger Ranch at the Gate of the Mountains on the Missouri River eighteen miles north of Helena. It was one of the first ranches taken up when Father was Clerk and Recorder in 1865. The original locator was Horace Clark and it is on a historic site as the famous explorers Lewis and Clark camped there. It had changed hands but once when we bought it and until it became a pleasure resort was enjoyed by our family during the summer months. On both sides of the river game was plentiful and during the game season we always had our share of deer, antelope, and mountain sheep. My brother David was a real hunter and the younger brothers soon took up the sport and delighted in camping on the trail. Father had cattle in those days and put up tons of hay. My oldest sister and I often went out and helped our men cook during haying. Every chance I got I would be out in the meadows raking hay with a gentle mare and sulky rake. My brother David was father's right hand man in those days and when he was not at school would be on the range with the men.

Helena's 2nd Disastrous Fire

In 1874, during a furious gale upper Main and Wood Streets was leveled to the ground. Cinders and flaming shingles were carried and started fires in different parts of the city and everybody was busy putting out fires on their own premises. Father nearly lost his life in that fire. He had offices in the same building as the Toole Bros. Lawyers. He saw that the fire was heading in that direction and immediately began carrying, valuable books and records connected with the Probate Office and storing then in the fire proof cellar. He finished rescuing his valuables and as the Tooles were away at Virginia City trying some cases he undertook to save their books. He made trips back and forth and was about to leave the building. The fire had undermined and the floor broke through. He caught onto two rafters and shouted for help. Others near by rushed to his rescue and not a minute too soon as he was about overcome with smoke. This fire was the means of building better and fireproof buildings and procuring better apparatus to fight future fires.

Miller's *Illustrated History of the Sate of Montana* gives added insight into the man, Nicholas Hilger.

Nicholas Hilger

NICHOLAS HILGER, a highly honored citizen of Lewis and Clark County, Montana, is a native of Luxemburg, Germany; born October 28, 1831, of German ancestry. His father's name was Daniel Hilger, his and mother's maiden name was Susana Evert.

Mr. Hilger acquired his earlier education at the state schools of Luxemburg, continuing in school there until his removal from that place in 1847, at which time the entire family, comprising of his parents, grandmother, brothers and sisters, emigrated to the United States, the great mecca of enterprising people from the old world. On arrival in America the family first located at Buffalo, New York, where they remained resident until 1857. The Father, although in the old country he was a machinist and wine manufacturer, after settling in Buffalo purchased a farm near the city and engaged in agricultural pursuits. In 1854, young Hilger removed to St. Paul, Minnesota, but after a short time settled at Henderson, that state, where he was soon appointed Justice of the Peace for the district in which he resided. To this office he was afterward elected, and after that again he obtained a position in the United States Land Office. After filling this position for a time he accepted a position in the Census Department of the Territory, preparatory to its admission into the Union as a state. After completing his duties in that relation he was elected County Auditor, and he served in that responsible capacity for three consecutive terms, namely, from 1857 to 1864; and while he was serving in this office he was elected Captain of a regiment of the State Militia, which office he held until the year 1864, when he resigned to join a train then starting across the plains for the great west. This train afterward joined the Sully Expedition, which was then sent against the Sioux Indians. Following the course taken by this expedition the party arrived at Helena on the twenty-seventh day of September, 1864. At this time Last Chance Gulch had not reached the zenith of development, and Mr. Hilger and others passed on to Montana City, which was then the county seat of Jefferson County, where they remained during part of the ensuing winter. While there Mr. Hilger was appointed the first Deputy Recorder for Edgerton County, by H. H. Eastman, the Recorder of the county. Mr. Hilger served in this office until June 1, 1865, and then returned to Minnesota for his family. After being delayed in that State for some time by his business interests, he at length returned overland to Montana, with his family, in 1867, since which time he has been a resident of this state. During this period he has served as Justice of the Peace and as Probate Judge for several terms, and also, during this time, he purchased his present home and farm on the Missouri River, and began to engage in the rearing of livestock. This departure proved successful, and Mr. Hilger is now one of the solid and prosperous farmers of Missouri Valley.

It was in the year of 1857, that Mr. Hilger was married, taking for his wife Miss Susannah Moersch, of Minnesota, and they have had ten children, eight of whom are still living, —four sons and four daughters—and several of these are married and have children.

Mr. Hilger is still hale and hearty and an active business man. For a number of years he has run a pleasure boat from his hospitable ranch to the Gates of the Mountains on the Missouri River. The trip to that point is one of the most beautiful in the west.

Hilger's partner in construction and operation of the toll road, William "Billy" Johns was also remembered in Miller's work.

WILLIAM JOHNS, a farmer of Little Prickly Pear Valley, was born in Germany, October 15, 1835. He received his education in his native land, but after reaching manhood came to the United States, landing in New York in 1856. He afterward began his career as a farmer near Chicago, receiving $7 per month and board, and remained in Illinois three years. During the Pike's Peak excitement Mr. Johns crossed the plains with ox teams to that place, where he mined for two and a half years, and received from $1.50 to $2 a day and board. In the fall of 1863 he located in Bannack City, Montana, and three weeks later went to Virginia City, arriving there during the trial and hanging of the road agents. In the spring of 1865, Mr. Johns engaged in freighting between Helena, Fort Benton and the different mining camps, also purchased and hauled salt from Salt Lake City to Helena, for which he paid seven cents a pound and received seventy cents per pound. Five years later he assisted in building the toll road in the Little Prickly Pear Valley, managed the same for seven years, and then preempted 160 acres of land where he now resides. In addition to his farming interests, Mr. Johns kept the stage station until the railroad was built, and since that time has been engaged in raising cattle and horses on a large free range near his farm. He raises a grade of Durham cattle, of which he keeps about 600 head, and also has both work and road horses. In 1891, he built a good frame residence on his place and has piped good spring water through his house, milk house, and barns. Mr. Johns was married October 11, 1866, to Miss Margaret Hoffelt, a native of this country but of German descent. To this union was born four children–Annie L., David F.,

William J., and Florence. The wife and mother died in 1879, and March 16, 1880, our subject was united in marriage with Miss Elizabeth Wallendorf. Socially, Mr. Johns is a member of the I. O. O. F. and the A. O. U. W., and, politically, he supports the Republican Party. He takes a deep interest in the welfare of Montana, of which he is a worthy citizen and an honored one.

Toll Bridges

In addition to the many bridges constructed by King and Gillette; and Hilger and Johns across the Little Prickly Pear on their respective toll roads, the Dearborn and Sun River crossing were also graced by toll bridges constructed by local inhabitants.

Evan J. Thomas, keeper of the Dearborn stage stop built a stone bridge across the Dearborn River and charged $1.00 per team to cross. It was rumored that some days, in spring time, when the river was running high, he would take in $100 a day in toll charges.

In 1867, John Largent and John J. Healy constructed a toll bridge of wood at Sun River Crossing. Largent lived on the Lewis and Clark County side while Healy resided in Choteau County. Coincidentally, they each ran stores and hotels on their respective sides of Sun River. The bridge replaced a ferry which had been operated by Healy.

In 1868, another toll bridge was built across the Sun River near Sun River Leavings. By 1870, a third toll bridge was added near the Churchill Ranch. Neither of the two latter bridges earned enough money to keep them in repair and were eventually abandoned and then destroyed by ice and high water.

Sun River Toll Bridge and House

Missouri River below Fort Benton

Missouri River from the Fort Benton Levee

Lime Kilns above Last Chance Gulch

Miners Cabin on Main Street in Helena

Chapter IV

Supplying the Mines

The Benton Road took one heck of a beating from the freight wagons that moved supplies and equipment from the river boat terminus at Fort Benton to the mines near Helena and beyond. It seems incredible that in 1866, from the first landings of the steamers in spring, until the docks were empty in the fall, an estimated 2,500 freight wagons, pulled by 20,000 oxen, and led by 3,000 men, traversed the just completed road from Fort Benton to the Helena area.

The *Montana Post* for February 3, 1866, stated that after the completion of the King and Gillette Toll Road "Freight next season can be laid down at Helena from Fort Benton in from five to seven days and for much less than it has heretofore cost; besides, the road will be as available in winter as in summer. The discovery of gold to the north will then tend to make Fort Benton, or its vicinity, the great depot of supplies for the territory, while the natural position of Helena will make it the distribution center."

Helen Sanders' *History of Montana* supplies us with the following insight into early freighting in Montana.

As the miners were distant from Benton, from about 150 to 250 miles, a large wagon transportation was demanded and sprang into existence. In 1865, John J. Roe and Captain Nick Wall organized the great Diamond "R", train, which they sold to Messrs. Carroll and Steele and MaClay and Broadwater in 1870. Then Garrison and Wyatt, Baker and Brothers, Henry A. Shodde, W. S. Bullard, Hugh Kirkendall and a score of smaller freighters covered the roads leading from Benton with their wagons, distributing to the mines the freights discharged from the steamboats, and for a time, owing to the limited means of transportation compared with its needs, commanded their own terms, and some times received as high as ten cents a pound in gold for the 140 miles from Fort Benton to Helena. But this did not continue for long, for in a short time freighters were plenty on the road. A. K. McClure wrote in 1867: "Just now the territory is drained of one million greenbacks to pay freights."

Bull Train

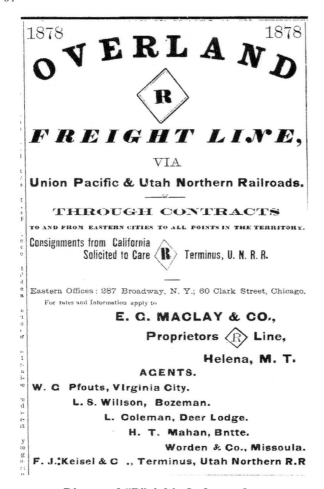

Diamond "R" Ad in **Independent**

There were numerous freighters that traveled the Benton Road. Three of the most important were, the Diamond "R", the Montana Freight Line, and I. G. Baker and Co.

Another freight line which started small in the early 1860s, but became more important with the advent of the railroad in Helena, is that which belonged to Hugh Kirkendall.

Histories of the Freight Lines

The Judith Basin County Press provided an article for the Montana Newspaper Association insert of January 18, 1937, which tells us much about the Diamond "R" freight line.

THE DIAMOND "R" Transportation Co., the biggest mule and bull team freighting outfit that ever operated in Montana came as the result of the suggestion of a 19-year-old Virginia City bookkeeper to his employer, that the latter place a number of mules, oxen and wagons which had been turned in to him by creditors in payment of their accounts; on the road

I. G. Baker Ad in **Independent**

freighting in an effort to make them pay for their winter's feed, instead of the owner having to feed them at a dead loss.

The suggestion was made by Ed G. MaClay, who, in November, 1863, arrived In Virginia City from St. Louis in company with Capt. Nick Wall, an early day merchant of that place who had become a member of the Missouri contracting and merchandising firm of John J. Roe & Co., of St. Louis, and who at the time was representing that concern in Montana.

MaClay had hot been long on the job when he discovered the dead weight of livestock and vehicles that were being carried on his books.

Murphy and Neel Ad in **Independent**

He called Wall's attention to the fact that they had a lot of livestock. "What are you going to do with it?" he asked.

Wall scratched his head. He himself had started as a merchant in a log shack at

Hugh Kirkendall Ad in **Independent**

Virginia City and had become affluent through his own efforts.

It was already well into the winter when MaClay made the proposal to start a freighting outfit and it took some time to make the necessary arrangements, but in April, 1864, they were ready to operate, and in that month the first load was hauled by the Diamond "R". The, "R" in the brand stood for Roe. So far as can be ascertained, there was no particular reason for putting the diamond around it except to make the trademark more outstanding.

Became Large Outfit

From that modest start, the Diamond "R" grew into an outfit which at the period of its greatest prosperity, just before the advent of the railroads in Montana, owned 350 mules, 500 yoke of oxen, scores of wagons, besides saddles, harness and buildings valued at more than a quarter of a million dollars. The first load hauled consisted of merchandise and hides. The merchandise was taken to Helena for Major Boyce and Colonel Vawter, then doing business in Last Chance Gulch, and the hides were hauled on to Fort Benton, from where they were shipped down the Missouri river by steamboat.

The Diamond "R" did not take on formidable proportions until a year or two later, when lines were established connecting Missoula, Fort Benton, Virginia City, Helena, Bowman, Deer Lodge (then Cottonwood) and Walla Walla, Wash., touching at Idaho points along the way.

When, in 1869, the Union Pacific railroad was completed connecting the Atlantic and Pacific seaboards by rail, the influence of the Diamond "R". Transportation Co. began to be felt all over the west. A route was established from Corinne, Utah, to Montana points. The completion of the Union Pacific sounded the death knell of river transportation to and from Montana. It continued, however, until 1882, but in constantly, diminishing volume. After that year the business was small and cared for mostly by boats which the government kept in commission.

Montana points could obtain goods and merchandise from the east much quicker and easier by having them sent to Corinne, by rail, and freighted from here, than they could by having them sent to Fort Benton by boat and then transferred to the freight wagons.

Hauled Helena's First Piano

The first piano in Helena was hauled into that city on a dead ax wagon by the Diamond "R". It carried the first church organ to Bowman and the first silks brought to this state were freighted in by it. In 1866, it hauled into Helena the first church bell that city had, that of the First Methodist Church, of which the pastor was Brother Van Anda. One night the church burned and the bell cracked in the fall from the bell tower.

Charlie Conrad and Frank Bateman lugged it out, of the ruins and hung it in the fire watch tower which for many years overlooked the town from the promontory between Wood Street and Broadway. The bell was later remove to Great Falls, but to what end is not known.

When on one of its trips, a long delayed freight train pulled up where the Lewis and Clark County Courthouse now stands in Helena, it carried a 25 horsepower engine which had been shipped from Philadelphia to the National Exploring and Mining Co., Unionville, four miles south of Helena. For years that engine supplied power to run the stamps at the mill of the Union mine, it was the first engine in Lewis and Clark County, although the year before two small engines were freighted through the town from Fort Benton, both of them consigned to the Hope Mine at Philipsburg, which had the first stamp mill of any consequence in the state.

In the summer of 1871, several weeks passed without the arrival of a train in Helena. Groceries were getting low and prices were advancing accordingly. One day a schoolboy who had been sent in the direction of Montana City to hunt for a cow that had strayed, returned and said he had seen in the distance a big bull train coming toward the camp.

Daniel Searles, later editor of the old *Butte Miner*, was teaching school in the "academy," located where Renig's store afterward stood, when the news reached him. He dismissed school and the children as well as all the townspeople were on hand to welcome the bull train when it reached the city.

Delay Due to Drunken Party

The price of tobacco dropped and a sugar and coffee famine were forestalled by the arrival of the train. The delay of the train, it developed was due to the fact that the bullwhackers got on a big drunk at Corinne, and refused to leave that place, despite the entreaties of the wagon boss. It was a month before he could induce the half-dozen bullwhackers with him to take up their bull whips and start on the trail northward to Montana. Nor could he hire anyone to take their place. The whole town was enjoying the party.

He finally won the argument by rolling a barrel of whisky into one of the wagons, tapping it, and telling the boys that it would go along with them on the homeward trip. Progress was slow until the barrel was emptied. Many of the bullwhackers and muleskinners that worked for the Diamond "R", by the way, had the firm's brand tattooed on their arms or some part of their bodies. It was also stamped of every wagon, canvas cover, wagon bow, harness, saddle, and animal owned by the company.

Remnants Scattered Over State

For years after the Diamond "R" went out of business there could be found on ranches in every part of the state; saddles, harness, wagons and all sort, of equipment which had belonged to the concern and which were sold when it was dissolved.

In 1868, MaClay, George Steele and Matt Carroll bought from Nick Wall and Roe & Co. the entire equipment of the Diamond "R". Headquarters were established at Helena, to

Matthew Carroll

Charles A. Broadwater

which point MaClay had moved several years before. Although the brand was retained, the company was officially known as E. G. MaClay & Co.

It not only enlarged its freighting operations, but maintained an information bureau, which gave out facts and figures relative to opportunities existing in the state in regard to business mining and stock raising. It also did what it could to bring new settlers into the territory.

At that time the general superintendent of lines was Col. C. A. Broadwater, who in 1883 founded the Montana National Bank at Helena and built the famous Broadwater Hotel and natatorium a few miles out of the capital city and for many years one of the most fashionable resorts, in the northwest. It cost $700,000.

Born in St. Charles, Mo., in 1840, Broadwater went from his home state to Colorado in 1861, and came to Virginia City in 1863, engaging in freighting. He at first handled a pack train for King & Gillette, later entering the employ of the Diamond "R" as its general superintendent.

When MaClay and his associates took over the Diamond "R", they retained Broadwater as

superintendent. He later became a partner in the company, continuing as such until 1879. By this time the construction of the Utah & Northern from Ogden to Butte, and the building of the Northern Pacific into eastern Montana had begun to make tremendous inroads into the business of the Diamond "R".

Reaped Profits

Broadwater saw an opportunity in military and railroad contracting and purchased much of the new surplus Diamond "R" equipment with which to engage in that line of work. One of his first jobs was supplying material for the construction of Fort Assnniboine on a six months time limit. He took a similar contract when Fort Maginnis was built in Fergus County, and made a big profit on the job.

Colonel Broadwater also became the leading partner in trading posts that were established at both forts. At Fort Assinnboine he was associated with C. L. McCullough, later vice president and cashier of the Montana National Bank at Helena. At Fort Maginis he was associated with C. J. McNamara.

Broadwater, who had been made Montana manager and representative of the Great Northern Railroad, which James J. Hill was building across the state, was also made president of the company organized by Hill to construct the Montana Central from Havre to Butte. Broadwater did much contracting on the building of the Great Northern.

Colonel Broadwater acquired banking interests at Great Falls and Neihart and was a heavy stockholder in the Great Falls original townsite company. At the time of his death he also had mining and cattle interests in many parts of the state. Tom Marlow, president of the Montana National Bank in Helena, a nephew of Colonel Broadwater, was appointed executor of his estate after McCullough resigned following two years of service in that capacity.

With the advent of the Northern Pacific and Utah & Northern Railroads into Montana the Diamond "R" Transportation Co. went out, of business. It gave up the ghost in 1881, six years before the Great Northern reached the state. During the years it operated it was an important factor in the development and settlement of Montana. The transportation methods of that day were crude, but the Diamond "R" had the best there was and it was organized, operated, and directed by men who were real pioneers.

Among the wagon bosses who worked for the Diamond "R" were: Simon Pepin, afterwards associated with Broadwater in the stock business in Chouteau County; Jim Adams, later a stockman near Cascade; and Robert Chestnut after whom Chestnut Valley near Cascade was named.

On April 22, 1876, the *Helena Independent* ran this article:

Montana Freight Line

Their promises to be lively competition in the freighting business this summer. Messrs. Murphy, Neel & Co., of this city, and owners of the Montana Freight Line, have arranged with the Northern Pacific Railroad and the reliable Coulson Line, of steamers from Bismarck, and will enter into through contracts to and from eastern cities to all points in the territory on very favorable terms. The satisfaction that shippers in past seasons have received at the hands of the Northern Pacific Railroad, and the splendid Coulson steamers, is again promised to shippers by the Montana Freight Line, Murphy, Neel & Co., fine mule and ox trains

will run in connection with steamers at Benton, and having the capacity of carrying 400,000 lbs. a trip, is a guarantee that freight will be forwarded promptly and expeditiously. Special inducements will be given for ores, base iron, wool, etc. The advertisement of the Montana Freight Line will appear in the next issue of the *INDEPENDENT*.

I. G. Baker

John G. Lepley in his article "Fort Benton's I. G. Baker - First of the Free Traders," which was printed in the *Montana Magazine of the Northern Rockies* for November–December, 1978, provides us with some insight into the company's freighting operation.

The I. G. Baker and Brother Company began in Fort Benton in 1864, as an Indian trading company. Isaac Baker had taken in his brother, George A. Baker to head the St. Louis office. They would trade goods to the Indians in return for hides and furs which would then be shipped down river to St. Louis for distribution in the states.

Early in the company's existence, Isaac brought his new wife to Ft. Benton, housing her in a splendid [for its day] two room adobe house located next door to his store on Front Street. The couple's daughter was born in that house, but shortly thereafter the town became too dangerous for his wife and child, so, the brothers swapped cities. Isaac went to St. Louis while George came to Fort Benton.

In the mid 1870s I. G. Baker and Company entered the freighting business. Lepley states that "From early spring until late fall they employed nearly a hundred bullwhackers and muleskinners and owned more than 500 yoke of oxen and several hundred mules."

Although their principle freighting was to Canada in the north, in the year 1877 alone they moved 4,648 tons of freight valued at $1,394,000. In that same year 50,000 buffalo robes and $1,000,000 in ore were shipped downstream.

Between 1879, and 1880, the robe trade virtually came to a halt with the number going down the Missouri dropping from 20,000 to 500. Arrival of the railroads spelled doom for merchants who had prospered so well at Fort Benton. The

Missouri was no longer the principle route for goods coming to Montana.

Freight Line Operators

From Joaquin Miller's *Illustrated History of the State of Montana* we glean information on the following early day freight operators.

William L. Bullard was born in the state of Virginia, July 26, 1812, and in the Old Dominion he was reared and married, the lady of his choice being Miss Annie F. Burruss, whose birth occurred there, March 26, 1815. Mr. Bullard emigrated with his family to Missouri, in 1838, and in La Fayette County he engaged in the manufacture of agricultural implements. To him belongs the distinction of having established the first foundry in Kansas City. He continued to reside in Kansas City, until 1860, when be removed to Buchanan County, same state. From 1861 to 1863, inclusive, he was engaged in freighting between St. Joseph, Missouri, and the Black Hills. In 1864, he removed with a part of his family to Montana, his family at that time consisting of his wife and four sons; Oscar M., Walter S., William F. and Massena. Oscar, his oldest son, was then in the Black Hills. This journey was made in one of their freight trains, the wagons being loaded with merchandise and drawn by oxen. They reached Virginia City in September, and remained there until Christmas, he in the meantime continuing his freighting between that point and Salt Lake City. The family spent some time in the Gallatin and Prickly Pear Valleys, camping in the latter valley in April, 1865. During the winter of 1864–5, Mr. Bullard had the misfortune to lose all of his freight oxen, except one, they having been snowed in on the Snake River, and died there. He then settled down on a farm, and while he continued freighting, his good wife did what she could on the farm. Produce of every kind was high. She purchased $69 worth of potatoes, at thirty-three and a third cents per pound; cut the eyes from them for seed, and then sold the hearts for seventy-five cents per pound, and made a profit of $40, on the transaction; she planted the seed and raised a crop that brought her $1,500. One particularly fine potato sold for $1. Every hill of potato crop was like so much pure gold to them. Bullard continued freighting up to the time of his death, which occurred December 24, 1868. His wife still survives him, being now in her eightieth year. She is a faithful member of the Christian Church, as also was her worthy husband, he having had the honor of freighting into the county, free of charge, the first Protestant Church bell.

EDGAR GLEIM MaClay, one of Montana's pioneers of 1863, and a pioneer merchant of Great Falls, was born near Johnstown, Westmoreland County, Pennsylvania, August 26, 1844, and traces his lineage to the clan MaClay of the highlands of Scotland, one of Scotland's most noted clans. The first of the family to come to America was Charles MaClay, in 1635, who settled in the Keystone State, where eight generations of the family have since been born, and where Mr. MaClay's father, John MaClay, was born, in September, 1792.

Mr. E. G. MaClay, of this sketch, the ninth of eleven children, was educated in the common school at St. Louis. In 1863, at the age of nineteen years, he came to Montana, with Captain N. Wall, a member of the firm of John J. Roe & Company, who were sending a stock of goods to Montana; and Mr. MaClay accompanied the expedition as its bookkeeper. They arrived at Virginia City, November 1, 1863, and opened a store.

After a residence of three years at Virginia City, Mr. MaClay moved with the firm to Helena. In 1868, he was one of the three gentlemen who bought out the firm, and the following year Mr. Broadwater became a member of the firm, and, in addition to merchandising, they did a large freighting business to Bozeman, Missoula, Deer Lodge, Helena and all the military posts in the territory. In 1881, Mr. MaClay sold out to his partner, Mr. Broadwater, and remained out of business for a year, in which time he made a trip east to improve his health. He then returned to Helena and formed a partnership with J. T. Murphy, Sam Neel and Dr. W. W. Higgins, opening a general merchandise store at Fort Benton. Mr. Neel died in 1882, and Mr. Murphy purchased the interest of Dr. Higgins, and the firm name became Murphy, MaClay & Company, in which form it has since continued. They continued the business at Fort Benton, meeting with satisfactory success.

In 1884, when the city of Great Falls was started, they opened a branch establishment there, that being the first general store in the town. The business at Great Falls increased so rapidly that in 1886, they decided to consolidate the whole business at Great Falls. In 1893, they disposed of the general stock and embarked in the hardware trade exclusively, in which they now carry a large stock and enjoy a successful business. Mr. MaClay has also been engaged in lumbering, with Ira Myers as partner, is one of the owners of the Diamond "R" mines at Neihart, and has other investments. When the Great Falls National Bank was organized he became one of the first stockholders, and was elected vice president, which position he has since held. In company with Paris Gibson, Ira Myers and others, he formed the Great Falls Water Company, which now furnish the city with an excellent water system. Indeed, he has aided in all other enterprises which have had for their object the improvement and advancement of the city of his choice, and so has acquired the reputation of being one of her most successful, public-spirited and enterprising citizens.

In 1882, he married Miss Blanche Murphy, a cousin of his partner and a daughter of Joseph Murphy, now of Montana. Mr. and Mrs. MaClay have had three children, one of whom they lost by death in its infancy. The living are: Theodora J. and Edgar G., Jr.

Mr. MaClay's political affiliations have always been Democratic, but he has never sought office, preferring to give his whole attention to his business interests, in which he has met with earned success.

John T. Murphy was reared to farm life in Missouri and received his education there. In 1859, when seventeen years of age, he started out in life on his own responsibility, coming as far west as Colorado, and there securing employment as a clerk. In 1860, he went to Nevada City, Colorado, and engaged in business on his own account. He conducted a general merchandise business there for a year and a half. Then he sold out and engaged in the wagon transfer business. In 1864, he came to Virginia City, Montana, with a wagon train of merchandise, and after selling out he returned to Nebraska City, Nebraska. The following spring he loaded a wagon train with merchandise, also shipped goods by steamer on the Missouri River, and brought all to Helena, where he opened a store July 1, 1865. His stock brought good prices in gold dust, and

John T. Murphy

he did a prosperous and remunerative business. As his trade and capital increased he established several branch stores, and conducted a successful mercantile business until the fall of 1890, when he disposed of his business in Helena. He is still, however, interested in merchandising at Great Falls. He had not been long in Helena until he discovered that there was money to be made in the stock business, and he has all these years been more or less interested in raising sheep and cattle. In 1890, he became one of the organizers of the Helena National Bank, and was elected its president. He was also one of the organizers of the Montana Savings Bank, and one of its directors. After the death of Col. C. A. Broadwater, president of the Montana National Bank, the directors looked about for a suitable financier to succeed him, and after much thought and the due exercise of judgment in the matter, John T. Murphy was selected as the man best adapted for the important position. He therefore resigned the presidency of the Helena National Bank and entered upon the duties of the presidency of this great financial institution, for which by large experience it is conceded he is so admirably fitted.

In 1871, Mr. Murphy was married to Miss Elizabeth T. Morton, a native of Clay County, Missouri, and the daughter of William Morton. They have four children, all natives of Montana, their names being: William M., Francis D., Addie M., and John T., Jr. They reside in one of Helena's beautiful homes.

Mr. Murphy is in politics, a Democrat, but politics has only claimed enough of his attention to enable him to vote intelligently, which is the duty of every good citizen. He has during his long business career in Helena made a most enviable record, and few men in the state are held in higher esteem than he.

Hugh Kirkendall from *Progressive Men of the State of Montana.*

A life of signal usefulness and exalted honor was merged into the immortal when death set its seal upon the mortal lips of Hugh Kirkendall, one of the pioneers of Montana and long one of the sterling citizens and business men of Helena, where he maintained his home for a long term of years. He was born in Allegheny County, Pa., on December 21, 1835, the son of Andrew and Nancy (McCreary) Kirkendall, both of whom were natives of the Keystone state and of German and Irish lineage. They were among the early settlers of northwestern Pennsylvania, where the father was a pioneer farmer and where they reared their seven children.

Hugh Kirkendall, the oldest child of his parents, in connection with active labor on the farm had instruction in the primitive public school of the neighborhood and then served a three years apprenticeship at the carpenter trade, becoming a capable artisan and receiving for his services as an apprentice the sum of seventy-five cents and a suit of clothes. Fully realizing that he must be the artificer of his own fortunes, Mr. Kirkendall gave prompt evidence of his self-reliant spirit by setting out for the west. He followed his trade in Missouri and Kansas, and early in 1858, entered the employ of the federal government, accompanying Col. Rollins and a party of government engineers to the far west to locate the headwaters of the Yellowstone River. Thus, he made his first visit to Montana, though the

territory was then Idaho. He remained in this country nearly two years and returned eastward in the government service under Gen. Wilson, manager of transportation, and was stationed at Fort Leavenworth, Kan. During the Civil War Mr. Kirkendall was in charge of the quartermaster's department, was at Fort Scott during the fight there, and later was sent to the battlefield at Springfield, Mo., arriving the second day after the conflict, and taking charge of the wagon train. He was an able officer, true to duty and showing self-abnegation and bravery. He remained in the employment of the United States until the war closed and then outfitted for Montana, bringing with him a stock of groceries. He came by the Bozeman route to Virginia City, and thence to Helena late in 1866. He purchased land on the east side of Last Chance Gulch, built the log structure yet standing at the corner of Ewing Street and Sixth Avenue and here conducted trade during the winter. From that time until the close of his life, Helena was his home, and his affectionate interest in the welfare and advancement of the city never flagged and was manifested by the earnest aid and cooperation he gave every worthy project. During his second trip to Montana his party had several conflicts with the Indians, but repelled the attacks.

In 1867, Mr. Kirkendall took a government contract to deliver supplies to the army posts and Indian agencies and held it for several years in connection with contracting for supplies. He also, under another contract, erected Forts Ellis, Missoula and Shaw. In 1877, when occurred the trouble with the Indians under Chief Joseph, he was manager of transportation for Gen. Gibbons, and after the memorable battle of Big Hole was assigned to bury the dead and care for the wounded, taking the latter to the hospital at Fort Shaw. Mr. Kirkendall for a time engaged in freighting between Fort Benton and Bannack, and from Corinne, Utah; to Helena. He was a man of great energy and business capacity, and his varied operations gave him a wide acquaintance among the pioneers and government representatives. He finally made contracting his sole business and aided as a contractor in the building of the Montana Central Railroad. The last contract work he accomplished was the installation of the large dynamos at Canyon Ferry and railroad work in the Big Bend country, and at the Cascade

Mountains on the main line of the Great Northern Railroad. He was also one of the firm of Larson, Keith & Co., who built the road from Helena to Butte for the Great Northern and constructed a number of other lines in Montana and Washington for the same company. He also raised highbred horses, owning a valuable ranch in the northwest part of Helena, and later owned ranch property in the Prickly Pear Valley, contiguous to the city.

In politics Mr. Kirkendall gave allegiance to the Republican party, and fraternally lie was identified with Morning Star Lodge No. 5, A. F. & A. M., of Helena; Helena Chapter No. 2, R. A. M.; Helena Commandery No. 2, K. T.; and Algeria Temple of the Mystic Shrine. He was also a member of Capital Lodge No. 2, A. O. U. W., while he was prominently concerned with the organization of the Montana Pioneer Society. On Easter morning, April 18, 1897, this honored pioneer passed away after a brief illness, unable to rally from an attack of pneumonia. His death caused universal bereavement in his home city, while throughout the northwest many who had known this brave and lovable man felt his loss. He was a man of loyal friendships and was true to all of his ideals. On January 26, 1862, Mr. Kirkendall and Miss Isabella Jeffrey, of Leavenworth, Kan., were married. She was born in Ashland County, Ohio, in 1839, the daughter of Alexander and Isabella (McCardy) Jeffrey, both of whom were natives of Scotland, whence they came to the United States in 1835, locating in Ohio and later removing to Leavenworth, Kan., where they passed their lives, dying at the ages of seventy-three and seventy-six years. Mrs. Kirkendall and four children survive the husband and father, the children being: Thomas B., who was associated with his father in business and now city treasurer of Helena, Nettie E., Bessie B., and Clara L. Mrs. Kirkendall is a member of the Baptist Church.

Freighters and the Indians

Freight trains in Montana were always an open invitation to Indian raiders. The Blackfeet-Piegans and later on the Nez Perces raised havoc with freighters on the roads as well as at the depots. Freighting on the Benton Road was not without its risks. The oxen, horses, or mules were always fair game for the ever hungry Indians. The enormous value of livestock in that day prompted many freighters to do whatever had to be done to retrieve lost or stolen animals. Hugh Kirkendall in 1869, experienced such a loss and went to inordinate lengths to find compensation for his missing mules. Ultimately, a day in court resolved the issue, almost to his satisfaction. Testimony by Kirkendall's wagon master to the Court of Claims for the December Term 1896, described the event.

MARTIN DONOVAN Testimony:

I have lived in Montana since the year 1866 except six or seven years; have been engaged as a teamster in 1869, I was wagon master for the claimant. About the 14th of December [1869], as near as I can recollect, I was camped on the Dearborn River with Kirkendall's train of 30 mules and one horse, they were a very fine lot of mules and were worth from $250 to $300 apiece. They were run off that night by the Blackfeet Indians. We followed the train for quite a number of miles, 10 or 12, and I went to Fort Shaw and reported the matter to the commanding officer, and I telegraphed to Mr. Kirkendall at Helena. The Indians were supposed to be at peace.

Mr. Kirkendall employed me to go north with a trading party known as Hamilton and Healy and try to recover the mules. I went there and stayed there all winter. I do not know whether it was in this country or in the British Possessions. It was on a stream known as the Belly River. I had very poor luck in getting any of the mules back. We found the mules up there and offered to pay the Indians for them if they would bring then in. I think we got three head. We offered to pay for them because we could not get them in any other way. I stayed there from sometime in January to along about the first of April. We offered no reward, but the pay was to be whatever they asked in trade.

Under Cross Examination:

I did not use any precaution because I did not suppose that there was any danger from the Indians. When we camped at Dearborn Crossing, the mules were allowed to roam. I drove them down to the water and stayed with them until dark. Came back to the camp, ate supper and went to bed and found the next morning that the mules were gone. I had no reason to expect danger from the Indians at that place; there had been no depredations in the vicinity that we had heard of.

Interesting testimony considering the widely publicized slaying of Malcolm Clark in August of that same year. Clark was murdered less than twenty-five miles south at his ranch on the Little Prickly Pear Creek.

On September 29, 1878, The *Helena Independent* reported an attack by the Nez Perce Indians on the depot at Cow Island, about fifty miles east of Fort Benton on the Missouri River. When the river boats could not make it all the way to Fort Benton, due to low water, they would discharge their freight at Cow Island.

INDIAN NEWS

Fifty Tons of Freight Destroyed by the Nez Perces.

Two Citizens Seriously Wounded in a Fight at Cow Island, [*Benton Record Extra.*]

BENTON, Sept. 25.—The Nez Perces crossed at Cow Island on the 23. They attempted to approach the rifle pits in a friendly manner, but were ordered off by the detachment in charge of the freight. They attacked the rifle pits at sundown making seven charges, and continued the fight until 10 o'clock the next morning. They then drew off and are now probably on Milk River.

The Indians burned the freight pile on Sunday night. There were 30 tons of government and 20 tons of private freight destroyed.

Col. Clendennin and citizens Weimer and Walter were at the Island and took part in the fight. Weimer and Walter were seriously wounded.

All the trains, as far as heard from, are safe.

The Benton parties arrived at the Island on the 24th, at 6 p. m.

LATER.

FORT BENTON, September 26, 1877. Murphy, Neel & Co., Helena.

GENTLEMEN: The Nez Perces attacked the rifle pits at Cow Island on Sunday, the 23d inst., and the fight lasted until 10 o'clock on the morning of the 24th. Twelve soldiers and four citizens were in the pits. No one was killed, but two of the citizens were seriously wounded.

The Indians burned 30 tons of government freight and what private freight was there, which we think was only four or five tons.

Ilges got to Cow Island at 8 o'clock on the evening of the 23d, just after the Indians left, and would follow sharply at daylight in the morning.

Cooper and Farmer's train, with four ladies and Dr. Brown, of Fort Shaw, had left Cow Island on Saturday morning, the 22d, and it is feared the whole outfit is taken in.

The Indians numbered about 300 warriors, 500 in all, with about 1,000 horses.

Yours in haste,
WM. H. TODD.

Another report came out on October 3.

A letter was received by T. C. Power Co., last evening, dated at Benton on the 30th, which says that, Fred Barker and Ed Bradley were killed by the Indians when Barker's train was attacked recently. Farmer & Cooper went to look for their cattle and have not since been heard of. Mr. Barker was well known in Helena, and was father-in-law to Gus Senieur.

By October 4, more information was available.

THE COW ISLAND OUTRAGE

Fred Barker the Only Man Killed.

From letters received here last night by E. G. MaClay & Co. and Gus Senieur from Cow Island, we gather the following particulars: The Indians crossed the river in three parties—above, below and at the Island. They destroyed all the freight that they did not want, except about ten tons of iron, steel, nails, etc. They numbered about four hundred. They cut loose and sent adrift all the boats and skiffs, except one that happened to be on shore, The Silver City will land her freight at Carroll, or at the point where Captain Kirtland's company is stationed.

The following are the facts in regard to the killing of Fred Barker. His train, together with Cooper and Farmer's, was encamped on Cow Creek, about two mile; above Cow Island, and the Indians camped about one mile above them, but did not offer to molest them. After dark, fearing that the Indians might come upon them in the night, the men took to the hills with their blankets, where they slept. In the morning they all returned to the train and cooked their

Gus Senieur

breakfast. Cooper and Farmer started after the cattle and passed through the Indian camp, but concluded not to drive them through the camp, but around it. As they were leaving the train Mr. Barker said he would follow them as soon as he ate his breakfast. When he finished his breakfast he started on horseback with another man on foot, but as soon as they got to the Indian camp they concluded it would be safer to go back to the train. Three Indians accompanied Barker on the return, while the other man made a cut off by crossing the creek. After Barker had rode a short distance, one of the Indians dropped behind, fired and shot Barker in the back, and the others fired upon him as he made for the brush. Cooper saved all the cattle of both trains. Mr. Cooper's letter says nothing about the wagons being destroyed, and it may be they were saved.

A report was issued from Fort Shaw on October 6th and printed in the *Helena Independent* on the 9th.

FIGHT WITH THE INDIANS

Seventeen Nez Perces Killed and Forty Wounded.

GENERAL MILES CAPTURES SIX HUNDRED HORSES.

Two Officers and Twenty-two Men Killed.

[SPECIAL TO THE *INDEPENDENT.*]

FORT SHAW, M. T. Oct. 6, 1877.

General Miles surprised the Nez Perce camp near the Bear Paw Mountains, on the 30th of September, killing 17, including Looking Glass, Joseph's brother, and three other chiefs, and wounded 40. He also captured 600 ponies. He has the Indians now closely invested. General Miles' loss in killed are Captain Hale and Lieutenant Biddle, 7th Cavalry, and 22 men. The wounded are Captain Mayhew and Captain Godfrey, 7th Cavalry, Lieutenants Baird and Romeyn, 5th Infantry, and 40 men. None of the officers wounded are dangerously so. Miles says these Indians fight more desperately than any he ever saw.

John Gibbon, Col. 7th Inf.

A closure report, at least for that current year, came out in the *Helena Independent* on October 11, 1878.

THE END OF THE MARCH

The most remarkable of wanderings recorded in modern times has just been ended. We refer to that of Joseph and his band of Nez Perces. After they left Clearwater, Idaho, and until their capture, they traversed a distance of over twelve hundred miles over the worst country on the continent, and all this time were pursued and harassed by from one to three armies, each of which was larger than their own. The band was hampered with women and children and a very large number of horses, yet notwithstanding all these hindrances they succeeded in eluding their pursuers, and even in outgeneraling those who sought to cut them off. They passed entirely around the settled portions of the territory, and, strange to say, the amount of injury done to settlers has been trifling. While smarting under severe chastisement they committed perhaps a dozen murders, but it was in their power to have committed hundreds and to have driven off thousands of head of stock, and why they did not do so will probably always remain a mystery. They even treated the prisoners they took in the most humane manner, not even offering indignity to females. Joseph has shown the most remarkable generalship that has been witnessed during the century, save in the last days of his travels, and then his prudence seems to have deserted him. He crossed the Missouri four or five days in advance of General Miles, and why he permitted the latter to overtake him is the most singular part of the whole affair as he could have kept on three or four days longer and been upon British soil and out of harm's way. This remarkable march will place him among the most notable of the red men and his deeds will be remembered so long as our history lasts. It is probable that the remnants of the band who escaped will join other tribes and their identity be lost forever.

What will be done with Joseph and his band is uncertain, but it is more than likely that the women, children, and warriors will be put upon some reservation and the chiefs sent to Florida. But we trust that Joseph will be treated the same as the rest of his tribe. That he has committed grievous wrongs we know, but certain it is that he has done many things that no other Indian would have done—spared the lives of his captors. His tribe has been severely punished and is now thoroughly subdued, and nothing can be gained by making a frightful example of the noblest warrior the Indian tribes have produced.

The following year a sad note appeared in the *Helena Independent* for February 15, 1879.

A RUNAWAY SON

One of the Victims of Nez Perce War.

Edmund Bradley an Assumed Name

In the list of the killed in an engagement between United States forces and the Nez Perce Indians last summer there appeared the name of Edmund Bradley, of Fort Benton, and it has just been ascertained that this was the son of a gentleman named Richardson, who removed to New Haven from Norwich. The son left some eight or ten years ago on account of some slight error, and until last September there was no trace of him. The Norwich Bulletin says that Mr. and Mrs. Richardson were both of them persons of fine taste and feelings and highly respected. Parental love and solicitude had been unusually vigilant to trace the boy, but the only clue ascertained was that simple announcement in the death-list. A letter written by Capt. Constant Williams, of the 7th Infantry, to Edmund Bradley Richardson, described the appearance of the young man, which was identical with that of the missing son, and added further, that one of his friends tells me that he had several times seen him write the name of Edmund Bradley Richardson, New Haven, Conn., and that Bradley told him that before he left home his knee was badly injured and that he was cured by Dr. Sweet, who came front a distance to attend him. The letter added the details of a severe fight with the Indians, in which Bradley perished bravely fighting, shot through the head. A later letter informs the parents of evidences of a careful education observed in the young man, which struck those who met him and that he was always a welcome visitor at his captain's tent. *The Fort Benton Record* of Dec. 13 states that young Bradley, as he was called, having been exhumed and brought to that town, was buried with military honors on the 8th of that month.

The Dangers of Freighting

The Montana News Association's Insert for September 30, 1935, relates the story of a freight outfit that was blown to pieces, authored by Al H. Wilkens, who knew the story first hand.

The scenes of the early steamboat and freighting days at old Fort Benton are still being reflected through the minds of a very few sturdy old-timers who are still living and have seen and gone through many trying ordeals that the present generation will never experience. The danger, privation and exposure that the early trailblazer was subjected to would fill the pages of a mighty book.

There are but a few of the people of the early seventies left to tell their stories of the past. Some are still able to rehearse their past experiences; some are past that stage.

It was my good fortune to meet and mix with many of the pioneers of Montana 61 years ago. I was a boy then, but was carrying a Winchester to protect my scalp at that early age. Father owned a freight outfit, consisting of two 10-mule teams. Freighting was a profitable business those days. The first steamboats plying the upper Missouri usually arrived at Fort Benton about the tenth of June, this being the only resource of freight. The place took on new life and activity. I usually rode on the spring cattle roundups and rode the range in the fall, but during the summer season I ran my father's freight teams. It was while I was freighting that I became acquainted with the Emerson brothers. They owned and operated four 10-mule teams on the northern road.

I found the Emersons to be very agreeable men and their drivers likewise were splendid fellows. I believe it was the summer of 1881 that we traveled most of the season together. The Emersons kept a night herder whose duty it was to take the stock to good feed and herd them until morning, when they were driven back to camp. In this way there was no time lost hunting stock and the animals were much safer. While we were traveling together my mules were night herded with the Emerson stock, and when I wanted to help pay the night herder they would simply say, "Forget it, kid."

I well remember the fateful trip together when we loaded out at the steamboat wharf at Fort Benton. I was loaded with furniture for the A. P. Curtin Company of Helena, and the Emersons for a Missoula firm. One of the Emerson teams was loaded with black powder and giant powder. This was a very dangerous cargo, but Ben Topp [Evan C. Shipley], the driver, was a carefree lad and didn't seem to realize his danger, and many times jokingly stated that he could have a blowout any time he wanted to.

My team was the first one behind Topp's [Shipley's]. All went well until we reached Helena and the Emersons went on to Missoula. This fateful morning I seemed to have a presentiment, and warned Topp [Shipley] to be careful. We had just got our cargo unloaded in Helena when word came in that the whole Emerson train had been blown to atoms. This was a great shock to the little mining town of Helena. Many of the town people rushed out to the scene of the explosion, which was eight miles out on the Missoula road.

We rushed into camp, threw off the harness and I mounted my saddle horse and struck out for the scene of the terrible blast. Before I reached the spot, however, I met John [James] Emerson driving one of his teams [hitched] to a freight wagon, and in it he had the charred remains of Topp [Shipley] and John's [James'] brother, Tip [William], who was badly shaken up by the explosion. John [James] told me in haste to go on and help his other driver in any way I could. He was rushing his brother to a doctor.

About half a mile further on I came to the spot where 10,000 pounds of powder had been exploded. I beheld a sight that would be hard to describe. While the first report had been greatly exaggerated, to the effect that the entire train had been blown up, still, it was a dreadful sight to look upon. There were only fragments of the sturdy freight wagons, while five of the mules were laying here and there, with parts of their harness still hanging to them. They, with their driver, had pulled their last hill; they had crossed the Great Divide. The fourth driver and night herder were walking from place to place, hardly conscious of what they were doing. Five of the mules of the ill-fated team recovered, or partly so. Parts of the wagons were found a full quarter of a mile from where the explosion took place. When the two men in charge got quieted down they told in detail all they knew about the affair. They said there was no warning; the first they knew of it they felt a terrific jar. Looking back, all they could see was a cloud of earth and smoke that seemed to reach to the sky, and they could hear the cries of Topp [Shipley], hollering for them to catch him. This he kept up till he died a few minutes later.

We laid over a day to pay our last respects to Topp [Shipley], who was laid to rest in the Helena cemetery. The next day we visited Tip [William] Emerson in the hospital and found him much better than we expected. That is the last time we met.

I was told later that the Emerson brothers sold their train and went in the stock business at Missoula. The freighter's life those days was a hazardous one. They were out in all kinds of weather, exposed to the ravages of Indians and road agents, besides, the roads were about as nature made them.

Through the [Little] Prickly Pear Canyons those days the road was very rocky and it was just a drop of the wagon wheels from one rock to another. Here is where it was thought the powder kegs were jarred and caused to leak and finally blew up the Emerson outfit. About a year later Dad Martin lost his entire freight team in this canyon. His team jack-knifed on him and the 10 horses, cargo, and three wagons went off the grade and down over the boulders about 300 feet into Prickly Pear Creek. There was not enough of the outfit left to pay for getting it out; the cargo was wet goods and the kegs and barrels were burst on the rocks and their contents lost. A year later I had a similar close call while on a dangerous grade in the big [Lower] canyon. I was caught in a severe hail storm which caused my animals to buckle back on me, but it was my good fortune not to go off the grade. If the old canyon walls could talk they could tell many interesting stories of bygone days

Horace Clark's father [Malcolm Clark], an Indian trader, was killed and Horace wounded by the Indians in this canyon.

These Prickly Pear Canyons in the early days were called the "Freighters Hell," deriving the name from the many accidents that happened there.

Both Helena Newspapers carried articles on the explosion. The *Herald* had a long article on August 22, 1881, while the *Independent* covered it in their issues of August 21, 23 and 26. The gist of the story matched perfectly with the way Wilkins described it in 1935. The principle difference was that Wilkins changed the individual names; probably to "protect the innocent." Another discrepancy was that both papers thought the wagons were headed for Helena and had come from the south. The *Herald* did say that the event occurred near Three Mile House which happened to be north of Helena and three miles south of Silver City.

Both papers reported that Evan C. Shipley died at Sister's Hospital on Sunday, August 22, 1881. He was interred at the now Benton Avenue Cemetery, location C3L, alley.

The Freighters Successes

The *Helena Independent* of June 13, 1876 told of a passing train in downtown Helena.

It was Murphy, Neel & Co.'s train which passed through Main Street yesterday the fine appearance of which excited general comment. It consisted of 20 wagons and 180 oxen. It is on the way to Benton.

On August 4, 1878, the *Helena Independent* reported that:

Governor Potts returned from Fort Benton yesterday, and reports an immense amount of freight at Benton and on the road to Helena.

An article in the same paper on the status of ox teams in Montana appeared on December 31, 1882.

The Devons are, on the whole, the most beautiful cattle of the world, and it is claimed they will make more beef for the same feed and care than any other cattle. The Devons make the best work oxen in the world. They are hardy and good travelers. But the bull train has gone out in Montana and the mule and horse have taken the place of the ox in the freight train and farm work. Nevertheless it is hard to beat a team of good, well trained Devons.

Some insight into the massiveness of items actually moved by the freight teams is gleaned from the following item in the *Helena Independent* for August 8, 1882.

Three teams of seven yokes of oxen each passed through town yesterday with timbers from Holter's saw mill for the new Gloster hoisting works. The largest of these timbers measured forty-four feet in length and was sixteen inches square. There were other timbers twenty-four inches square, but not so long as those mentioned above.

The days of freighting, in Montana, on a large scale, ended abruptly with the coming of the railroad. Helena's dream of being on the main line came true in 1882 with the arrival of the Northern Pacific Railroad.

The *Helena Independent* of May 22, 1883, told the story from the mules perspective.

Hugh Kirkendall announces himself in the field for transfer business from the depot. The streets have been blocked with freight teams for the past few days, but the mules look rather sad-eyed and their ears have a lonesome droop. Evidently the whistle of the locomotive discouraged them, for they have neglected to furnish the city with their usual music.

By November 23 of that year, the same paper noted that freighting to isolated places was still a money maker for those who stuck with the profession.

Marysville Matters

To the Editor of the *Independent*.

Marysville, November 20—The much advertised heavy piece of machinery, weighing twenty thousand four hundred and seventy pounds, bound for the immense compressors of the Montana Company Limited sailed triumphantly through Marysville today on the hurricane deck of a prairie schooner. Thirty well-fed mules for a motive power, and the boss Montana freighter Hugh Kirkendall, assisted by four true and tried mountain and plains navigators, in three days time from Helena, have at last safely landed the above cargo on a shelf hewn from the steep mountain side overlooking this picturesque village. With the extensive work now going on, Cruse Hill is a perfect bee hive of industry. In spite of wind or storm the building of air compressor and tramway and grading the site for the big mill is going ahead as fast as skill and muscle can accomplish such huge undertakings.

Kirkendall Freight Train in Little Prickly Pear Canyon

Kirkendall Mule Train in Little Prickly Pear Canyon

Main Street in Helena−1866

The Warf on Front Street, Benton, Montana

Murphy, Neel Freight Company

I. G. Baker & Company

T. C. Power and Brother at Fort Benton

I.G. Baker Train in Front of Record Building, Fort Benton

Old Malcolm Clark Cabin on Sieben Ranch

Malcolm Clark Family Graveyard Below Medicine Rock Mountain

Dearborn Crossing Cemetery

Commanding Officers' Quarters at Fort Shaw

Chapter V

The Indian Menace

Located in a region frequented by the Blackfeet, Bloods, and Piegans, it is not too surprising that the Benton Road would have its share of incidents with the native population. At first it was just a case of the Indians stealing livestock from the sparse settlements or freighting operations.

Although formal warfare never developed, in April of 1866, the Piegans attacked the Indian Agency and farm at Sun River Crossing, burning the buildings and sending the agent and his helpers into full flight. Within days a party of twelve men left Fort Benton on an Indian hunt. Three Piegans were executed by hanging them from some trees not far from Sun River Crossing.

At that same time other Piegans were busy killing a well liked young man by the name of Hunicke and his companion, Petit Cris. They had been on a mission to gather up some stolen horses, which were located at a Gros Ventres camp. When the young men failed to return to Fort Benton, the Gros Ventres started a search for them. The victims' bodies were not found until late in the winter. Charles Carson met the same fate on the Dearborn River in the winter of 1865–6. This Carson does not appear to be related to the famous Kit Carson although popular opinion has him as a nephew to Kit. An exhaustive check of Kit Carson's siblings and their descendents does not turn up a nephew with the name Charles.

A herder for the Diamond "R" freight outfit, by the name of Clark, lost his life at the hands of two Piegan warriors and their squaws in the spring of 1868. The culprits were tracked down and when questioned it was learned that one of the warriors had committed the murder over the strenuous objections of the other three Indians. The guilty brave was tried by the tracking party and hung. Most of the white men wanted to hang the other brave as well, but for the time being he was confined to a blacksmith's shop adjacent Largent's store at Sun River Crossing. The next night he was taken out of his confinement and shot repeatedly by parties unknown.

The tempo of ruthless acts was increasing on both sides and something had to be done to convince the Indians that the whites were there to stay. Nothing shows permanency better than a well manned fort with well armed soldiers.

Fort Shaw-Protector of the Road

Edith Rolfe Maxwell provides us with a fascinating history of Fort Shaw and its relevance to the Benton Road in an article from the *Fergus County Argus*, dated May 30, 1938.

To the many who now drive up Sun River Valley to see the fine new public school building at Fort Shaw, partly remodeled from one of the original stone structures of the old fort, it is hard to visualize the scene as it was when the military post was established in 1867. At that time there were no permanent settlers along the entire course of the river. True, the Blackfeet Farm, founded in 1858 at the Crossing by the terms of General Steven's treaty with the Blackfeet tribes had been occupied until the previous fall [1866] when it was burned by the vengeful Piegans. A small log cabin erected by a free trapper named Goff stood on the south of the river at the crossing. Another log cabin two miles down the river on the north side was built and occupied at times by Little Dog, a Piegan chief, friend of the whites and hated by members of his tribe because he tried to emulate the white man. About eight miles above the site of the fort was the former location of St. Peter's Mission of the Society of Jesus established March 13, 1860. Two log cabins were built and then the place was abandoned Aug. 9 of the same year. Later, Malcolm Clark had a trading post there doubtless using the same cabin, until he removed to his ranch on the [Little] Prickly Pear now known as the Sieben Ranch.

Nevertheless, the valley was not lonely. It was a favorite place for Indian encampment, for mighty herds of buffalo wintered up in this region providing a never-failing source of food. White and mixed blood trappers and hunters spent the hunting season there. Herders in charge of the horse herds belonging to the fur trading post of Fort Benton grazed their stock in this valley.

Seven years earlier Lieutenant Mullan had completed the military road from Walla Walla to Fort Benton. That spring [actually, July] Major Blake, commanding 300 troops, bound for Fort Colville in Washington, arrived at Fort Benton and was the first to traverse the Mullan Road after its completion through Montana. In 1862, the great overland train of emigrants led by Captain James Fisk marched in military style up Sun River Valley along the Mullan Road on the way to Oregon. Most of these immigrants turned aside on reaching the Prickly Pear Valley to try their fortunes in the newly discovered Salmon River and Beaverhead mines. The following years saw many other wagon trains come over the northern route and the Mullan Road. Steamboats came up river to Fort Benton to bring more and more men and goods destined for the rich gold mines west of the main range of the Rockies. They followed the sharp grade of the road from the Missouri river bottom at Fort Benton to the high plains above; then over the plains skirting the steep-sided "breaks" or plunging down the upper, more shallow extremes; plowing through adobe flats, passing north of Prairie or Benton Lake to wind down to Sun River Leaving, near present day Vaughn. From the Leaving they passed up the north side of Sun River to the Crossing, now the town of Sun River, thence up the south side of the river to the site of Fort Shaw, then turned south to the Bird Tail Divide, through the Prickly Pear Valley to Helena and the other gold camps.

Some Walked, Some Rode

Emigrants driving plodding ox teams, freighters driving mule teams with wagons piled high with flour, bacon, tools, and whisky and other necessities of the frontier; men on horseback and men walking; each helped to reach his destination without an encounter with the dreaded Blackfeet or the road agents both of whom infested this region. No tavern with its promise of cheer greeted the travelers; there were no stables to shelter their weary beasts. The best they could hope for was a camping place with sufficient water and grass and the company of other honest wayfarers for protection against marauders.

The influx of whites caused great resentment among the northern Indian tribes. They saw their hunting grounds invaded and the buffalo slaughtered and driven off. So they began a series of depredations attacking the trading posts, wood-yards and freighting outfits. They would stampede the stock and murder the men in charge, looting goods and burning what they did not want. They must destroy what they thought was destroying them. There were plenty of retaliatory acts on the part of the whites. Indians found singly or small parties were ruthlessly murdered by white men whose outlook was primitive as that of the savages. Others employed the more effective plan of calling upon the government for protection against the Indians. This resulted in the restriction of the Blackfeet to their reservation and the establishment of Fort Shaw midway between Fort Benton and Helena to keep the Mullan Road safe for travel.

According to the *Virginia Tri-weekly Post* of May 30, 1867, troops had been stationed along the Benton Road prior to the establishment of Fort Shaw. "We have been informed by Mr. Huntley, stage line operator, that troops have been permanently located on the road from Helena to Fort Benton. Maj. Horr is at the Dearborn, with 67 men, and will guard the route between Kennedy's and Sun River. Lieut. Hogan is stationed at Sun River, with another detachment, and will guard the road between that point and Benton. Ten men will be posted at each station and no danger need be apprehended."

First named Camp Reynolds, Fort Shaw was established June 30, 1867, by four companies of the 11th Infantry under Major William Clinton from Camp Cook, at the mouth of the Judith River. Pursuant to department orders of July 1867, the name was changed in honor of Col. Robert O. Shaw of the 54th Massachusetts Volunteers who was killed at Fort Wagner, July 18, 1863. His regiment was formed in response to a call from President Lincoln to recruit the free colored men. Captain Shaw, then serving in the south, was appointed Colonel.

Benefit in Square

The post is built around a square of 400 feet inside in accordance with plans drawn up by General Reeves. Adobe bricks 6x12x4 inches were used for the walls, covered on the outside with drop siding and within with lath and plaster. The material for the brick was procured from Adobe Creek, a mile east of the fort. The mud was mixed with wild hay for strength. The fort was constructed under contract by J. H. Hubbell. When Thomas J. Mooney, now of Glasgow, came up the river in 1868, his first job was helping with this construction. He was paid $4 per day. In the east his wages had been $10 a month, so the 16-year-old tender-foot felt his fortune practically was made. Charles D. Ladd, who for many years, until his death, was a resident of Great Falls, also helped in the construction of the fort. He was a private soldier in the 13th infantry, having enlisted in 1866.

The post established a camp at Beaver Creek on the North Fork of Sun River to get out logs. These were floated down the river to the saw mill set up at the fort, which sawed them into the rough lumber used in construction. On the old trail from Hannon Gulch to Medicine Springs, now the Allan Ranch, can be seen trees still bearing the scars made by ropes used to hold back the wagons on their descent of the sharp declivity at that place. These scarred trees and many rotting stumps are all that remain of the lumber operations of the Fort Shaw soldiers.

Finishing materials, quarter-sawed oak for interior woodwork, flooring, nails, paint, and tile for the handsome fireplaces in the officers quarters, came up the river by steamboat and were freighted overland from Fort Benton

Before winter set in one-half of each set of company quarters, a part of the hospital, a storehouse and three sets of officers' quarters were erected. Early the following spring the building resumed and the remaining buildings were built and roofed. The work was completed in 1869.

Facilities at Fort

The buildings consisted of double sets of officers' quarters of four rooms each, four barracks each 102 feet front length, hospital, store, chapel, mess hall, stables which extended outside the quadrangle to the river, and an icehouse at the river bank. The cemetery was located a short distance west, citizens as well as soldiers were buried there. *Lesson's History of Montana* gives the following information concerning those buried in the cemetery in 1867: "Daniel H. Lee, private of the 13th U. S. Infancy was found dead Nov, 26 on the prairie about three miles from the fort. He was last seen alive on the evening of Nov, 24 at Sun River Crossing, five miles from the fort. At that time, he was patronizing the tavern at the crossing, and was intoxicated. Those facts, with the want of marks of violence, led to the conclusion that his death was due to exposure while in a drunken condition. John Hanson, another private of the 13th Infantry committed suicide by shooting himself through the head, July 26. William Collins, of the same regiment died from acute dysentery, Dec. 9. Christopher Nelson (Dalager), a citizen, died from typhoid dysentery, Oct. 6, and was buried in the cemetery. So also was Daniel Smart, another citizen, Sept. 29."

Fort Shaw and its military occupants arrived just in time. Real Indian problems intensified the winter of 1867−68. The *Virginia Tri-Weekly Post* on February 15, 1868, stated the following:

INDIAN MASSACRE—Wells Fargo & Benton coach, of Tuesday last, brought in from Dearborn Station the body of a man named Charles R. Scott who was murdered by Indians Sunday night last. The deceased and his brother, Amos, who have been mining during the past season in the vicinity of Big Indian and Tucker Gulches, started out on a hunting expedition, and had pitched their camp some five miles above the Dearborn Crossing. They had with them five head of horses, together with guns, ammunition, provisions, etc. On Sunday afternoon last, about sundown, two Indians, one, an old and the other a young buck, came into the camp, exhibiting a friendly bearing, were treated kindly and took supper with the Scotts. After the meal, one of them complained of being ill, and lay down before the fire, and his example was soon followed by the two white men and the other Indian. About twelve o'clock, the eldest of the Indians sprang up with a yell, seized one of the guns and shot the deceased, the ball entering above the heart. Immediately on the Indian giving the yell, and firing, both men sprang from their blankets, thus scaring the Indians who ran off and hid in some willows on the bank of the river. After staying in camp about an hour and seeing no sign of the red devils, Amos started for assistance, to the station. On his return, he found that the Indians had come back and stripped the camp of nearly everything movable in it, as well as driving away the stock. In their haste to make off with their plunder, they did not scalp their victim. Pursuit was out of the question, as no horses were to be had sufficiently fresh to over-take them. It is supposed the Indians were either Bloods or Blackfeet, although they told the Scotts, when asked in camp what tribe they belonged to that they were Pen d'Oreilles. The carelessness displayed by the two white men in this instance, was almost unheard of, and will no doubt prove warning to small parties who may be out in the future.

On the same date that paper added this better news:

THE INDIANS—PROTECTION FOR THE ROAD—The rumor brought to town on Saturday night to the effect that Kennedy's Ranch [near Wolf Creek] had been attacked and burned, and the inmates either killed or prisoners in the hands, of the Indians, happily turned out to be without foundation. The fact that the Indians have been creating disturbances along a portion of the road between this point and Fort Benton of a serious nature is sufficiently alarming to give rise to all sorts of rumors. The coaches of Wells Fargo & Co. have received the attentions of our red brothers to a considerable extent. The last affectionate greeting was tendered on Sunday evening last to the down coach, a few miles beyond the Dearborn. It came in the shape of a bullet, which penetrated the driver's seat. Hereafter the road no doubt will be safe, as will be seen from the following

communication, which Mr. Gillespie has kindly permitted us to copy.

FORT SHAW, M. T., Feb. 15, 1868.–Dear Sir : As the Indians have troubled your coaches between Kennedy's and Tingley's several times, Major Clinton, Commanding Officer of this post, has ordered the mounted company (seventy men), which I command, to patrol the road between those points. We will be on the road every day, a portion going up and the other down, so that I hope we may prevent any further depredations.

Yours, respectfully,
J. L. STAFFORD,
1st Lieut. Com'd'g Mounted Co.

R. T. Gillespie, Agent W. F. & Co., Helena M. T.

By February 20, the Indian problems had taken on a wider scope and the *Post* added the following notice:

APPEAL FOR ARMS

To His Excellency, Green Clay Smith, Governor of Montana the undersigned citizens of Trinity Gulch and Little Prickly Pear Valley, on account of the frequent raids and depredations committed by the Indians of late in this vicinity, do most respectfully petition that we be furnished with arms and ammunition whereby we may be better enabled to protect our lives and property.

F. Ralston, Geo Detwiler
Chas Marley, Henry Klindt
R. Graham, Chas Green
H. Letherage, F. H. Thomas
O. Williams, L. Sturgeon
J. R. Rush, M. Keating
M. E. Walton, Roger O'Hara
G. W. Reid, J. R. Carter
A. C. Welch, Jas McGlees
J. S. Roberts, C. S. Sears
F. L. Graves, Wm. Kinsely
M. Lainleiu, N. Contancin
F. Connor, C. Graves
H. Gethard, B. Zimmerman
P. Lynch , Lorenzo Mejia
P. McCann, J. E. Murphy
James Fraisey, E. M. Child
J. H. McCleary, J. H. Pooley

J. J. Argui, J. W. Bishop

O. M. Argui, R. C. Wood

Wm. A. Parker, L. Andrews

John Hathorn, B. F. Johnson

John Moss, M. Hosebay

H. T. Jacob, S. E. Jacob

S. Silverstein, H. Silverstein

E. M. Stanger, Chas L. Cary

John Means, J. Mullholld

S. A. Hade, J. Margue

F. R. Cooper, B. F. Bell

W. Boblin, Joseph Comssa

G. R. Leffingwell, W. J. Wilson

S. B. Harrison, S. D. MeCheny

S. E. Jacob, Wm. Russel

Chas Florence, E. Barnes

L. P. Hedlebrand, Thomas Flinn

Patrick Flinn, L. H. Herthern

A. H. Hart, E. Hart

P. Caruly, R. Farrond

J. W. Gipley, F. Gulden

P. Green, H. Brook

J. L. Lider, P. Owen

I. Sauchy, G. Vient

T. McForres, L. Castro

F. Guturres, J. Devereux

D. H. Freeraut, J. G. Douthett

Jos Chase, A. Mead

P. Henry, O. H. Carpenter

E. Baldesto, Thomas Hauley

E. A. Garido, A. E. Haskell

Thos Honeywell, Ed. Waken

Chas Strob, Wm. Haskell

David Bush, Peter Trucho

Emery Larche, P. Pierreault

V. Mancham, Luke Viges

Joseph Daraleau, E. Le Baron

B. Fellows, Fred Nutter

The above petition having been presented to Col. Scribner, aid-de-camp, at Helena, he telegraphed the Governor the fact, with additional information of the movements of the Indians. Governor Smith at once sent the following:

REPLY:

COL. SCRIBNER, HELENA :

Investigate personally. If necessary go to the threatened locality and furnish the citizens of Little Prickly Pear Valley with one hundred stand of arms and sufficient ammunition.

(Signed.)
Green Clay Smith, Governor.

The list gives us some perspective on who actually occupied the area north and somewhat west of Helena at that time. Most of these men probably lived in the Silver Creek area as it was reported to have over 100 residents in 1864.

By May 2, 1868, the *Post* reported another story about the Indian problems.

Another Indian Murder—
The Blackfoot Hostile

Editor Post: Yesterday the U. S. mail party from Camp Cook (which arrives here semi-weekly) brought the sad intelligence of the murder of Nathaniel Crabtree. Crabtree was one of the first of a few daring spirits who thought it advisable to penetrate the hostile country occupied by the Blackfeet Indians on the Missouri River below here, and open to the commerce of our territory the hidden wealth of coal which lies buried in the banks below. He passed the winter at the coal bank in safety. This spring he went from the coal bank down the river to Drowned Man's Rapids, for the purpose of hauling out pine knots and wood for the use of steamboats. On Friday last, (24th) while out hunting for his cattle, about one mile from his cabin, he was attacked by a large party of Blackfeet Indians, and shot six or seven times with arrows. He was conveyed to Camp Cook and died in the hospital the same night. He stated himself that the Blackfeet Indians killed him.

Nat. Crabtree was well known in this part of the Territory, as a high minded, honorable young man. He never interfered with the Indians (although no lover of them) and his death may be attributed to his carelessness and contempt for the red demons.

While this "murder" was going on, a portion of the same band, of Indians (Whom it seems numbered between 200 and 800) proceeded to Camp Cook (three miles below) and in full sight of 400 soldiers, well armed and equipped, proceeded to quietly appropriate 23 head of government horses and nine head of mules.

After securing these trophies, they proceeded to an adjacent hill and gleefully proclaimed their great victory. All this was done while still in the range of the guns of the Fort. It is needless to say that the Indians have said horses and mules now on herd, but will probably return them when called upon.

Another item in the *Post* of May 16, 1868, told the story of yet one more incident.

INDIAN RUMORS

A gentleman from Lincoln Gulch reports that twenty miles north of that place, near the Benton Road, three prospectors were attacked by Indians. Two of the three men managed to escape from the "Friendlies" and ran to Lincoln Gulch to give the alarm, while the third one is missing. A party of well mounted and armed miners are now in search of the missing one, with a slight desire, we have no doubt, of giving the red skins a severe drubbing, if they can catch any.

The *Weekly Montana Democrat* for May 29, 1868, chimed in with a copy of an article appearing in the *Post*.

Indians Captured

On Saturday noon an Indian thievery expedition, consisting of twenty-one Blackfeet, made their appearance at the station of Wells Fargo & Co. at the Leaving of Sun River, on the Benton Road. Each one of the savages was on foot, well armed and provided with a rope. The employees of the stage company immediately secured their stock within the enclosure and prepared for war. Seeing that the whites were in readiness for battle, the Indians, with their characteristic display of bravery, sneaked off. A messenger was sent to the Sun River Crossing for men to pursue the Indians. A company of thirteen was raised, which under the leadership of Messrs Largent and Hamilton, came upon the Indians as they were eating by the river bank, and surprised and captured them. They were delivered over to the military authorities at Fort Shaw on Monday, and the citizens are now waiting to see what action will be taken in the case of the savages. If they are treated leniently the settlers threaten to deal out justice in their own manner the next time a scion of the Lo family falls into their hands.

Robert Vaughn in his book *Then and Now, Thirty-Six Years in the Rockies, 1864–1900*, describes an attack near Fort Benton which occurred in the summer of 1868, to a friend of his.

Jim Matkins was wounded by Piegans, near Benton, in 1868. Mr. Matkins was one of my best friends. At the time he was shot by the Indians he was an employee of the Diamond "R" Company, a firm that had several ox teams engaged in hauling freight from Fort Benton to various towns and points in the territory. He related to me the following particulars of the chase he had with the Indians at the time he was shot. He said: "One day at Fort Benton I loaded sixteen of the company's wagons with freight for Helena. Tom Clary and J. C. Adams had charge of the outfit. They pulled out that day and camped the following night at Eight Mile Spring. I was clerking for the company at the time. I could not get the bills of lading ready at the time they left; so, late in the evening, after dark, I got on my saddle horse and started for their camp. After I had gone about three miles I heard the clatter of horses' hoofs, and, looking back, I saw eight Indians coming as fast as their horses could carry them, and bullets began whizzing by me; but what frightened me the worst was their fearful 'Indian yell.' I put the spurs to my horse and rode for dear life towards Clary and Adams' camp, which was five miles further. I had a Winchester rifle that had sixteen loaded cartridges; I fired several shots at the Indians. In this way I kept them at bay for a while. But there was one who had a very fast horse and he was the only Indian that could keep pace with me, for mine was a good runner; but this redskin could run up to my side whenever he wanted to. After running in this way for about three miles, and in a shower of bullets, I discovered that I was shot in the hip. I could see but one Indian and he had slacked up his pace to load his gun. I dismounted and took as good aim as I could in the dark and fired four shots. I believe that I wounded him or his horse, for he came no further. I could feel that my boot was filling up with blood and I was getting very weak; it was as much as I could do to mount my horse. When I arrived at the camp I told all that had occurred. I was put in a wagon drawn by two yoke of oxen, and Clary and Adams, with two other men took me back to Benton that night, and my wound was dressed. The bullet is still in my hip."

Mr. Matkins afterwards died from the effects of this injury. He is buried in the Highland Cemetery at Great Falls.

Robert Vaughn also mentions another man by the name of James Quail who was killed near Silver Creek in 1869. James was on his way to get his horse which was grazing on the slope of a hill near his cabin. There he was shot and killed by an Indian who robbed him of his horse and gold watch on which his name was engraved. The watch was later spotted on an Indian at a Piegan camp near the Marias River.

The settlers had just about had their fill of illicit Indian activities and were ready to take matters into their own hands. Even the media was ready to fight using sarcasm and innuendo.

The situation with the Indians grew worse and by the summer of 1869 the territory seemed to be aflame with murder and robbery. To that point the victims were not well known throughout the region. Suddenly, a high profile pioneer was made victim of the outrages. Fur trader, rancher and treaty negotiator, Malcolm Clark was killed by his wife's relatives, who were also Indians. According to the *New Northwest*, dated August 20, 1869:

ANOTHER INDIAN OUTRAGE
Murder of Malcolm Clark

There arc few people in the territory who did not know Malcolm Clark, old pioneer and trader, whose farm is on the Little Prickly Pear, about half a mile this side of the upper toll gate, on the Benton Road. Many years ago he came to this territory, married into the Piegan tribe and raised a family of half breed children, whom he had educated and instructed with great care. On Tuesday night, about twelve o'clock, Mr. Clark was treacherously murdered by a raiding party of Piegan Indians—a tribe whose interests were dearer to him than those even of his own race, and in whose favor he was ever ready to argue. The circumstances are these: About two months ago the Indians raided off a lot of Mr. Clark's stock; and about election time—when they raided into Lincoln gulch and vicinity they also took some more from Mr. Clark. On Tuesday night a band of Indians, numbering about twenty-five, and most of whom were acquaintances of the family, rode up to the door, and some of them entered the house. They were very cordial in their manner; told him that some

Malcolm Clark

"young men" of their tribe had run off his stock two months ago, and some more two weeks since; that it was against the wishes and desires of the tribe; that they loved him; felt he had been their friend, and that they had brought back with them his stock, and if his son would go out to the road that they give him back his horses and help to drive them into the corral. The young man went out but had scarcely gone three yards from the house when Clark heard the report of a gun. He went out to see what was the matter, and as soon as he reached the corner of the house he too was shot. The wound was mortal, and we believe he immediately died.

His son still lives and the doctor went out there, twenty-five miles, yesterday. The Indians then deliberated about killing the whole family, but desisted at the entreaties of the old grandmother aided by some noise down the road which scattered them as if they thought white men were coming—*Gazette*, 19th.

Robert George Raymer in his book *Montana, The Land and the People*, offers the following account:

The Piegan War (1869–70)

Friction between the Indians and the white settlers continued; for the Red Men realized that they were fighting for their home. In the summer of 1869 four or five wagons of emigrants were attacked near Fort Benton by Indians, who were afterwards discovered to be Crows. This greatly excited the white settlers who were always in fear of an Indian uprising.

Just after this the brother of Mountain Chief, head of the Piegans, and a young Indian boy, a Blood, rode into the post [Benton] with special orders from Major Alexander Culbertson. These innocent Indians were shot down by excited whites, these whites who claimed to be civilized men and Christians. The Piegans were thoroughly aroused when the news of this murder reached them. Mountain Chief realized that he would not be able to check his young braves and so warned the whites and asked them to leave, saying he would not be responsible for what might happen.

Among these white settlers was a certain Major Malcolm Clark, a former agent of the American Fur Company who had retired from its service and had settled in the [Little] Prickly Pear Valley near Helena. Here he lived with his squaw, who was a daughter of a chief of the Piegans, and their five children: Helen, Horace, Nathan, Isabelle, and Judith. Because of his wife's being a Piegan and because of the high esteem in which he was held among the Indians, Major Clark was over-confident in his safety and did not heed Mountain Chief's warning.

A cousin to Major Clark's wife, Ne-tus-che-o, took advantage of this feeling among the Indians to take vengeance upon the Clarks for a personal grudge he had been harboring for a couple of years. In the spring of 1867, while visiting at Major Clark's home, Ne-tus-che-o's horses together with Major Clark's were stolen. Although some of the Indian's horses were located they were not restored. Ne-tus-che-o felt that Clark was implicated in the robbery in some way, and so he brooded over the loss of his horses, which were more precious to him than life. Finally one night, he left taking with him a band of Major Clark's horses, among which was a favorite horse of Horace's. When the theft was discovered Major Clark and Horace rode in pursuit. When they came into the Indian camp, Ne-tus-che-o rode up on the favorite horse. Horace was so enraged that he took the pony from the Indian at the same time

lashing Ne-tus-che-o across the face with his riding whip. The Indian never forgave him.

Since the Indians were so aroused against the whites by the murder of Mountain Chief's brother, Ne-tus-che-o gathered a group of young braves and rode to Major Clark's house one night in August of 1869. He professed friendliness, even kissing Horace. He told them that their horses had been found and were a short distance away and asked Horace to go with a certain Indian to bring them. This Indian, after they had gone a little way, shot Horace and left him for dead. Ne-tus-che-o then called Major Clark out of the house on some pretext and killed him. Horace, who was not fatally wounded, crawled back to the house. The family barricaded themselves in a room thinking Ne-tus-che-o would exterminate them all but he was persuaded to leave.

This tragedy led to the so-called Piegan War of 1869–70, for the United States Government demanded the surrender of Ne-tus-che-o. Mountain Chief, the head of 1,500 Piegans, refused to comply with this demand.

Explanations of the act were prolific then, and since that time. They ranged from Clark having swindled the Indians for the last time to the "sudden end of a two year old family feud, as described above," to "this was retribution for the killing of two Piegans in Fort Benton a few weeks earlier." In any event, the military made an abrupt switch from defensive to offensive actions.

By December, the Army was out in full force searching for the evil perpetrators of the deed. Forces from Fort Ellis, near Bozeman, and Fort Shaw joined in an attempt to run down the elusive Mountain Chief and his followers. He was reported to have led the band of Piegans and Blackfeet who participated in many murders of whites and theft of horses over the summer of 1869.

Major Eugene Baker, Commandant at Fort Ellis, led the combined group. The winter was one of the harshest on record and the soldiers camped out over Christmas day in Little Prickly Pear Canyon while the mercury dipped to minus 40 degrees.

The two forces marched only at night in an attempt to surprise Mountain Chief's camp, thought to be on the Marias River north of Fort Benton. Scouts and captured Indians swore that the first village encountered was indeed that of Mountain Chief. On January 23, 1870, Baker jumped at the opportunity to deal a decisive blow to this group of thieving murderers.

The only problem was that Mountain Chief was miles away and the Indians they had found were led by Heavy Runner, a documented friend of the whites. The die was cast and there was no turning back for the nearly frozen soldiers. After nearly an hour of pouring lead into the lodges along the Marias, 173 Indians, including Heavy Runner, lay dead or dying and another 100 plus women and children were in captivity.

Even Malcolm Clark's son, Horace, participated in the massacre. Years later he would testify that Baker was too drunk to know what Indians he was killing or to even lead the soldiers on the right village some fifteen miles away. In rebuttal, Captain J. W. Ponsford would write in the December 19, 1903, edition of the *Montana Daily Record* that it had been fortunate no liquor was allowed on the march as many soldiers would have died from hypothermia. "I don't remember what we had to eat, [on that Christmas Eve] but I do remember what we didn't have to drink. Our Colonel had been very careful to see that no spirits were taken along on the trip, and that proved to be a mighty good thing. If the troopers had been allowed to drink what whiskey they had wanted, many of them would have been frozen to death that night. Whiskey is alright in its place, but its place is not on a long march when the mercury is trying to crowd out the bottom of the thermometer."

Federal Marshal, William F. Wheeler, provided his opinion of the so called "Baker Massacre" a decade later in the *Helena Daily Herald* for January 1, 1880.

PIEGAN WAR OF 1870

An Unpublished Chapter
BY COLONEL WM. F. WHEELER

The campaign of Major Eugene M. Baker, Second U. S. Cavalry, against the Piegan Indians (a band of the Blackfeet tribe) in northern Montana, in January, 1870, although denounced at the time by the eastern press as a wanton massacre, was one of the most necessary punishments, as it was one of the most, important events, that has ever

transpired in the annals of border warfare. It is the object of this paper to briefly relate why and how it occurred. In the summers of 1868 and 1869, as everybody then resident of the territory, well remembers, murders of white men by the Blackfeet (Piegans) were almost of daily occurrence, and the stealing of horses of settlers was carried on by wholesale. It was unusual if the daily papers did not record some Indian deviltry in nearly every issue. The people of Choteau, Meagher, Lewis, and Clark, and those residing on the borders of Deer Lodge and Gallatin Counties, were the principal sufferers. Almost every freight train between Helena and Benton during the summer of 1869 was attacked. Garrison's herders were killed by the Indians within three miles of Fort Benton, and McQuail and his partner were murdered while working their mines in sight of Silver City. Horses were stolen from the valley in sight of Helena in broad daylight, and the whole herd was stampeded from Boulder Bar, within half a mile of Diamond City, at daylight one morning, and the yells of the Indian horse thieves were heard by the citizens of town as they were driven away. Hugh Kirkendall's whole train of thirty-two splendid mules were stolen early one morning while camped at the Dearborn. Every stage passenger, freighter, traveler, or prospector on the road between Helena and Fort Benton and through Meagher County was compelled to carry his rifle and revolver, not withstanding, which fifty-six white men were murdered during the year 1869 by savages who mostly ambushed and killed without warning.

On the 23d of August, 1869, these Indians (Piegans) came to the ranch of Malcolm Clark, who lived near the mouth of Prickly Pear Canyon, on the place now owned by James Fergus, twenty-five miles from Helena, and by lies about returning his stolen horses drew, him out of his house in the night and shot him dead. They also shot his son Horace through the face and left him on the ground for dead, but he subsequently recovered and is now living at Highwood in Choteau County. They intended to carry off Clark's wife and three daughters, but were too busily engaged in securing the thirty to forty head of horses, owned by Mr. Clark, to do it that night.

The next morning Miss Ellen P. Clark, his oldest daughter, (now and long an honored teacher in the public schools of Helena) gave

General Alfred Sully

the news of the murder of her father to the white men at King & Gillette's toll gate, and the survivors were brought into Helena and cared for by the citizens. Major Clark had lived among the Blackfeet twenty-eight years and had married into their tribe, which rendered his murder remarkable, as he had spent a fortune in administering to their wants and was always their great friend and counselor. Private revenge was supposed to be the cause of his sacrifice. Major Clark was personally known to nearly every settler of Montana and had displayed hospitality with a liberal hand to many weary immigrants, who were out of means, on their way from the states to the rich gold fields of the territory. His murder, in the center of the most populous county in Montana, and near the largest town site, awakened the people to the necessity of some prompt action by themselves or the government, and letters were sent by scores to the military and civil authorities in Montana and at Washington, giving details of the murders committed by the Indians. The newspapers teemed daily with articles setting forth the dangers of our situation and demanding protection.

I had been qualified as U. S. Marshal on the fifth day of July of that year, and proceeded at once to procure the evidence necessary to indict and convict the murderers in the numerous cases which had occurred during the year. The only case In which the murderers could be identified personally, or where they could be indicted for the murder, was that of Malcolm Clark. His daughter Ellen and son Horace knew personally, and by name, five chiefs who had participated in he killing of their father. With their evidence I went before the U. S. Grand Jury at the October term of the Third Judicial District Court, which met in Helena, and there the five leaders were indicted for the willful murder of Malcolm Clark. They were as liable to personal punishment by the civil authorities as white men would have been for the same offence.

Before the meeting of the Grand Jury, I had searched through every number of the *DAILY HERALD* from the first of January to the day court met, and the Grand Jury was informed of the exact number of white people killed and the number of horses stolen by the Indians, and as near as I remember, I found that fifty-six whites had been murdered and over one thousand horses had been stolen by the Blackfeet in 1869. At the request of the Grand Jury, I drew up a report of these facts for the use of the court which every member signed with request to the court that certified copies should sent to all military and civil authorities having any jurisdiction or authority to punish the Indians for their misdeeds. I forwarded copies to President Grant, the General of the Army and Acting Secretary of War, General Sherman; the Secretary of the Interior, General J. D. Cox; to General Sheridan, at Chicago; General Hancock, at St. Paul; and General, DeTrobriand, commanding the U.S. forces in Montana, at Fort Shaw; and wrote letters to each, setting forth our perilous situation. I also gave General Alfred Sully then U. S. Superintendent of Indian Affairs for Montana, copies of the warrants of arrest for the five murderers, and made a demand for their surrender. He acquainted the President and Secretary of the Interior with these facts, and asked for instructions. Upon this information a Cabinet meeting was called, at which our then Delegate, Hon. Jas. M. Cavanaugh, was invited to be present. The condition of Montana was fully discussed. Mr. Cavanaugh wrote me that General Sully was instructed to demand the murderers from their tribe, and if they failed or refused to surrender them on his demand, they were to be, by him, notified that the Government would send its soldiers and take them by force or make war on the Indians. Attorney General Hoar was the only Cabinet officer who dissented from this decision, and he called him a Massachusetts humanitarian! Cavanaugh himself was a native of Massachusetts.

General Sheridan was instructed by General Sherman, then Acting Secretary of War, to detail the officer in Montana best fitted for the purpose of conducting an Indian campaign, to proceed against them in case they refused to comply with the demands of General Sully. He promptly chose Major Eugene M. Baker, Second U. S. Cavalry, then in command of Fort Ellis, and assigned him to this duty. He was chosen for his brilliant campaign against the Indians in Oregon. His instructions were to the point. Sheridan's telegram to Major Baker said: "If you have to fight the Indians, hit them hard." The sequel will show that he fulfilled his instruction literally. All Montanans agree that, no better commander could have been selected for the purpose.

I accompanied General Sully to Fort Shaw to make a demand of the Indians for the surrender of the five murderers of Malcolm Clark. We happened to arrive there on Christmas day, 1869, and were invited by Capt. Cutter, post sutler, to a magnificent Christmas dinner given by him to the officers of the post.

The next morning, December, 26th, runners were sent off to notify the chiefs of the Piegans to meet Gen. Sully in general council. In a few days the council met at the Blackfeet Agency, on the Teton, and Gen. Sully informed the council of the object of his visit. After a long consultation the council agreed to deliver the murderers to General Sully at Fort Shaw within twelve days. General S. waited for the fulfillment of this promise, but soon found that the murderers had been sent north to the British boundary, and the interpreters said that the Indians laughed at the idea of surrendering their brethren to be hung by the whites and the soldiers they did not fear. They had never come in contact with them yet. As soon as General Sully became satisfied that the Piegans were acting in bad faith, he notified General DeTrobiand, commanding the district of Montana, who in turn communicated the order of government to Major Baker to march at once against the Indians. He accordingly marched from Fort Ellis, a distance of 190 miles, to Fort Shaw with five companies of his glorious 2d Cavalry. His force was about 250 strong. At Fort Shaw be was joined by a company of the 13th U. S. Infantry.

After a short rest, Major Baker. with his whole command, about 800 men, in the middle of January, 1870, the mercury indicating nearly 40 degrees below zero, made a march of two nights and one day against the Piegans who were encamped in their winter village on the Marias river, 80 miles from Ft. Shaw.

Major Baker surrounded the village just at daylight on the morning of the second day, January 23d, I believe, and got between their camp and herd of horses before an Indian was seen. A soldier, a little in advance of his company, rode near to a teepee, when an Indian, hearing the tramp of horses, stepped out with his gun across his arm and without any warning shot the soldier dead off his horse. At this Major Baker ordered his men to fire as long as there was any resistance. In an instant every warrior was out of his teepee, firing at the soldiers. Being completely surrounded the Indians sought shelter inside their teepees, and with their knives cut holes through their sides and fired from within. As long as they kept this up the soldiers fired into the teepees. When the Indians ceased firing Major Baker ordered his soldiers to cease, and called upon the Indians to surrender, which they did at once.

The result of the fight was 800 ponies captured and 178 Indians killed and some wounded. About 150 women and children left alive and eight warriors escaped. Unfortunately, about fifty women and children were killed. But this was unavoidable as the Indians fought from their teepees where families were, and the soldiers had to fire into them until resistance ceased. Not one of the murderers was found among the dead Indians. When inquired for they answered that they were living north of the line [in Canada], thus proving that the Indians did not intend to surrender them, and had acted in bad faith towards General Sully.

It was found that the Indians were suffering severely from the smallpox. So Major Baker left Lieut. Doane, with one company, with instructions to attend to the wounded, to leave them sufficient teepees, provisions, robes, and camp equipment for their comfort and to burn the rest, of the infected camp with all contents, including the dead, while he immediately marched to another Indian village 15 miles away. When he arrived there every Indian had fled, having been notified of his approach by those who escaped from their first village. Their teepees were standing and with their contents were all burned to prevent the spread of the smallpox. After this the command returned to Fort Shaw. The soldiers suffered severely from the intense cold, and conducted themselves most gallantly in the battle and on the march.

A great number of vagabonds, regular camp followers, accompanied Major Baker's expedition from Fort Shaw. As soon as the fighting was over they at once commenced to plunder the Indian camp of buffalo robes, of which there was a large number, all infected by the small-pox. Major Baker observed this and immediately ordered Lieut. Doane to seize and destroy the last one, to prevent the infection from being sent abroad. This order was carried out most faithfully, by Lieut. Doane; and the scavengers were sent back to Sun River and Fort Benton empty-handed. They and their friends and backers at once raised the cry that Major Baker had wantonly murdered a large number of defenseless women and children, and flooded the east with their letters in order to be revenged on Major Baker and his command and bring them into disrepute. The eastern press and the humanitarians took up the cry, and Major Baker and his gallant soldiers were denounced as fiends and worse than murderers. The result was that the control of and management of Indian affairs was taken away from the officers of the army and turned over to various religious bodies, with such results since as have culminated in the massacre of the gallant Custer and his entire Command, the Nez Perce War of 1877, the murder of Major Thornburg and his gallant soldiers, and Agent Meeker and his employees.

The people of Montana felt indignant at the abuse and injustice done Major Baker and the Second Cavalry, and the citizens met spontaneously in every town and camp in the territory, and with an unanimity unequaled and in burning language thanked their gallant soldier friends for their heroism in fighting and

General John Gibbon

subduing the cowardly murderers of their friends and neighbors and the despoilers of their homes and pilferers of their property. His Excellency, President Grant, General Sully Sherman, General Sheridan, and all the principal military authorities of the government fully sustained Major Baker and his gallant command in all the efforts that were made to displace the one or to disgrace the other. The Second Cavalry still serving Montana, and in connection with the brave Seventh U. S. Infantry and John Gibbon are now and always will be remembered for their uncomplaining, unrequited and gallant services in our defense for the past ten years.

The results of Major Baker's campaign are not underrated by the people of Montana and cannot be appreciated by eastern people, for they do not know the danger which was averted in our case and have forgotten their own Indian wars. Ever since January, 1870, the Blackfeet tribes, who, from the descriptions of Lewis and Clark, were then (and until subdued by Major Baker) the most treacherous and blood thirsty of all the Indians they encountered from the mouth of the Missouri to the mouth of the Columbia, have been peaceable and quiet, and it has been safe to travel all over their country. Very few white men have since been murdered by them, and they were generally whisky traders and characters dangerous in any community and caused their own calamities. The punishment of the Piegans had a most salutary effect on the conduct of all the other tribes in Montana. The Sioux massacred Custer and his command, and the Nez Perces raided within, our borders, but their wars originated out of our boundaries.

I have written this article not in defense of Major Baker and his command, nor in defense of the military management of the Indians by General Sully, for they need no defense, but to show that by proper efforts to enforce laws against Indians as well as against whites, when fully seconded by the whole power of the government, backed by its brave military force, that the Indians can be subdued, ruled, and probably eventually civilized and at least protection can be given to our hardy and adventurous settlers on the remotest frontiers. One year of management by military officers has given us far better results in Montana than nine of church mismanagement.

I also write to show that the Grand Jury in indicting the murderers of Malcolm Clark rendered it necessary for the government to arrest them by military force, or to punish the tribe for refusing to surrender them, or to give up all control over them. They were subdued and peace has been the result among all our Indians.

If they were turned over to the management of military officers, the salaries, of the numerous agents would be saved, and I believe the Indians would be better controlled and their affairs better managed than now. But, I did not intend to discuss this question of Indian management, on which many of our best men differ.

I have shown why and how the Piegan campaign originated and how it resulted and its after effects.

Wheeler's argument that there was a need to burn the Piegan Village to stop the small-pox epidemic among the Indians is an issue entirely overlooked by those in sympathy with the Indians.

General DeTrobriand, commander of Fort Shaw, was the focal point for explanations of the occurrences surrounding the so called Baker Massacre. These explanations were at the request of the Inspector General and de Trobriand's immediate commander.

In a letter to the Inspector General, dated February 3, 1870, de Trobriand makes at least two good points. First, as to the issue of the number of women killed, he points out that many of those women actually died at the hands of their husbands who might have anticipated similar treatment of their wives by the white soldiers as would be guaranteed if the roles were reversed and white women had been captured by Indians.

Secondly, he mentions that although many friends of the Indians claimed that most of the warriors were out on a hunting trip, it was common knowledge that when the temperature dipped as low as minus 40 degrees, most of the hunters would have been huddled around their campfires.

Prior to the conflict, General de Trobriand's correspondence to citizens in the territory did not support Wheeler's concern for the safety of its settlers. In fact, a careful examination of the *Helena Weekly Herald* for the period mentioned by Wheeler does not indicate serious Indian problems beyond the murder of Malcolm Clark and the theft of Kirkendall's mules.

The debate rages on, even to this day, but one fact remains clear: to the Blackfeet and Piegans the blow was devastating and they would never again bother the travelers along the Benton Road.

Edith Maxwell's story of Fort Shaw continues:

The military reservation of 32,000 acres was set aside in January, 1870. It extended east within a mile of Sun River Crossing and west a mile above Simms Creek. It laid in both Edgerton and Chouteau Counties, the river forming their boundary line and also the southern boundary of the Blackfeet reservation, so that that portion of the military reserve, which lay in Chouteau County, was part of the Blackfeet reservation. Edgerton County was renamed Lewis and Clark County and the part of old Chouteau County north of the Sun River is now Teton County. The military reservation is, in the main, a level valley bottom from two to three miles wide between steep bluffs. Its southern part slopes up to the high plain with the bluff called Shaw Butte to the south and Square Butte southeast. The elevation at Fort Shaw is 3,930 feet.

Largent Opens Store

There was much stirring in the valley while the fort was building. John Largent came in 1867, to the crossing with a stock of goods and opened a store in Goff's cabin. Thus, the town of Sun River was started. A mail route from Corrine, Utah, at the end of steel on the Central Pacific Railroad, to Fort Benton via Helena and Fort Shaw was opened by Wells-Fargo and Fort Shaw became a post office. Nat Pope, nephew of General Pope, was the first post trader at the fort in September, 1867. A telegraph was built from Helena to Fort Benton by way of Fort Shaw to connect the military posts. A good deal of annoyance was caused by buffaloes, which knocked down the poles by using them for rubbing posts. They tangled up and carried off the wire and no doubt were heartily cursed by the "swaddies" detailed to repair the damage.

In 1870, the 13th Infantry was succeeded by the 7th Infantry, commanded by Gen. John Gibbon, brother of the famous cardinal. The 3d Infantry under Col. John R. Brooks relieved the 7th in the spring of 1878, remaining until 1888, when it was succeeded by the 25th Infantry (colored) commanded by Col. J. J. Van Horne. This regiment occupied the fort until it was abandoned in 1890, and the reservation reverted to the Interior Department.

The soldiers at Fort Shaw took part in every important military campaign in Montana: Baker's massacre on the Marias in 1870, Baker's battle on the Yellowstone in 1872, the campaign against the Sioux on the Little Big Horn in 1876, and the battle of the Big Hole in the campaign against the Nez Perces in 1877. General Gibbon was in command of the military district of Montana with Fort Shaw as headquarters.

The laws of 1870 relating to the introduction of liquor in the Indian country made the work of this and every other frontier post largely that of policing the reservations. The old time fur traders had degenerated into whisky peddlers seized every opportunity to slip into the reservations with their wares. Details of soldiers were constantly on the alert to arrest them or drive them off the forbidden ground. Canadian Indians came to hunt and must be chased back over the border. Indians who had strayed from the Blackfeet reservation had to be rounded up and returned to their homes, cattlemen's herds which grazed on reservation lands had to be driven off. Prohibition and traffic laws were as difficult to enforce in those days as in modern times and as bitterly resented by those who felt their liberties thus invaded.

Soldiers' Life Hard Grind

For the most part the life of the enlisted soldier was a hard, monotonous one. When payday came he eagerly sought relaxation and amusement. That too frequently was debasing, gambling, honky tonks, and whisky, chiefly because no other attractions were offered by those who catered to his trade. Sun River never lacked saloons to supply the wants of its floating population of freighter, soldiers, cowboys and tinhorns. Whisky Cursed Brown had a saloon famous in these early days at the southern extreme of Shaw Butte on the Bird Tail Road, just outside the military reserve.

Hunting was a favorite sport. The lakes and sloughs nearby teamed with a great variety of ducks. In the earlier years the buffaloes were plentiful and close enough to the post to afford good hunting.

Music had an important part in the pleasures at the fort. Each morning, the weather permitting, the band played for the military exercises on the parade ground. It played for the dances and entertainments and was known as the finest band in the army. Services were held in the chapel when ministers could be secured and there was always an excellent choir. There were frequent theatricals and entertainments; at one time the fort was fortunate enough to have a family of actors take up their residence there and play soul-stirring dramas with the help of talent drawn from the enlisted soldiers. The late Mrs. O. H. Chowan of Great Falls was the youngest of this gifted family.

Lively Social Life

Mrs. Roe, wife of Lieut. Faye Roe who was stationed here for a number of years, gives in her *Letters of an Army Officers Wife*, a most lively picture of social life at the fort when the companies returned from their arduous summer campaigns.

"Almost every evening there is some sort of an entertainment, German dinner, luncheon, or card party," she wrote "I am so glad we gave the first cotillion that had ever been given in the regiment, for it was something new on the frontier; therefore everyone enjoyed it. Just now the garrison seems to have gone cotillion crazy, and not being satisfied with a number of private ones, a German club has been organized that gives dances in the hall every two weeks. So far Faye has been the leader of each one. With all this pleasure the soldiers are not being neglected. Every morning there are drills and a funny kind of target practice inside the quarters, and of course there are inspections and other things."

The Western Montana tribes were probably not nearly as much of a menace to Montana settlers as were the Apaches and Comanches in other parts of the west. The abundance of troops and a great concern at the federal and territorial levels for the mines of the region provided some level of security to Montana's pioneers.

Other tribes such as the Nez Perces and the Sioux would continue to threaten the population along the Benton Road. Their acts there were minimal compared to the trouble caused by the Blackfeet, Piegans, and Bloods.

Lt. Colonel Eugene M. Baker and Officers at Fort Ellis 1871

The Infantry at Fort Shaw

Bird Tail Butte on the Benton Road

Dearborn River Crossing

Sun River Crossing

Chapter VI

Operating the Stage Lines

E. M. Pollinger, in a letter to Col. J. E. Callaway, and those interested in early stage coaching in Montana, left a few brief comments about his recollections on the subject. Since 1866, Pollinger had been driving a stage coach and providing supplies and accommodations for passengers for Wells Fargo on their Virginia City to Helena run. When Gilmer and Salisbury bought the stage lines in Montana, he drove the Helena to Fort Benton route until 1878.

I am not positive which C. C. Huntley started the first Concord Stage from Helena. Just one coach to Fort Benton Summer of 1866, operated by a man named Joe Kinney, old stage man. Last I knew of him he was clerk & recorder of Umatilla Co., Oregon at Pendleton. The first United States mail from Helena to Fort Benton, C. C. Huntley got the contract for short time 3 or not over 6 months, spring of 1867, George Baker of the firm of I. G. Baker & Co of St. Louis was the first United States Postmaster at Fort Benton. I stocked the road from Helena to Fort Benton for Wells Fargo & Co. Started the first coach from Helena also Fort Benton the 5th day of June, 1867, tri-weekly first of July 1867. Bought C. C. Huntley out & established 6 horse daily coaches between the two points. Could give whole lot of details but would be too long however the road cleared $42,000 dollars that season. Loaded Steam Boat down with gold dust taken from Highland and Diamond City and various other Placer Mining Camps. Capt. Sam DeBough (Debow) steamboat, the Guidon by name, was owned by Capt. Simms, old Mississippi Steam Boat man. Wells Fargo collected about $10,000 dollars for carrying gold dust at one (1) per cent commission. That Steam Boat on that trip, Guidon, made the fastest time from Fort Benton to St. Louis that has ever been recorded 9 days & 11 hours I think [it] was the time Wells Fargo &

Co sold out to Gilmer & Salisbury, August 1st, 1869, but the deal hung fire and was not completed until the first of October. When completed it dated back to August 1st. Some very strange things took place during the deal. However, Wells Fargo & Co was robbed of the stage road & its equipment.

It didn't take long after the opening of the King and Gillette Toll Road, through Little Prickly Pear Canyon, for an astute businessman to start a stage line from Helen to Fort Benton.

Charles Clarence (C. C.) Huntley was just the man for the job. His early life was well documented in a biographical sketch published around 1871, in the book *American Biography Containing Sketches of Prominent Americans of the Present Century*.

CHARLES CLARENCE HUNTLEY, the subject of this sketch, was born in Ellicottville, Cattaraugus County, N. Y., in 1844. Two years later his parents removed to Illinois, and founded the township, which now bears the family name. Strictly speaking, the Huntleys were not in poor circumstances; yet they discouraged from the first boyhood days of their son any inclination upon his part to seek absolute freedom from a share of the ordinary labors and duties which the household required. As young Huntley grew in years, his active disposition revealed itself; and he longed to escape the restraints which his quiet home imposed upon him. Fully determined to engage in the busy scenes of life upon his own responsibility, he made known his intentions to his father, and begged that the latter would permit of his leaving the parental roof. The aspirations of the youth did not at first meet with the approval of the elder Huntley, neither did the mother appreciate the arguments advanced by her son in reference to his immediate future projects. They thought him too young to go forth into the world without additional counsel of their own, and did not fail to express their fear that they were acting unwisely when at length, after persistent and earnest appeals, they yielded consent to his wishes. It was arranged, however, that he should first enter the Chicago University, and it was at this institution that he received his education. At the age of eighteen, and at the breaking out of the Civil War, he entered the army as Lieutenant in the 16th Illinois Cavalry, and served in the department of the Ohio, then under the command of Burnside. He was engaged in the siege of Knoxville, and as a reward for his heroic conduct, exhibited in several instances before the enemy's works, he was promoted to a captaincy. Soon after this event, he was taken a prisoner of war, while engaged in a skirmish at Jonesville, Tennessee. His capture, however, was not easily affected, and it was not until he and his few companions had become isolated from the main body of the column, and surrounded by a greatly superior force, that they ceased to offer resistance. The captive was speedily conveyed to Richmond, and assigned quarters in the Libby Prison. Here he was held for five months, at the expiration of which he was sent to Macon, Ga., thence to Savannah and Charleston, and lastly to Columbia. While at the latter place he attempted to escape; but bloodhounds were put upon his track, and he was again captured. In December, 1864, after an experience of eleven months of prison life, his exchange was effected. At the close of the war he resigned his commission, and went to California to join his parents, who had gone thither to regain failing health. While here he heard of the wonderful gold discoveries in Montana, and without hesitation resolved to visit this famous locality. To defray the expenses of the trip he conceived the idea of filling two large wagons, each drawn by six horses, with teas and tobacco, and proceeding with the same to the gold fields. The commodities sold at a very high price, and Huntley had the satisfaction of placing in his pocket a good round sum as profits. He made his headquarters for the most part at Helena, and it was, while on one of his visits at this place that he took steps to establish a stage line between it and Fort Benton. Having succeeded in his undertaking, he proceeded to Washington, and was successful in obtaining

several large mail contracts for the territories. He then returned to Helena, and at once made arrangements for establishing various stage routes between important points in Montana, the most noted of which is the Helena and Fort Abercrombie line. These enterprises were by no means free from difficulties and dangers; and unwilling himself to hazard the lives of the men in his employ, without a display of courage on his own part, it was his practice when opening a new route to seat himself upon the box with the driver, and share with him all the perils of the journey. Not infrequently did it occur that they were made the target for the bullets and arrows of hostile Indians. And the record of Huntley shows that no less than eight of his men were killed during the first year of his arduous undertaking. Mr. Huntley still remains in the service, and at the present time can point with pride to 2,000 miles of mail route under his control in the territories. Aside from the merit of individual enterprise, which can be justly claimed by Mr. Huntley, it must not be overlooked that his services in the far west entitle him to take first rank with our public benefactors. Each day reveals more clearly the importance of regular and connected mail transit in our territories, and the time is rapidly approaching when the pioneer efforts of Mr. Huntley in this direction will be still more highly prized by the Government, and the whole territorial population. The unprecedented progress of the great west within the last decade is mainly due to the energy and enterprise of a few daring spirits; and it is but just to claim that Mr. Huntley, by indefatigable efforts in his special field of labor, has contributed largely towards its prosperous development. Suffice it to say that Mr. Huntley's work has been appreciated, and he has been well recompensed for his labors. He commenced life with comparatively nothing, and although quite young, has already amassed a handsome fortune, and promises well for greater work in proportion to greater wealth in the future.

Charles Huntley was not alone in his efforts. Within a year, his cousin Silas S. Huntley arrived on the scene and together they managed to control the vast majority of the stage lines and mail contracts for the Territory of Montana. A section in *Progressive Men of Montana* affords an excellent insight into the life of S. S. Huntley.

S. S. Huntley

Silas S. Huntley was born in Ellicottville, Cattaraugus County, N. Y., May 2, 1831, the son of Daniel Huntley, who was a native of New York and married a Miss Hawkins, of New England. Both represented old families of the early epoch in our national history. Daniel Huntley occupied a high position in the community, owned much real estate, and in his church, the Episcopal, held the office of senior warden. His wife was, however, a Presbyterian. This worthy couple lived useful lives and both died at their New York home. Their son Silas was a student at Springville Academy when the dark cloud of Civil War rose from the national horizon. Ever responsive to the call of duty, the young man abandoned his studies to participate in the greatest internecine strife in history, enlisting in the Thirty-seventh New York Volunteer Infantry. He was rapidly promoted, served on the staffs of Generals Berry and Kearney, and was with each of these officers when they were killed. He was in service in the first and second battles of Bull Run, the conflict at Williamsburg, the sanguinary Seven Days' fight, and other early battles of the contest. At the close of the war he was mustered out of

service, a valiant and loyal veteran, and returned to New York.

In 1867, Mr. Huntley came up the Missouri river to Montana, and here his initiative and progressive spirit was soon in evidence. He organized the stage lines between Helena and Fort Benton, from Helena to Diamond City, Lincoln, Virginia City and Bannack, also from Helena to Fort Abercrombie, and those between Missoula and Walla Walla, Wash.; Virginia City to Bozeman, and from Bozeman and Helena to Tongue River. He and his cousin, Charles C. Huntley, and Bradley Barlow, then president of the Vermont Central Railroad, controlled all stage lines in Montana save that from Helena to Salt Lake City, and held all mail contracts over the great stage lines of the west, the longest being between St. Louis and Walla Walla via Boise, Idaho. The stage line between Missoula and Walla Walla was sublet to Senator W. A. Clark, and through its successful operation was created the nucleus of his immense fortune. The most important line in both passenger and freight business was the Old Shasta Stage Line, which handled all travel between Oregon and California. These partners originated every stage line in Montana and controlled an immense business until the expiration of their mail contracts, when occurred the failure of Mr. Barlow, entailing great financial loss to the Messrs. Huntley. They were then making arrangements with the Emperor of Brazil to operate stage lines in that South American empire, but abandoned this project after their losses.

Mr. Huntley retired from the stage business in 1878, and in company with P. B. Clark, now of Helena, engaged in raising standard-bred horses near Toston, Meagher County. The Huntley and Clark ranch soon became famous far its fine grade of horses, and a number of them soon made conspicuous records on the turf in the east. When the depreciation of the horse market came, Mr. Huntley directed his great energies and executive abilities into other channels of enterprise, though he still retained his ranch property. In 1891, he became the organizer and manager of the Yellowstone Park Transportation Company, which he conducted until his death. He advanced this enterprise to the important position it now holds, that of providing transportation and other accommodations for the greater portion of the tourist business in this splendid "Wonderland." Early in 1901, this company acquired from the Northern Pacific Railroad all its hotels in the park and conducted them in connection with the transportation business.

In politics Mr. Huntley was from the first a Republican, deeply attached to the principles of his party, and believing in the beneficence of their application in the government of his country. He was a faithful follower of President McKinley, with whom his personal relations were intimate and tender, so much so, in fact, that the violent death of the President profoundly affected Mr. Huntley, it being to him a keen personal bereavement. He was also warmly interested in his soldier comrades, being a zealous member of Wadsworth Post No. 2, G. A. R., at Helena, and also of the Loyal Legion. Some twenty years before his death Mr. Huntley was united in marriage with Anna Dean, who was born in Madison, Wis., a daughter of Simeon and Ellen (Watson) Dean. Simeon Dean belonged to the prominent Dean family of Massachusetts, where he was himself born. Ellen Watson Dean was a native of New Hampshire. The eminent ancestors of both came from England.

Mr. Huntley's executive ability was almost phenomenal, and his name is indissolubly connected with Montana history from early pioneer days until death placed its seal upon his brow. He was well known and honored by many eminent public men of the nation, had a wide acquaintance in the national capital and counted among his intimate friends such men as Whitelaw Reid and Murat Halstead. His last illness was of brief duration, and his life ended at his cottage, at Mammoth Hot Springs, in the Yellowstone National Park, on September 11, 1901, from whence his remains were brought to Helena for interment. His death came as a personal bereavement to his hosts of old time friends in Montana who deeply appreciated his noble and useful life. He had to an eminent degree the quality of making steadfast friends, and the memory of his life rests as a benediction on those nearest and dearest to him.

By July, 1866, the tri-weekly stage between Helena and Fort Benton made its first trip. Huntley's line was short lived, at least with respect to the Benton Road. By June 29, 1867, Wells Fargo had purchased the mail contract from Huntley and although this did not give them exclusive rights to stage coaching on the route, ownership of the mail contract was usually the only guarantee for financial success in the stage coach business.

In spite of Indian problems along the route, Wells Fargo's line flourished from 1867 until the fall of 1869. A couple of examples of Indian problems were recorded in undated and unnamed sources tucked away in the vertical files of the Historical Society under "Stagecoach Travel." The first came with the obituary for "Dad" Ross who had driven the Wells Fargo stage in 1867.

He was on his route between Fort Benton and Sun River in 1867 when twenty-five Indians swooped down upon his coach. Ross defended the treasure and lives under his care with shotgun and pistol. After a running battle of several miles, the Indians withdrew less five of their number, who were dead.

The second had to do with Charlie Rowe who drove stage for Wells Fargo in 1868.

A funny thing happened when I was driving stage for the Wells Fargo Co. over the Bird Tail divide between Benton and Helena. In the winter when traffic was light we layed off the concords and used the light wagons, which we called "snaks," and drove only one team of mules. I had the mules what I called "chain broke" that is I had whipped them with a chain that I always carried and as it hurt very much they were deathly afraid of it. They dreaded that chain so much that I had only to rattle it with my foot and they would run like the wind.

One day in December, 1868, I was driving to Twenty-Eight Mile Spring: and just as I was going up a slight incline six or eight miles from the station, a war party of 14 Indians came riding over the hill. When they reached the top, they stopped a minute for a pow-wow. Pretty soon eight of them came toward me, and when they were within about 25 yards, they shouted, "How?" and came dashing around me in a semi-circle to the rear, wheeled about and followed me.

I put my lines across my shoulder so I could guide the team, took up my repeater, as if to take aim, and while my passenger turned so he could keep his eye and gun on the eight, kicked the chain. The mules, already anxious to get home, heard the rattle of the chain and they lit out like lightning. I started them to the right of the six Indians who were coming down the hill from the front of us. As soon as the mules commenced to run, two of the party rode on to intercept us. As one of them rode to my near mule and reached for the rein I took aim at him and he threw up his hands and wheeled to the rear. By this time the whole party was following us on the dead run, but they were without firearms and thought better than to fight us with their arrows. Although I could have picked every one off with my rifle they knew I would not attempt to unless forced and that they might bluff me, into submission. They would have taken our guns and team and probably our scalps as was being done all around, but we soon outdistanced them as the mule were grain-fed and could run at break neck speed for a couple of miles.

When we got to the station we found the three stock-tenders barricaded in the barn. The same party of Indians had attacked the cabin and the men had retreated to the stage barn, which was built to withstand an attack. The Indians had eaten what they wanted from the cabin and had thrown the rest into the snow.

A distance card published in 1868 revealed the location of the stage stops along the Benton Road. The first was called simply "Toll Gate" which presumably was the toll house located at the southern opening to the Little Prickly Pear Canyon near Malcolm Clark's ranch. Second was "Kennedy's" at the ranch belonging to William Kennedy near present day Wolf Creek. An interesting account of an Indian scare experienced by the Kennedys appears in his biography in Michael A. Leeson's *History of Montana-1739–1885*.

Returning to Helena with them [his family] in 1865, he took up a ranch on the Prickly Pear which is still called "Kennedy's Ranch." In August, 1866, he sold out on time and went to Benton, where he kept a hotel and restaurant. The ranch not having been paid for came into his possession again in 1867. He therefore disposed of his business in Benton and returned to the Prickly Pear Valley with his wife and one child and accompanied by one man and a half-breed Indian. As they reached the top of a hill near the Dearborn, they were surprised and captured by sixteen Indians, who took a vote as to whether they should kill them or set them free. The result of the vote

30	WELLS, FARGO & CO.'S OVERLAND EXPRESS.				
From Helena to Fort Benton, 140 Miles.					
	MILES.				MILES.
HELENA	0	0	Sun River	16	84
Toll Gate	25	25	Leaving Sun River	8	92
Kennedy's	12	37	Springs	20	112
Dearborn	16	53	Coolie	16	128
Bird-Tail Rock	15	68	FORT BENTON	12	140
From Fort Benton, Mon., to Helena, Mon.					
	MILES.				MILES.
FORT BENTON	0	0	*Bird-Tail Rock*	16	72
Coolie	12	12	Dearborn	15	87
Springs	16	28	Kennedy's	16	103
Leaving Sun River	20	48	Toll Gate	12	115
Sun River	8	56	HELENA	25	140
From Helena and Virginia, Mon., to Salt Lake City.					
	MILES				MILES.
HELENA	0	0	Eagle Rock	10	299
Ten-Miles	10	10	*TAYLOR'S BRIDGE	9	308
Beavertown	12	22	Cedar Point	10	318
Little Boulder	11	33	Yampatch	9	327
Basin	11	44	Black Foot	11	338
White-Tail Deer	15	59	*Ross Fork*	12	350
Jefferson Bridge	15	74	Pocatello	12	362
Spring Creek	14	88	Black Rock	10	372
Indian Creek	12	100	Robbers' Roost	13	385
California Ranch	12	112	*Carpenter's*	12	397
*VIRGINIA	12	124	Marsh Valley	14	411
Stinking Water	12	136	Devil's Creek	9	420
Slatestone	12	148	*Malad City*	10	430
Sweetwater	12	160	Henderson Creek	9	439
Black-Tail Deer	14	174	Mound Springs	11	450
Toll Gate No. 2	8	182	*BEAR RIVER (Junc.		
Sage Creek	12	194	with Boise Road)	12	462
†*Junction*	12	206	Mormon City	13	475
Summit	10	216	Brigham City	10	485
Pleasant Valley	9	225	Big Dam	11	496
Dry Creek	12	237	*Ogden*	11	507
Hole in the Rock	14	251	Kay's Ward	15	522
Kamas Creek	8	259	Centerville	12	534
Desert Wells	12	271	*SALT LAKE CITY	12	546
Market Lake	18	289			

NOTE.—Capitals, Terminus of Division. Italics, Home Station. * Telegraph Station. † Junction with Bannack and Salmon River Roads.

Wells Fargo Distance Table

was a tie. They then allowed the half-breed a vote and he cleared them and they were set at liberty, but afraid to leave for fear some of the Indians would follow and massacre them, it being 9 o'clock at night before they were given their freedom. He, however, sent the half-breed for the chief, who ordered two Indians to get the oxen and attach them to the wagon, and informed Mr. Kennedy through the half-breed that his safest plan was to go on. This he did, arriving with his family safe at their former home. The same band murdered a man at the same place the following day. He remained on the ranch until 1869, when the Indians became so troublesome that he took his family to Corinne [Utah] and sent them to the states, himself returning to Helena.

Third was "Dearborn" at the crossing of the Dearborn River. Fourth was "Bird Tail Rock," which was a home station for the stage line.

During 1868, it was run by Daniel Campbell but by 1869 it was in the hands of Steve Spitzley.

The fifth stop was "Sun River" managed by John Largent. Next there was "Leaving Sun River," conveniently named for the place where the stage left Sun River Valley.

The seventh stop was the "Springs" or Twenty-Eight Mile Springs. The eighth and last was "Coulee" or Eight Mile Station located on the Teton River. It was the only spot in the vicinity where one could descend from the plateau, on which the road was located, down to the Missouri River.

Apparently, some customers were unhappy with the quality of service provided by Wells Fargo on the Benton Road. The *Helena Weekly Herald* for May 28, 1868, had the following comments on the subject.

Wells Fargo & Co.'s Line-A Gross Imposition Upon the Public

BENTON CITY; May 24,1868.

I arrived here this morning at 8 o'clock, forty-eight hours out from Helena! The stage stock on the route from Kennedy's to Sun River is wholly insufficient to draw empty coaches, to say nothing about passengers, mail, or express matter. Bull teams of freighters were called upon twice to take the coach out of mud-holes and up hills. Passengers, the first night out, walked nearly the entire distance from Dearborn to Bird Tail Rock. Last night, in the darkness mud and rain, passengers were called upon, to walk through the country, bordering the "Lakes," and this morning we are in a plight to, be imagined but scarcely, to be described.

The manner in which a portion of this line is run, I regard as a cheat upon the public, and unless speedily remedied in supplying the necessary stock, will be anathematized by every passenger, compelled to pass over it, as little less than downright robbery. I call the attention of Mr. Pollinger to the contemptible cattle on the Benton division, the absence of grain at a number of the stations to feed his "stock." and their pitiable condition from over work, and nothing to eat. The traveling public demands a remedy at once.

On September 2, 1869, it was announced that Wells Fargo had sold their stage line running from Corinne, Utah [connection point for the Union Pacific railroad] to Helena, Montana to the company of Salisbury and Gilmer, stage line operators out of Salt Lake City, Utah, who provided stage service over the Benton Road for the next eight to ten years. Aware of future competition from the railroads, Wells Fargo & Co made a wise choice in getting out of the stagecoach business in Montana and most of the western portion of the country.

On March 15, 1878, William Rowe of Fort Benton was awarded the mail contract from Helena to Fort Benton. His sureties were Thomas C. Power and Joseph S. Hill both also of Fort Benton. The contract itself was signed by the Postmaster General, D. M. Key, and Thomas Power's brother, John W. Power who was postmaster for Fort Benton at that time. Gilmer and Salisbury continued to run the stages and carry the U. S. Mail from Helena to Benton until July, 1878, at which time William Rowe and Company took over. The transition was not abrupt as Gilmer and Salisbury continued to carry passengers for awhile after that. Rowe started off on July 1, carrying the mail on a daily basis, but only carried passengers three times a week. On "mail only" days, he would use a small mail wagon on the run.

Of particular interest is the fact that on June 15, 1878, John W. Power, William Rowe and Joseph Hill as trustees created the By-Laws for the new corporation known as the Benton and Helena Stage Company. By November 20, 1878, the Benton and Helena Stage Company, with John W. Power as President began to acquire land in Fort Benton as well as the stage stables and corrals at Leaving Sun River and Twenty-Eight Mile Springs from Gilmer and Salisbury. Clearly, the intent was to take over all the stage business on the Benton Road.

On May 29, 1879, the now termed "Helena and Benton Stage Company" advertised in the *Helena Independent* stating that they ran a "Daily Line of Four Horse Coaches to the Head of Navigation." The route was through "Silver City, Fort Shaw, and Sun River crossing, carrying the United States Mail." As an added caveat, the ad noted: "Passengers and express matter carried at reasonable rates, and fast time guaranteed. This line is one of the best appointed in Montana, and due attention is given to the comfort of its patrons."

The book, *Montana-Its Story and Biography*, gives a full and insightful story of this incredible man, William Rowe.

William Rowe. Nearly eighty years have dissolved in the mists of the irrevocable past since William Rowe, venerable pioneer, first saw the light of day. He has lived through one of the most remarkable, and in many respects the most wonderful, epochs in the world's history. There will never be another like it, for it embraced the period when the strong-armed home-seekers from the eastern states and from the western countries of Europe invaded the great west (he being among the number) and redeemed it from the wilds, bringing it up through various stages to the present high state of civilization. To all this he has been a most interested, and by no means a passive, spectator, having sought to do his full share in the work of progress in the locality, which he finally selected as his place of abode. He talks most interestingly of the early days, when customs and manners were different, everything, in fact, unlike what our civilization is today. Because of his sterling qualities of character and his splendid record he enjoys the respect and esteem of all who know him.

William Rowe was born in Cornwall, England, on February 2, 1840, and is the son of James and Julia (Williams) Rowe, both of whom were also natives of Cornwall. The father was born in 1801, and died on April 28, 1877, when seventy-six years of age, while the mother, who was born in 1802, died on December 29, 1876, when seventy-four years old. Of the thirteen children born to this worthy couple but two are living, the subject of this review and Mary Ann, the widow of William Davis and who lives in Fort Benton, Montana. James Rowe was reared and educated in Cornwall, England, and later went to work in the mines. After his marriage he went to Honolulu, and still later to California, whence he drifted into Mexico. In the spring of 1844 Mr. Rowe returned to England, and then brought to America his wife and their children, seven or eight in number, landing at Quebec. Their trip was made by a slow-going sailing ship, between ninety and a hundred days being consumed on the voyage. On the way across one of the children died and would have been buried at sea had it not been for the protestations of the mother, who was

permitted to bring the body the rest of the way. From Quebec they continued their journey up through Montreal to Detroit, Michigan, thence to Chicago. From there they proceeded to Elizabethtown, Jo Daviess County, Illinois the entire trip from Quebec having been made with a four horse team and wagon. Mr. Rowe engaged in mining, in which he was prospered and was soon enabled to build a home for the family. He was adept with many tools, being not only a carpenter and shoemaker, but was even able to make his own clothes. He later engaged in farming and stock-raising for a time, but after the death of his wife and while on his way to Montana to visit his son, the subject of this sketch, he died on the steamer Benton during the trip up the Missouri River. His remains were buried at Fort Beaufort. He was a faithful and honored member of the Methodist Episcopal Church.

William Rowe was a lad of four years of age when the family emigrated from England to America, settlement being made at Elizabethtown, near Galena, Jo Daviess County, Illinois. The schools of that place he attended in winter, but at the early age of eight years he became a wage earner, his first work being dropping corn, for which he received twenty-five cents a day, working from sunrise to sunset. He was but a small boy at a small job, but he stuck faithfully to his work, and in that way earned enough to pay for a cow. In December, 1849, he left home and obtained employment at watering horses, but in the following spring he went to work for his brother-in-law, Henry Roberts, at farm work. Later he was employed at cabinet work in Galena for a time, but later went to work again for Henry Roberts, with whom he remained until seventeen years of age. Then he was employed to mix mortar and carry a hod, for which he received one dollar a day, but later obtained a chance to work for his board and opportunity to attend school. He then entered the employ of a Mr. Coleman, who was to pay him $160 for a year's work, but at the end of nine months he went to British Hollow, Grant County, Wisconsin, where he drove a team, hauling lead for Hymar & Vance. He was sent to Fairplay, where he bought lead for that firm, and later he went to Portage Lake, in the northern peninsula of Michigan, where he obtained work in the Franklin Iron Mine. From there he went to Detroit, Michigan, thence to Chicago, and to Galena, Illinois. During the following year he was engaged in driving for the Wisconsin Stage Company, after which he took eighty head of horses to LaCrosse, Wisconsin, for the Minnesota Stage Line, the J. C. Burbank Company. After breaking the horses, he took them to Winona, Minnesota, where on October 1, 1861, he put them to work on the road. During the following winter Mr. Rowe drove on the river between St. Paul, Minnesota, and LaCrosse, Wisconsin, but in the following spring he was sent to St. Cloud, from which place he drove the route to Elk Creek or Bailey Station. His next location was at Abercrombie, Minnesota, then at Campbell's during the summer of 1862. He was then called back to St. Paul with his teams and drove the stage between Henderson and St. Peter, Minnesota. In the fall of that year he witnessed the hanging of thirty-nine Indians who had been convicted of murdering white men, women and children during one of their uprisings at or near Mankato, where the hanging occurred. During the winter of 1862–3 Mr. Rowe drove stage between St. Paul and Redwing, and the following incident shows somewhat the character of the route he drove. On March 23, 1863, on his way up from Redwing, he was compelled to cross the Mississippi River. The ice had broken up and a ferry boat was used to transfer them to the other side. This time he did not want to cross on the boat, as it was exceedingly dangerous, but two of his passengers were very anxious to get through to St. Paul, so they decided to attempt the crossing. The stay line on the boat was made fast to a big boulder on the shore and Mr. Rowe drove his team onto the boat. The horses were on board, but as the wheels of the coach struck the edge of the boat they pushed it from the shore and the coach went into the icy water, the two men being drowned. The other six passengers were rescued. Later Mr. Rowe drove between St. Anthony and Anoka, Minnesota, and between Clearwater and Mantoville. Then Mr. Rowe changed his vocation and for a time engaged in the operation of a saloon and billiard hall in St. Cloud. In the spring of 1864, he bought a team of horses, harness and a wagon, and loading up with eleven barrels of flour, he headed for Selkirk, Canada. There he sold his flour and his watch and returned, to St. Cloud, where he found his partner in the business there had sold his interest. Mr. Rowe then sold his own interest and went to St. Paul, where he entered the employ of the Minnesota Stage Company. About

this time he met with a serious misfortune, losing the sight of both of his eyes for about two years. He went to visit his family in Illinois and while there had his eyes treated, with successful results, the sight being restored.

For one year Mr. Rowe was in business in Grant County, Wisconsin, but in June, 1867, he landed at Fort Benton, Montana, having come up the Missouri River from Omaha on the steamer "Deer Lodge." From there he went to Helena, walking the greater part of the distance, and there bought a horse, with which he went with the stampede to Blue Cloud Gulch, where he engaged in prospecting and mining. Eventually he gave his claim away for a tin cup and a butcher knife and returned to Helena, where he engaged in mining. Later he drove a six horse stage outfit between Helena and Canada Ranch, but a year later returned to Fort Benton and engaged in the feed stable business. In the spring of 1869, he bought a span of mules and started for Silver Creek, but his mules got away and he chased them to Wolf Creek, thence to Helena, where he engaged in hauling dirt for $20 a day. He sold his wagon for $125 and neck-yoke and whiffletree for $25, and went to Pioneer City, where he worked in the mines as long as the water lasted, after which he engaged in prospecting and mining on French Gulch, where he was successful in finding gold and mined there for about a year. He then sold out and spent the winter at Arkansas Springs, Arkansas, in the hope of recovering his health. He then went to Deer Lodge, Montana, where he was appointed under sheriff, under West Jones, and night watchman. After two years' service he opened a billiard hall, which he later sold and in the fall of 1872 returned to Fort Benton and engaged in the hotel business.. He was appointed Sheriff of Chouteau County, serving two years, and then was elected for a similar period. He then was appointed United States Deputy Marshal, serving about six months, following which he was appointed United States Mounted Revenue Inspector for Montana and Idaho, holding that position for about one and a half years. He then continued the operation of the hotel at Fort Benton and at the same time took a contract to carry the mail between Fort Benton and Helena daily for four years at $8,000 per year, also a special contract to carry the mail between Fort Benton and Fort Assiniboine for two years at $6,000 per month.

William Rowe

He soon afterward sold his contracts for $26,700, [to J. M. Powers] and in the fall of 1884 he began buying horses, having his headquarters at Fort Benton. Then for about one and a half years he was engaged in the livery business and in the operation of a cattle and horse ranch, in which he has continued ever since. He is the owner of 340 acres of splendid land near Fort Benton, of which about 200 acres are, in cultivation. At one time he was an extensive breeder of English shire horses, having paid as high as $3,500 for a stallion of that breed. He also bred Shorthorn cattle, and in all his operations has been progressive and enterprising. He also owns a number of pieces of city property in Sioux Falls and elsewhere.

On January 18, 1876, at Fort Benton, Montana, Mr. Rowe was married to Katie Jane Babbage, who was born on May 1, 1860, in Vancouver, Washington. Her parents were John and Catherine (Cullinane) Babbage, the former a native of Devonshire, England, and the latter of the city of Limerick, Ireland.

To Mr. and Mrs. Rowe have been born sixteen children, seven of whom are deceased, all passing away in infancy except Harry, who died at the age of twenty-four years.

Politically Mr. Rowe is an earnest Republican, while fraternally he is a member of Chouteau Lodge No. 25, Ancient Free and Accepted Masons, of which lodge he has served as master two terms. He also holds the distinction of being the first Mason raised in Chouteau County. Quiet and unostentatious and ever attending strictly to his own affairs, he has made better all who have come with the range of his influence, so that his career is eminently worthy of being recorded on the pages of the history of the state of his adoption.

William Rowe had been a stock grower in Bannack according to the 1870 census. The *Helena Independent* of January 13, 1925, provides an obituary that tells a few more interesting facts about his life. At that time he was one of the oldest pioneer residents of Fort Benton, having arrived in Montana in the early 1860's on the same boat that brought T. C. Power. For many years he was a stage driver from Fort Benton to Helena. Finally, he worked his way up to mail contractor and actually ran the stage line between those two places. He also was identified with several other business adventures. He owned the Overland Hotel in Benton, the Emerson in Jefferson City and the Grand Union in Benton.

William Rowe's brother, Charles Rowe was involved with William in the operations of the stage line and drove the stage frequently.

Fisk Ellis gives us a rare insight into the operations of a stage station in his article about the Dearborn Country carried in the *Great Falls Tribune* of February 24, 1935. His mother and father ran the Flat Creek Station just three miles northwest of Dearborn Crossing from 1879 to 1882, during Rowe's ownership of the line.

The stage station was still at the Dearborn Crossing four miles toward Helena from Flat Creek when spring opened [1879]. Here the driver from Helena stopped. Horses were changed; the coach greased and passengers ate supper and settled themselves for the night ride over Bird Tail Divide with a new driver to Sun River Leavings.

But this location did not make an equitable division of the work between Rock Creek and Eagle Rock for it made the drive only 13 miles between Rock Creek and the Dearborn over comparatively good roads, while it was 17 miles between the Dearborn and Eagle Rock, over Bird Tail Divide, the hardest stretch of road between Helena and Benton. Every week, teams on the long drive were switched to the short drive and vice versa, to save horse flesh.

To equalize this, the stage line management decided, the year of which I write, to move the station to Flat Creek, making the easy drive 17 miles and the Bird Tail drive 13. Possibly absence of a saloon at Flat Creek may also have been a contributing factor.

Built a Cabin

When father knew for certain that we were to get the stage station he began his preparations at once. Two things were required, a cabin for the stock tender and drivers and a barn for 10 horses. The cabin was built of logs cut on the hillsides near the mouth of Flat Creek; the barn of lumber hauled from Bob Ells' sawmill in Prickly Pear Canyon, three or four miles above Kisselpaugh's saloon, which was not far from the site of the present town of Wolf Creek. By midsummer the buildings were ready.

The evening of Aug. 1, a 14 passenger coach, loaded almost to the limit, came rolling over the bench-land from Helena. It was an hour earlier than usual, for it had not stopped the customary time at the Dearborn, as formerly, but had come through to Flat Creek to change horses and drivers and for the passengers to have supper.

A driver named Gibson brought it in. There were 15 passengers and the boots were crammed with baggage. Four horses was the usual team, but that night there were six and, when the coach rolled out for the trip over the Bird Tail, there were six.

What a wonderful sight for a 9 year-old boy leaning against the garden fence to see Gib, as he was called, swing the six horses in a graceful circle and bring the coach up beside our front gate for the passengers to alight. It was then that I abandoned being a cowpuncher, muleskinner or bullwhacker and determined to be a stage driver driving six horses.

Little did anyone think that poor Gib was coming to Flat Creek his first and last time. Two nights later, too sick to drive farther, he climbed off the boot at Rock Creek and staggered to a bed, telling the stock tender to "take her through." The stock tender had formerly been a stage driver so he arranged for someone to care for his stock, mounted the boot and turned the stage over to the next driver on time.

Died of Smallpox

"Smallpox in its worst form," said the Doctor sent from Helena. Gibson was isolated in a cabin nearby under care of an old man who had formerly had the disease. In a few days Gib was dead. The old man buried the body, then burned the cabin, Gibson's and his own clothes, had a thorough bath in the creek and donned fresh garments that had been laid out for him on the prairie. So far as I remember, there was no further spread of the disease.

These were extreme disinfecting methods, but dread of smallpox was such that no one took chances. We were too close to its ravages of Civil War days to regard smallpox as light as we do today.

Concord coaches such as I have mentioned were particularly well adapted to their work. Strength was built into them at every point. The body, with its big boots, front and rear, was mounted on thorough-braces that permitted it to roll or rock back and forth, taking much of the strain off the wheels in gullies and chuck holes. If the front wheels came to an abrupt stop against the bank in a gully, the coach body rolled forward on the thorough-braces and stopped slowly instead of with a blow as did the ordinary wagons.

Years of experience had taught their builders how to get the most possible capacity into the bodies of these old coaches. Under the driver seat and feet was the front boot. In it were carried the mail, treasure box small express and, on occasions, a little baggage. The rear boot extended back from the coach body four or five feet, had a heavy cowhide apron to cover its contents. as did the front boot, and held from 500 to 1,000 pounds of baggage. The large coaches had four seats inside, each one long enough for three passengers, with room on the driver's seat for two more, so these coaches were known as 14 passenger wagons.

An iron rail around the top permitted light baggage to be carried thereon. Some times passengers, too. I saw, now and then as many as 17 passengers in and on a coach, three perched on top holding firmly to the iron rail. When so loaded, six horses were used if the time schedule was maintained.

Stage station routine was simple. The coach from Helena arrived, if roads were good, about 6:30 in the evening, staying long enough for the passengers to eat supper, usually about an hour. The one from Benton came about 3 in the morning, stopping just long enough to change horses. The stock tender's job was to have the horses fed, watered and harnessed, ready for the change when the stages arrived, and to see that the drivers were awake and ready.

My folks bought the Flat Creek Ranch off Bob Thoroughman in 1871, and moved onto it in early spring of that year. Thoroughman had not lived there for some time and the place had run largely to rattle snakes and packrats. The barn was a log affair with a rattle trap board roof back of the barn was a log corral; in front, a pole corral. All in all, it was not much of a place, but it did not cost much, $400 I believe, and it was at the least a start in the range country.

On May 5, 1882, William Rowe agreed to sell his stage line to Jacob Powers, a rancher from Meagher County. By May 23, 1882, the *Helena Independent* carried the following information.

Jacob Powers, the new mail contractor on the Benton line bought the coaches, stock, etc. from the former contractors at the following prices: coaches, $500 each; stage stations, $500 each; horses, $135 each; four horse harness, $100 per set.

Jacob had been born in Maine in 1842, and is listed in the 1850 census as living with his parents, Phillip and Stephanie Powers, brothers Hannibal, Francis and Ammi and sister, Texas. They all resided in Pittsfield, Somerset County, Maine. By 1860, five more offspring were added to the family, making a total of ten children.

Brother, Francis, and sister, Texas, came to Montana with Jacob who supposedly migrated for health reasons. The three are listed in the 1880 Census as living in the Missouri River Valley in Meagher County. The two brothers were said to

Jacob Matthew Powers

be stock farmers while Texas was keeping house for them.

In the year 1885, Jacob Powers exhibited the kind of stamina, courage and conviction so typical of western transplants from the eastern states. His stage was held up near today's Sieben Ranch and Jacob took it personally. He wanted to make sure that the perpetrators did not get away with such an audacious act.

The story was well documented by Powers later on as he lived out his life in Great Falls. Finally, it was published in the *Montana Magazine* for autumn, 1980.

On the 27th day of May, in the year of 1884, while engaged as superintendent of the Helena and Benton Stage Line, I left Helena at 3 o'clock p.m. to go to Mitchell's Stage Station [now Sieben], which was twenty eight miles from Helena.

When I arrived at Silver City, I found the Mitchell Station stock tender there, who informed me that the stage that left Helena that morning had been held up and robbed about six hundred yards beyond that station. He had come there to telephone me and John Fallon (the stage agent at Helena) had informed him that I had left town a few minutes before and that William Steele, a Deputy Sheriff, was in the office and would start for the place of robbery immediately. Steele and [George] Conrad, two deputies, took a short cut through the hills and arrived at the station just as I did.

We ate supper, then went down and looked over the ground where the stage was robbed. John Mead, who was working for Mitchell and was in charge of the ranch for a few days while Mitchell was away, informed us that on the morning before, two men had come to the station just after sunrise, put their horses up and stayed until afternoon, and that their horses showed by the mud on their legs that they had crossed creeks instead of following the road; this and other circumstances aroused his suspicions, so he took particular notice of everything they had about them; he said they wore cowboy hats, and had on chaps, and each had cantanas on his saddle, one had a bay and the other a black horse, also gave the brands on their horses, [and] could give full a description of their clothing; the slimmest one had a black mustache, wore boots with high heels and one of the boots had a cut two or three inches long in the instep which had been sewed up.

A half-breed stopping in the neighborhood had seen two men answering this description, about three miles east of the station, riding away very fast, about an hour after the stage was held up. We believed these to be the parties that we wanted. Steele and Conrad stopped at Mitchell's that night, while I, thinking that the men might cross the Missouri River at Canyon Ferry and go over into the Judith Country, started for Helena at 10 o'clock. That night was very dark as it rained a little occasionally, made the trip in four hours, hired a livery team and started for Canyon Ferry, which is eighteen miles east of Helena.

At the crossing of Prickly Pear, at what is now East Helena, I looked through the stable at the station but did not find the black and bay horses that I was looking for, reached the Ferry about 6 o'clock in the morning, and found that no horseman had crossed there. I fed my team, ate breakfast there and then turned back, at Spokane Creek, I turned to the left and went up to the Half Way House, (an old stage station on

the Helena and Bozeman stage road,) about fourteen miles from Helena, on the way, I talked with several ranchmen but learned nothing. The Half Way House, at that time was kept by Bruce Toole. Here I had my team put up and stayed till afternoon. After telling Mr. Toole that our stage had been robbed, he informed me that about a week or ten days before that, a man had stopped at his place, several days, whom he believed to be a horse thief, and gave this reason, the day that the man left his place, he went into Helena and saw this man with Con Murphy, they had changed horses, Murphy was riding this man's horse and he was riding Murphy's, and Mr. Toole knew that Murphy was a horse thief. He also told me that the man claimed to be unwell while staying at his house, but he was satisfied that there were other parties connected with him, around there some of the time, for one evening this man bought a bottle of whiskey, went up over the hill back of the stable, and was gone until after dark, when he came back he did not have the whiskey, and Mr. Toole thought that he had taken it to some of his friends.

I asked about the color of the horses and he said, one was black and the other was a bay, also gave me a description of the men which tallied with the supposed stage robbers. Mr. Toole told me that Con Murphy stopped the winter before with John O'Neil, who lived on Spokane Creek about a mile and a half northeast of the Half Way House, but could not give the name of the other man, for he did not register, but heard him say he was formerly from Texas. I had never seen Con Murphy but knew him by reputation as a horse thief connected with the Edmondsons who were noted horse thieves.

I reached Helena about 3 o'clock and reported to [Stephen C.] Gilpatrick, the Sheriff, what I had learned, also told him that they were a part of the band of Edmondson horse thieves. Without taking any sleep, in twenty-four hours I had ridden nearly one hundred miles, found out who robbed the stage, and felt sure that they would be captured in a short time. Steele and Conrad had come into Helena without learning any thing after I left them the night before.

The next day about noon, Steele and I started for Edmondson's Ferry, which is about ten miles above Canyon Ferry, and owned by

Edmondson, the father of the thieves. When we got as far as the Half Way House, we met a man by the name of Reed, who told us that on the morning before, two men traveling toward Radersburg on horse back had stopped at Mr. Gallagher's place near Bedford, and got something to eat, but he could not tell us much about them, so we concluded to go over there and get the particulars. Mr. Gallagher said that one of them came to his house very early in the morning and got something to eat, which he took out to where the other man had stopped, about half a mile from the house; while they were eating, he examined them through his glasses and saw that each one had a gray horse. Steele said that they had received word at the sheriff's office that two gray horses were stolen at Clancy, Jefferson County, night before last and these were probably the thieves. We then turned back towards Helena, stopped at Beaver Creek for supper, and arrived at the Half Way House about 9 o'clock, where we put up for the night. We had traveled about forty-five miles since we left Helena.

Just before we got to Beaver Creek on our return, we met Conrad and another deputy, who informed us that a man had come into Helena, who said he had met the men about ten miles east of where the half-breed saw them riding very fast, on the afternoon that the stage was robbed.

Before retiring that night, we arranged that Steele and Conrad would get up at day light in the morning, go down and watch O'Neil's house, and that I, being acquainted with O'Neil, would eat an early breakfast, go down and go into the house. The next morning when I had almost reached O'Neil's house, Steele and Conrad came out of a side gulch and told me that they had watched the house about three hours and had not seen anyone around it. I told them to go and get their breakfast and I would go down and see if I could find anyone there. While going down into the gulch, I saw a man leave the house with a dish, and go towards some horses that were on a hill on the opposite side, about a quarter of a mile up the gulch. When I got to the house, I found O'Neil standing near the door, after passing the time of day, I asked him if he could tell me where I would be apt to find a horse that I had running on that range; he told me where it was the last time he saw it. While talking to him, the man who had gone up to the horses caught one, got

on it and started the others toward the corral but they ran across the gulch and went over where I had left Steele and Conrad, before he could drive them to the corral. As soon as he corralled them, he saddled a horse, rode up over the hill, was gone a short time and came back, he did not say anything about seeing anybody in my hearing but at one time, he and O'Neil were a short distance from me.

They were called in to breakfast and I went into the house with them. There was another man there, a ranchman, who was hunting horses and had stopped for the night. It did not take long to satisfy me that he was just what he claimed to be.

After breakfast, I had a long talk with O'Neil and his wife, and told them that the stage had been robbed. When I left, O'Neil walked up over the hill with me, and asked if anyone had come down with me; I told him that I had come down alone, he then told me that the man said there were two men near there, one of whom was armed with a rifle, and they had gone up toward the Half Way House. I told him Steele and Conrad had come to the Half Way House with me and probably they were the parties whom he had seen; he then said he could tell me who robbed the stage; and said it was Con Murphy and another man whose name he had forgotten but knew he was from Texas; I replied, "I know it and they are the parties whom I am hunting." [H]e said, "I would not have had you come here for anything." I said, "You know that Con Murphy stopped with you last winter, and as they came this way after they robbed the stage, I thought this might be a good place to look." Thinking that I might learn more by making a confidant of him, I told him what I had ascertained about them; he told me that about two weeks before, the Edmondsons had gathered up a band of horses on that range; these were the horses they had stolen during the fall and winter in other parts of the territory, and driven there and turned out, and had driven these horses away, a few days before; they had told him there was a park up in the mountains to which they took the horses, some place in Idaho, and in going there, they could cross Snake River, at a ford, when the water was low. He also said Con Murphy and this man came to his place the Saturday morning before and took breakfast; Murphy introduced the man to him and said they were going over that way to see what they could pick up, then they were going to follow the others into Idaho. ...

O'Neil requested me not to tell anyone that he had told me anything, also advised me not to try to capture them, but let others do it, if I did try to capture them, to shoot on sight for they had often said they never would be taken alive, subsequent events proved that he was right.

When I got in sight of the Half Way House they were all watching for me as they were getting anxious over my long stay. We then went into Helena and reported to the sheriff what I had learned, he sent Steele and Conrad to Deer Lodge that night, so they could take the Utah Northern train to Dillon, the next morning, to see if they could head off the Edmondsons before they got out of the country. The night that Steele and Conrad went to Deer Lodge, the gang stole about twenty-two head of horses, belonging to John Keating [a rancher], out of his pasture, which was about three miles above Edmondson's Ferry, drove them over into Crow Creek Valley, and camped there most of the next day; here they were seen by Lou Smith [another rancher in the area] who knew Henry Edmondson and Con Murphy, as they had hired him a short time before, to assist in branding some colts. ...

Smith did not know the two men who were with them, but noticed the brands on the horses they were driving, so, when he heard that Keating's horses were stolen, he could tell who had them and the direction they had gone.

Powers' efforts in the case ended at this point, but Con Murphy's story was far from over. From the *Helena Daily Herald* of July 19:

EXAMINATION OF CON MURPHY BEFORE JUDGE ALDEN

Both a Road Agent and a Horse Thief
He and George Munn, His Pard,
Robbed the Benton Coach
on the 26th of May Last.

Munn Killed in Idaho by the
Madison County

Party Composed of George Thexton, Jr.,
Hank Stewart, Jack Adams, and
Others, Who Followed the
Trail via Henry's
Lake Into Idaho Territory.

This morning the noted convict "Con Murphy," who escaped from the Deer Lodge Penitentiary and was rearrested several years ago at Dearborn, was brought before Judge I. R. Alden for examination this morning for robbing the U. S. Mail and the Benton coach on the 26th of May last. It appears that Murphy was a member of the noted band of horse thieves that raided Jefferson County last month, and that he and his pard, George Munn, were detailed by the robber band to hold up the Benton coach and get what money they could, and then join the thieves somewhere on the trail. On Thursday, the 26th of May, two suspicious characters came to Mitchell's ranch, 24 miles from Helena, on the Benton Road, and remained there until after they had taken dinner. These persons were scrutinized very closely by several who saw them, and so definite was the description given of the travelers that a cut in the side of the shoe was recognized in the shoe of the dead Munn who was afterwards killed at the house of Ricks in Idaho. The robbers while at Mitchell's gave out by inquiries about the round-up that they were cattle men. Some time before the arrival of the coach from Helena these men were noticed to go down the road towards the month of the Prickly Pear Canyon, and being suspicious characters their every action was noticed, and they were seen after that by several. The coach was held up and the passengers robbed about 2 o'clock on the same afternoon. The robbers mounted their horses that had been hitched in the brush and rode away Wring the road for the horse thieves that were to be found on the trail somewhere between Jefferson County and Henry's Lake.

Con Murphy was identified at the examination by Elijah H. Kates who saw him and his pard on the Bear Tooth road near Judge Hilger's on the evening of the robbery and was described particularly by the witness who also gave a close description of Mann.

Mr. Charles W. Cooper identified his gold watch and chain taken at the coach robbery and found on the person of Con Murphy by George Thexton, Jr., who arrested him at Rick's ranch about the 11th of June. Thomas J. Hartigan and Charles E. Dudley also gave important testimony. When arrested Murphy was compelled to surrender to his captor, George Thexton, Jr., who testified that Murphy handed over to him a 38-calibre Colt's revolver and the gold watch and, chain taken from Mr. Cooper. When arrested Mr. Thexton found under the lining of Murphy's hat the mask used at the stage robbery, which was made of dark berege—a soft woolen fabric used for veils—and which Murphy tore into three pieces, saying, "you have got enough against me already," one of which was produced at the examination this morning. The case was prosecuted by W. C. DeWitt, U. S. District Attorney, for the government, and Mr. Casey for the defense. The testimony was conclusive—almost proof positive. The attorneys declined to argue the case, and the prisoner was remanded to jail in default of $1,500 bail to await the action of the next U. S. Grand Jury.

The *Helena Daily Herald* for January 31, 1885 continues the story of this daring outlaw.

Two nights after this Con Murphy escaped from the Helena City jail by cutting his way through the roof and stealing a valuable horse and equipments from Dallas Haskill, of Helena and was 30 miles away before daylight and before his escape was discovered. Riding by night and laying in the mountains by day, he worked his way down the Yellowstone to near Big Timber, with a reward upon his head from U. S. Marshal Botkin of one hundred dollars. On the 6th of August he was recaptured near Big Timber and brought back to Helena, and was the first prisoner in the new steel-clad cells of Lewis and Clark County, on August 8, 1884.

To stop the mad career of this robber and desperado there were mutterings heard in Helena that the shortest way to do this would be to let lynch law be meted out to him. The contractor of the new cells; not yet completed, fearing an attack upon the jail before his contract was taken off his hands, prevailed upon the U. S. Marshal to send the prisoner, to the prison of Silver Bow County.

A CHARMED LIFE - MURPHY LEAPS FROM THE CAR WHEN THE TRAIN IS RUNNING 18 MILES AN HOUR

On Saturday, August 9th he left Helena for the jail of Silver Bow County, in charge of Under Sheriff George Conrad. On the way to the Silver City [Butte] and when the train was near Stuart, Murphy, with both feet shackled and handcuffed, made a leap for liberty from the car window while the train was going eighteen miles an hour. The deputy noticing the absence of the prisoner, who had stepped into the water closet, rushed in after him, and was just in time to see him going out of the window feet foremost. The train was stopped after a while and run back to the place of the escape, which consumed time enough to allow Murphy to hide in the brush, although it was daylight Sunday morning. Here the deputy was put off, who, with the assistance of some of the neighbors beat up the brush and soon found their prisoner lying in the mud close to a little stream of water. He had forced a bracelet from one hand by hauling it against a tree, taking with it the skin for some distance. When recaptured, the prisoner was marched ten miles in front of a revolver, with his shackles removed for fast walking, and safely lodged in the Butte jail, where he remained until transferred back to the Lewis and Clark County jail for trial at the November term of 1884. When sent for by the court on the second day after the election, November 6th, the court was informed that the prisoner was not to be found—that he had made his escape. Since which time and until his final recapture, fight, and death related in other columns of the Herald, he is supposed to have lived in the mountains near Helena receiving subsistence and succor from the remaining persons of the notorious band of horse thieves—only four of whom are known to have been captured, sentenced, and killed and coming into the city and causing the late fiendish incendiaries.

Murphy was finally taken into custody at the O'Neil House. Powers summarized what happen as Murphy was being returned to Helena.

A blizzard came up and they stopped over night at the Half Way House. The next morning while McFarland was getting his team ready to start, the policeman took the hand-cuffs off of Murphy, to let him put his overcoat on, then looked out of the window to see if McFarland was ready, as he turned towards Murphy, he saw that he had a pistol, they exchanged shots, and Murphy passed through a door, went up the stairs and entered a wardrobe that was next to the side of the house. The policeman was shot through the left hand, but Murphy was unhurt. Murphy's pistol had not been emptied, and he dared them to come up and face him, but in stead of doing so, they sent for O'Neil, who came with his rifle, stationed himself in a woodshed, on the side of the house that Murphy was on. O'Neil sent two bullets through the side of the house, which went close to Murphy, who seeing that they would soon get him if he stayed there, offered to surrender. ...

When it became known in town [Helena on January 26, 1885,] that Murphy had been captured, about two hundred men went out and meeting Murphy two or three miles from town, took him from the officer and hung him to a rail road bridge.

The stage coach era on the Benton Road ended shortly after the completion of the Montana Central Railroad in 1887. By then many had traveled the route and, fortunately, a few had recorded their experiences.

Partygoers on Stage near Helena

Stage Stopping at Wells Fargo Office on Bridge Street, Helena, Montana

Sun River Stage

Charley Rowe Driving the Mail Stage

Last Stage through Little Prickly Pear Canyon-Circa 1887

HELENA AND BENTON STAGE CO.

J. M. POWERS, President and General Manager.

A DAILY LINE OF

Four and Six-Horse Coaches

TO

FORT BENTON,

VIA

Cartersville,

Dearborn,

Fort Shaw and

Sun River.

CONNECTING WITH STAGES FOR

Great Falls of the Missouri,

Old Agency, Piegan Agency,

Florence and Augusta.

	Distances from Helena.			Fare.
FORT BENTON,	- - 145 Miles,	- -	-	$15 50
SUN RIVER,	90 "	-	-	10 00
FORT SHAW,	- 85 "	-	-	9 50
DEARBORN,	- 50 "	-	-	7 00
CARTERSVILLE,	- 38 "	-	-	5 50

SPEED, SAFETY and COMFORT ASSURED.

HELENA, - - - - **MONTANA.**

Last Ad for the Stage Company in the **Montana Gazetteer** *1886–87*

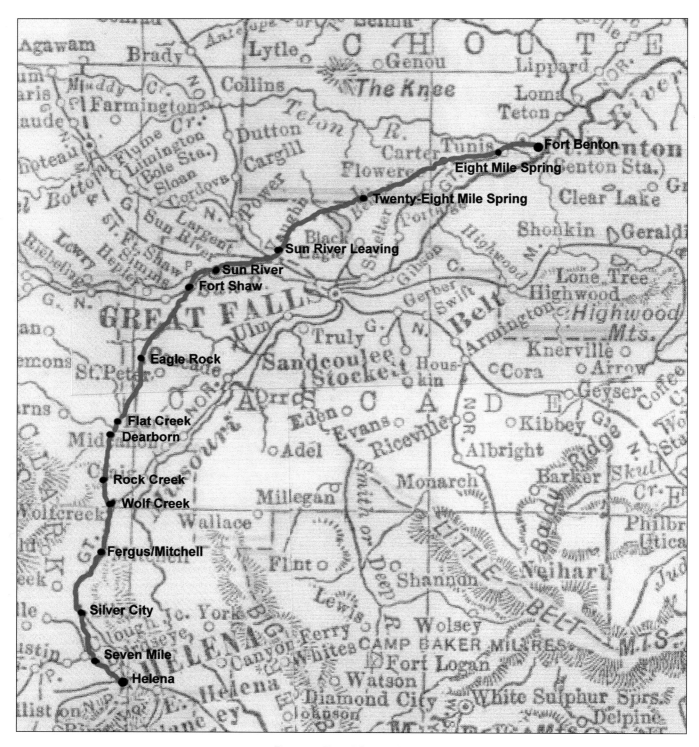

Benton Road Stage Stops

Entrance to Little Prickly Pear Canyon

Dearborn Crossing on the Benton Road

Bird Tail Divide on the Benton Road

Bird Tail Butte on the Benton Road

Chapter VII

Traveling by Stage Coach

During the twenty or so years that stage travel was available on the Benton Road, newspaper editors frequently printed stories of experiences on that route supplied by the traveling public. By following these stories, which span over half of the period during which stage travel took place, we can focus in on stage stops, scenery along the way and road and routing improvements

The *Helena Weekly Herald* for April 16, 1874, carried the following item:

NORTHERN MONTANA 1874

The "Judge," just returned from a tour through the Sun River and adjacent countries, looking after the interests of the *Helena Herald*, has the following remarks upon persons and things to offer:

After the start is made for a trip through northern Montana over the most direct route the first place of note coming under one's observation is Silver City, the oldest, and yet by no means the least mining camp in the territory. But little change is observed in the town since a year ago, but that little is for the better. John Green, the widely known and popular landlord and merchant is still at the Silver Heels House, and continues to dispense that courtesy and accommodation so natural to him and agreeable to his patrons.

John Green opened a miner's supply store at Silver City in 1867. The 1870 census shows John Green as "Inn keeper at Grizzly and Silver Creeks." John was at that time a thirty-five year old from Ohio. His wife Isabella from Canada was living with him.

A year later he had sold out to Andrew Glass, a twenty-seven year old Fort Shaw resident who

was born in Sweden. By 1878, the Silver Heels Hotel had been sold once again.

Just across the way where once we found Uncle Lemlein, we now are greeted by Fred Lindewedell [Lindwedel], who makes a splendid landlord, and is doing well as proprietor of the Silver City Hotel.

In the 1870 census for Silver Creek, Martin Lenline and E. M. Childs are noted as "hotel keepers." In that same year "Wait" Lindwedel is reported to be a thirty-one year old "gulch miner" born in Prussia and living at the South Fork of Canyon Creek and the Little Prickly Pear. In October, 1877, a ball was held at Fred Lindwedel's in Silver City. Apparently, Fred was also the local Postmaster as he resigned that position in July, 1878.

During the past winter large dumps of pay dirt have been taken from the bed of the stream, which are now being washed up. The usual amount of bar diggings, will be worked the coming season, and Silver Creek will contribute towards the national wealth at least its usual amount for the season.

A five mile drive from Silver City takes us across the Little Prickly Pear Basin to Billy Johns' station at the head of the Upper Canyon, where the traveler can find good refreshments for man and beast. The road through the seven miles of canyon below is a good one, and none who travel it grudge the toll charged.

William Johns is listed in the 1870 census as a "Toll Gate Keeper," age thirty-five and born in Prussia. Living with him was his twenty-two year old wife, Katharine.

That portion of the Benton Road for which his toll applied extended from Johns' ranch through the Upper Little Prickly Pear Canyon to the second toll booth belonging to King and Gillette which was located at the southern end of the Lower Little Prickly Pear Canyon. This toll road was laid out and built by Nicholas Hilger and Billy Johns in 1872. Nicholas Hilger was the father of the well known Montana pioneer, David Hilger.

Between the Upper and Lower Canyons is situated the ranches of James Fergus and Son, surrounded by a grazing country second to no other in the mountains; and possessing within the enclosed fields meadow land sufficient to supply hay for even thrice the number of their present large herds of stock. The Fergus ranch has the reputation of being one of the most hospitable, home-like stopping places on the Benton Road, and what everybody else says is corroborated by the writer hereof.

James Fergus' story was well told in Sanders' *A History of Montana*. His prominence in Montana for over thirty years demands a thorough accounting.

JAMES FERGUS was elected the first president of the Montana Pioneers Society, an honor fitly bestowed, when most of the prominent builders and makers of Montana were still alive and there were many other pioneers eligible to the same position. A brief sketch of his career is therefore a distinct contribution to the history of Montana.

He was born in Lanarkshire, Scotland, October 8, 1813, and died at the age of eighty-four in 1897. He grew up in a Scotch home, where the religious spirit was that influenced by a rigid Presbyterian father and mother of liberal views. He had a common school education, and at the age of nineteen crossed the ocean to Canada. He spent three years in a Quaker settlement and learned the trade of millwright. The first summer he spent in the United States he was employed as a millwright at Green Bay, Wisconsin. At that time, over eighty years ago, he also visited Milwaukee and Chicago, and in the late 1830s moved to eastern Iowa, in what was then the Blackhawk Purchase. He built and superintended powder mills at Savannah, Illinois, and at Moline in that state engaged in the foundry and machine business. He was also a member of the firm

James Fergus

Wheelock & Fergus, paper manufacturers, at Moline. But for ill health, he might have become one of the great industrial figures in the middlewest.

In 1854, he moved to Minnesota and in company with two other men laid out the town of Little Falls, owning five-twelfths of the town site. He built with his partners a dam and bridge across the Mississippi River. Later he became identified with Fergus Falls, Minnesota, owning half the town site.

From Minnesota he started west again, and while in Colorado in the winter of 1861−62 received reports from the new gold mines of the Idaho country. He joined Captain Fisk's expedition of 1862. His [Fisk's] account of the experiences of this pioneer expedition is preserved in the files of the Montana Historical Society and has been published in several works. He drove his own ox team from Little Falls, Minnesota, to Bannack, the first mining camp of Montana. Such were the qualities of his character and the vigor of his leadership that he was from the first looked upon as a man of prominence in the territory, and was called upon for many official responsibilities, including election as the first recorder of Alder Gulch, Virginia City, and as the first county commissioner appointed in the territory for Madison County. He afterward moved to Lewis and Clark County, near Helena, and was elected to serve two terms as commissioner of that county and as a member of the legislature. He also did some placer mining at Alder Gulch and Virginia City, owning the mine known as No. 13 Last Chance Mine and No. 2 Anaconda Mine near Butte. But his chief interest throughout his career was stock raising. In 1865, he located his ranch on [Little] Prickly Pear Creek and was in the cattle and sheep business there for sixteen or seventeen years. Seeking a wider range, he located about 1880 in the Judith Basin, where he founded what is known as Armells Ranch and grazed his herds over many hills.

His reputation as a public man followed him to the Judith Basin and he was soon prominent in public life. He represented Meagher County in the first Constitutional Convention and afterward in the State Senate. He was instrumental in getting a new county set off from Meagher. The bill, which he introduced, gave the name Judith to that county, but on the motion of two of his political opponents the bill was amended so as to make the county Fergus County. He was himself a Republican in politics.

James' son, Andrew Fergus, was a well known rancher who occupied a site near his father on Little Prickly Pear.

Continuing with the Judge's account of his travels:

> The bridges through the Lower Canyon are all in good repair, and the grades are immediately to receive the small amount of labor needed to place the whole line in first class condition. Mr. A. J. Stevens, a very pleasant gentleman and just the man for the place is found at the tollgate and takes your toll in that agreeable way, which leaves the impression upon you of having received a favor instead of having extracted a greenback.

This was the toll gate for the King and Gillette Toll Road. Within a couple of years, this portion of the Benton Road would be acquired by Lewis and Clark County.

> Emerging from the canyon and traveling three miles, and here we are at Bob Coburn's ranch. Everybody knows Bob Coburn, everybody who travels the road stops him and

Robert Coburn

> everyone is satisfied with the fare and treatment received and prices charged therefore. Bob is surrounded by herds of fat cattle and is generally prospering.

This would be about three miles north of present day Wolf Creek. Bob Coburn later on became a rancher in Sun River Valley. The *Helena Independent* of May 3, 1884, reported that Bob Coburn and Henry Sieben, both of Choteau County had last year, wintered their stock on the east side of the Snowies and that they had wintered well. They expected to have around 1,000 steers to market that year.

> Five miles further on we come to the station kept by Billy Moore, who has a good house and stable, sets a good table and gives your team proper care.

William S. Moore was a farmer who was born in 1844, in Kentucky. In the 1880 census he was living with his wife Hattie, two daughters and a son. According to Fisk Ellis in an article from the *Great Falls Tribune* dated October 3, 1937, and titled "Old Days in the Dearborn River Country," William and his wife were involved in a double murder in 1886. From the evidence found at the scene, it appeared that Williams wife, Hattie, shot

William in the abdomen with a rifle whereupon he retaliated by shooting her in the chest. William then shot himself in the head and lay dying in Hattie's lap while she wiped the blood from his brow. Both were buried at the Dearborn Crossing cemetery. The Lewis and Clark County Coroner's report, dated February 26, 1886, added the notation that "the deceased came to their deaths by gunshot wounds but whether inflicted by their own hands entirely, or the hands of others, we can not say."

> Next, we come to the Dearborn Crossing, over which immediate section Frank Galmiche long has had and still retains full sway. Frank has recently had left him a handsome legacy in France, and is desirous of selling out and going over to see about it. The place should be owned by a family and would be, if properly kept, one of the best paying stations on the road. Frank offers his ranch and improvements, toll-bridge cows, horses, blacksmith shop and many other useful implements at low rates.

Frank Galmiche was apparently successful at selling his property as the new owner, Nicholas T. Chemidlin, was in possession by July, 1878. Chemidlin did not last very long at his new occupation as he had returned to Helena, working as a printer, by the census of 1880. At that time he was living with his wife Mary, and a son and daughter. Nicholas was born in New York in 1845.

> Mr. James Lee has recently purchased the Bird Tail Station, and says he is going to improve and make of it a desirable stopping place for the traveler.

James Lee was a stock grower from the Bird Tail area. Lee was born in Missouri in 1841, and was living there with his wife Elisabeth according to the 1880 census.

> Between Bird Tail and Fort Shaw, we stop to chat with our friend John D. Brown, and receive his ever-ready cash for the *Herald*. Mr. Brown keeps a general assortment of groceries and provisions, and has a liberal trade.

> Arriving at Fort Shaw, we make our way direct for the headquarters of the Commanding General of the Sutler Department and are received by that functionary in the person of Joseph H. McKnight (who continues to preside

in that capacity to the satisfaction of the officers and enlisted men at the post and the citizen settlers far and near) with a geniality most agreeable, and only equaled by that extended by George Heldt, his popular, able, and ever-jolly assistant. Mr. McKnight has large invoices of goods now en-route by rail and river from New York, Chicago, and St. Louis, and will soon be prepared to supply every want of soldier and citizen at such rates as will defy competition.

Joseph H. McKnight was a "Trader" according to the 1870 census. McKnight resided at Fort Benton. He was born in Iowa in 1844. George Heldt had been a store clerk in Sun River Valley. George was born in 1839 in New York.

> A combined trip of pleasure and business was taken by Joe and myself down Sun River as far as the Leaving, and the result was a pleasant ride, several new subscribers a two hour hunt after wild geese (we only got away with one, although five shots were fired) a good dinner, and pleasant chat with Robert Vaughn. Some questioned the manner of our getting possession of that dead goose, but if friend Vaughn don't blow on us, their curiosity will never be further satisfied upon the subject.

> We also took a trip up the valley some forty miles through the South Fork settlements and found it both profitable and pleasant. Where, in 1866, the luxuriant bunch- grass was nipped only here and there by bands of wild sheep, antelope, deer, elk, and, an occasional herd of buffalo, we now behold thousands of cattle grazing, and where then not a white man dwelt, are today large, though not thickly settled, farming settlements, asserting the superiority of their valley over many others for producing either stock subsistence, cereals or vegetables. Mr. D. J. Hogan was in charge of the herd of cattle belonging to Con. Kohrs & Co., about 2,000 in number. Mr. Hogan has about 350 acres of meadow and pasture lands substantially fenced, and is otherwise prepared with buildings, corrals, etc., to care for his stock should a rigorous winter make it necessary. Mr. J. R. Cox, partner of Dan'l Floweree, has their herd of about the same number in charge on the north side of the main stream, and has a very desirable location for headquarters. Nearly every settler owns bands of cattle, numbering from 50 to 500 head each, and yet the ranges are comparatively unharmed and equal to support the increase

John Largent, Sr.

during the present generation. The whole Sun River Valley is now demonstrated to be equal to any other for farming purposes, as well as superior to most for grazing purposes, and I know of no better section for settlers to make homes in.

J. R. Cox was the brother-in-law of Daniel Floweree. Daniel was a very successful rancher, and business man, well known throughout Montana. He lived in Helena but had extensive land holdings in Lewis and Clark, Teton, and Choteau Counties.

At Sun River Crossing I note the completion of a two-story hotel, owned and kept by Charles Bull.

Charles Bull was born in Connecticut in 1836, and noted as a "hotel keeper" in the 1870 census. He was living with his wife, Cornelia, two sons and a daughter, at Sun River Valley.

Largent and Hill, and J. J. Healey & Co., are the merchants of the place, and Mr. Weicand manufactures for all that healthful beverage, beer. Healey & Co. have in running order a

flouring mill, half a mile from the crossing, said to be one of the most complete and best mills ever erected in the territory. This is an additional advantage this valley possesses over others. Largent & Hill have also a large steam saw mill located on the Missouri River about fifteen miles from the Crossing. The supply of logs comes from the river banks above, a large number having been; just run down, and the proprietors are now prepared to fill orders. The garrison at Fort Shaw will be further reduced during the present season, two more companies being under orders to move to the Muscleshell route for the better protection of that line. Company F. Capt. Williams in command, is to be stationed at Story's Fort, on Troutcreek; and company I, Lieut. Ammet in command, is to report at Carroll per first return steamer. Lieut. Benson is also going out in charge of a small expedition for the purpose of looking out the best pass through the Belt Range from Fort Shaw to Judith Basin, with a view to facilitate possible future military movements.

To properly close the trip to northern Montana, I paid a visit to the Blackfoot Agency, distant from Fort Shaw thirty miles. The Agency is located on the Teton, surrounded by a wide valley, and has plenty of timber for fuel and fencing within convenient distances. The new "father" of the Indians belonging to this Agency, R. F. May, has had the buildings newly whitewashed and repaired, giving them both a neat and comfortable appearance.

Richard F. May had been a "news dealer" in Helena according to the 1870 census. Richard was born in Delaware in 1823. By 1880, he had moved to Bozeman where he was living with his wife Clara and working as a merchant.

About fifty acres will be cultivated this year, mainly in oats and potatoes. There are over one hundred lodges of Piegans at the Agency, averaging eight or ten to the lodge. Rations are issued to these Indians every Monday for the ensuing week and, judging by the proportions of their stomachs and contented-looking countenances should say the Agent was liberal with the rations. Happening there on the Sabbath, I dropped in upon the Sunday School where I found Mr. B. W. Sanders, aided by other earnest workers; teaching some forty Indian children from the Bible to love one another. I was very agreeably surprised at the attention given to the lessons imparted and advancement already made by these children, and this part of the "peace policy" bids fair to yet overcome the prejudices of the many and accomplish the desired end, the civilizing and, if possible, the Christianizing of the Indians. Agent May is evidently carrying out the policy of the Government. over its Indian wards to the letter, and in my opinion time will demonstrate that that policy is in the main the right one.

Al Wilkins, of Livingston, was intimately acquainted with the pioneer highways around Fort Benton and had a part in some of the interesting experiences on the road in the stage coach days. This article, presented in the *Montana News Association* insert, dated February 18, 1935, was one of his favorite stories about those times.

Frontier Roads and Stage Coaches, 1876

The first Concord Coach line between Fort Benton and Helena that I remember was operated by the Gilmore and Salisbury Company. On the flat part of the road they used four horses to a coach, but over the Bird Tail Divide and through [Little] Prickly Pear Canyon six horses were used. This part of the road was very rough and there were steep hills to climb. In the summer season the road was lined with big freight outfits which camped wherever night overtook them. Many times, camping in the [Little] Prickly Pear Canyon, they merely pulled to the side of the road, leaving only room for the stagecoaches to pass.

One driver on the line, named Three-Fingered Mike, had the night stage drive through the canyon. He took great pleasure in popping his whip as he passed the freight outfits, waking all the drivers. Poor old Mike drove over the Great Divide at Helena about 1884.

In 1876 Father and I ran a road-house and stage station on the Benton and Helena Road at what was known as Eight-Mile Springs, eight miles out of Fort Benton. Another station was at Twenty-Eight Mile Springs, 20 miles further on.

During the year 1875, Twenty-Eight Mile Springs station was kept by Edward Kelly who, according to a "Traveling Correspondent" in the *Helena Independent* of October 16, 1875, "Keeps first class accommodations and has made this one of the most popular stopping places on the road." In 1877, he was still the station keeper and was

Ed Kelly

touted as having one of the best way stations in the country. Kelly was born in Ireland in 1846. By the 1880 census he was living at Fort Benton with wife Rosa and their son.

There was always more or less trouble along the line because of runaways and breakdowns. In the summer the coaches had trouble because of muddy roads and in winter from bad storms and deep, drifting snows.

About 1878, the late William Rowe got the stage contract from Fort Benton to Helena and stocked the line with new Concord coaches and new horses. Most of the horses were only about half broke, and there were many runaways.

The winter of 1878–79 was a very hard one with many severe snowstorms. In one of these storms, Ed Garrett had a runaway that turned into a real adventure, though no one was seriously hurt. Ed had driven about six miles toward Fort Benton from the Twenty-Eight Mile Springs when he heard a noise that warned him a trunk was loose on the rear boot of the stage. One passenger was with him on the driver's seat, and another inside the stage.

Garrett supposed the passenger on the seat with him knew a little about horses, so he handed him the lines and got off to fasten up the loose trunk. He had just reached the back of the coach when the horses started to run. The outside passenger threw the lines and jumped. The passenger inside, realizing he was mixed up in a runaway, opened the door and piled out into the snow.

The storm was heavy and the wind was blowing hard. The coach was soon lost to sight. Garrett and his astonished passengers started on down the stage road, hoping the team would be located after it had had its run. The trail was soon lost. So Ed, who was a tall, lanky fellow with a space-eating stride, lit out ahead of his two companions to walk the rest of the distance to our station at the Eight-Mile Springs. He got in about one o'clock in the afternoon. As I was usually the trouble man when anything went wrong, he asked me to go back and help find the runaway stage.

After Ed had a lunch; he, Billy Fox, and I started out with a team and buckboard, passing the two passengers on the way, still walking toward Fort Benton. They were elderly and were not making very fast time.

To show the perils of stage coaching in those days, it is interesting to note that the 1880 census shows William J. Fox of Choteau County being a freighter with the physical handicap of "toes froze off."

At Huntley Coulee, where the runaway had started, I figured the horses would turn down into the breaks along the main road. When we finally located the coach at the head of a coulee, the lead horses were down and the coach had turned over and lay in such a way that the horses couldn't get up.

We put a rope over the coach and righted it, and got the horses all on their feet. Strange to say, none of them was hurt. The only damage was two broken lamps on the coach.

We were, soon ready to start back. I got on the driver's seat with Garrett, and Fox took the buckboard. We soon had to cross the head of a coulee. I told Garrett the place he had picked didn't look good and we had better not try to cross there. He went on. As I had feared, there was a deep washout at the bottom. The leaders plunged in sinking about four feet into the

drifted snow, and as they plunged out and up the other bank, they jerked the coach into the hole, standing it almost on end. I was thrown over against the bank by the lead team. Garrett was thrown to the right, making a head-first dive into the deep snow. When I got up I could just see his legs, from the hips up, feebly wiggling in the air.

I rushed around and tried to pull him out. He was a big man and if I ever tugged and lifted in my life I did it then. I finally had to dig away the crusted snow before I could move him, and he was limp when I got him out. But he soon revived in the cold air after I had pumped his arms for a bit. By that time Bill Fox had caught up with us, and helped pull the stage, out of the hole.

When we were ready, to go again, Garrett left the driving to me and got inside the coach. The horses were raring to go. We drove to where the run away started and picked up the lost trunk. On the way to the Eight-Mile Spring, we picked up the two passengers who were cold, exhausted, and hungry.

At our Eight-Mile Spring Station we got a hot meal and changed horses. Garrett asked me to drive to Fort Benton for him, and we made that eight miles in about as fast time as I ever drove horses.

Both the passengers said they had frozen fingers and toes on our arrival. At the Fort Benton Stage Station we found Billy Rowe was there waiting for the coach. He called Dr. Turner to treat the two passengers. Fortunately, the doctor found the fingers and toes were only painfully frosted.

That winter one coach was pulled off its run and the company put on a one-horse two-wheeled jerky to carry the mail. The driver was a man named Casey. During one of the storms that winter Casey got lost and was out in the weather for about eight days. When Billy Rowe and others found him he was sitting in the cart holding his feet up to the dash board. Asked why, he replied: "I'm warming my feet."

The poor fellow was delirious from, hunger and exposure. The horse had broken the reins and was feeding through the snow on the buried grass.

Rowe rushed Casey to Fort Benton, where it was found necessary to amputate both legs at the knees. His hands were badly frosted, too, but he did not lose them. After be had recovered he was sent by the first steamboat to St. Louis, where the stage company had him fitted out with artificial, limbs, and in other ways repaid him for the loss of his legs.

Casey came back to Fort Benton, and was employed for some time about the stage office in one way and another.

Only the coming of the railroads brought an end to similar experiences on the pioneer highways of Montana.

Charles Higginbotham, in an undated and unpublished manuscript entitled *Life Lines of a Stage Driver* provides a wonderful insight into a trip he made as a stage sleigh driver. We don't know exactly what year this took place but it was probably the winter of 1877–78 when sleighs were running on many of the routes starting in the month of December. This story certainly speaks to the harshness of a Montana winter.

Benton to Rock Creek about 1877

While driving on the Benton Road, a fellow by the name of Wallace Taylor was on his way to his folks at Helena, to spend the holidays with them. I picked him up at Sun River Crossing, and he bought a bottle of eleven-year-old whiskey for him and me. We got to Fort Shaw, five miles further, when a fellow came around the corner, clad in a scotch plaid suit, and with his ears and hands done up in cotton batting.

You'd have thought he was just out of a hospital somewhere. The Weather Bureau man had failed to mail his daily report to Washington, and he happened along, just at that moment. It was 57 degrees below. When he passed my lead horses he said, "Driver, get down into your furs; the thermom's 57 below, and still a-fallin'." Just then the cotton-battin' man stepped up and asked if this was the Helena coach. "Yes, get on your overcoat, it's cold," I said. The gent in the ice cream suit with cotton-battin' trimmings replied curtly, "I've paid my fare, I can stand it if you can!" "Well," said I, from the depths of my buffalo coat, "They could pick you out of the snow with a caloric needle, but they'd sure need a hay fork to find me." Then I said to the agent, "Has this fellow paid?" "Yes. He hasn't clothes enough to flag a hand-car!" But the fellow

insisted that he was dressed warmly enough, so I took him under protest, and on his own responsibility. He piled in on the sleigh, and sat on a bare board though there was lots of hay in the bottom of the sled. We drove twelve miles to supper at Eagle Rock. Wallace's whiskey had frozen up, and we couldn't manage it. But there was a saloon at Eagle Rock, and there we warmed up, outside and in.

Eagle Rock Stage Station was located just southeast of Eagle Rock on Bird Tail Creek. The station was known at various times as Eagle Rock Station, Brown's Station or Brown's Hotel. At least part of that time it was owned and operated by John D. Brown, a stock grower. Brown was born in Ireland in 1831, and by 1880, was living with his wife Catharine, three daughters and a son.

When supper was announced, we had shed our buffalo coats and pants, but our prize passenger, of the cotton-battin' wrappings sat by the stove and wouldn't come in to eat.

It was ten miles from there to the top of the Bird Tail hill; we stopped there and changed horses. My new team was six slashing fine animals, quite fine enough to match this fine sleigh-riding night. There was a galorious big moon, only it was what you might call cold! Three hundred yards from the station we pulled a small hill with a crooked dugway, two feet in depth. Mr. cotton-battin' says, "How far is it to the next station?" "Eight miles" says I. "How long to make it?" "An hour and a half." We went down the long hill a-kitin', till we came to a bridge. "How far to the station?" says cotton-battin', shivering in his ice-cream suit. "Twelve miles." "How long"?" "Two hours." In a couple minutes we crossed another bridge. "How far NOW to the station?" "Sixteen miles and it'll take three hours and 15 minutes." We rounded a curve and drove on to the station.

It was the 23rd of December, just before Christmas, and a number of sheep men had come in, somewhat early, to celebrate. Already they were as well, lit up as the station was, which sent a blaze of warmth and hospitality from every window and chance-opened door. "Come in and drink," yelled Long Shorty, a six-footer who seemed to be the leader of festivities. After the team was unhooked, we went back to the saloon. Taylor had gone on in, but cotton-batting, answering "Long Shorty's" invite, replied, "I don't drink, thank you."

Shorty reached forth a long arm and grabbed him by the collar; a friend seized him by an arm, and. they lifted and dragged him into the saloon. Inside, Shorty took command. "Line up, right about face, and bellies to the bar." E. Z. [Evan] Thomas bolstered up to the lumber. Thomas ran the place, and he was the biggest devil I ever saw.

Evan Thomas was the inn keeper at Dearborn where he lived with his wife Rachel and five daughters. Evan was born in 1835 in Wales. He moved to this place, known as the Keystone House, in the summer of 1876 having purchased it from Galmiche.

He waited on us; Wallace and I drank before the rest. Shorty looked back over his shoulder and saw cotton-battin' standing by the stove, scorching his padded mitts, and said to him, "Excused me, pard, but won't you join us in a Christmas drink?" "I never took a drink in my life remarked he of the mitts, virtuously. "By gad, you'll take one now!" cried Shorty, and the fun was on.

They mixed him a hot one, and they used a funnel to pour it down him; then we staged a walk-around 'round the stove, till another called, "halt, bellies to the mahogany!" Cotton-battin' drank that time, with no special invite. By now the team was hitched up, and I cornered Wallace. "I'll slip out," said I, "and drive over to the office a half-mile. You make cotton-battin' think I've gone without you. I'll wait for you." So we did. Wallace knew the road, and knew I'd wait till they overtook us. But we had the passenger sweating for the first time since he came aboard. I greeted cotton-bat' as though I'd never seen him before. "Where are you going?" "Me? Why, I got on at Fort Shaw," he said in a tone of voice that implied that I must be crazy or drunk. At Rock Creek at breakfast I turned him over to the tender-mercies of Mose Gebo [Moses Gebeau], a Frenchman.

Moses M. Gebeau was a stage driver for many years. He was born in 1836, in New York, the son of French parents.

Rock Creek Station was located about three miles north and slightly east of the present town of Wolf Creek. Today the site is occupied by Rock Creek Ranch off of State Highway 287.

Mose hauled him as far as Silver City, twelve miles out of Helena but would not take him any further. He was by this time pretty near frozen, and had to lay over to thaw out.

Silver City was a "lively" mining camp on Silver Creek. Originally destined to become the county seat for Edgerton County, it was soon surpassed by Helena, just twelve miles away. Although Silver Creek was one of the first major mining areas, the richer diggings at Last Chance Gulch stole its glory and Silver City faded into obscurity.

When I went back to Fort Shaw, on the night of the 24th, I got in at 3 o'clock in the morning. The postmaster said it was 66 below zero.

I went on down to Sun River, and I ran across George Houck, who said he'd be damned if he'd leave before daylight, as it was too cold. That evening I met, and from here they went on with me, the Secretary of the line, the Division Agent and a Diamond "R" man, Ed. MaClay, all pretty well illuminated. Now, I like the smell of corn-juice, though I never drink any of it myself. We got into Fort Shaw that night, and the Secretary ran over to the Post Office, a couple hundred yards, to get the latest info from the Weather Bureau man, who told him that it was 68 below. Can you wonder that Fort Shaw has the name of being one of the coldest spots on the continent?

He had a flour sack two-thirds full of loaded booze bottles. When we got on top of the Bird Tail Divide, in rounding a curve, I turned the sleigh over. It hurt nobody and nothing, but a musical instrument, that went singing down hill. Hill, a small man of about 118 pounds, weight said, "You boys load up again, and I'll go back after the music box." He retrieved it, but found it too much of a task to climb back to us. So he yelled that he'd meet us at the bottom of the gulch, which he did. When we arrived at Rock Creek, it was Christmas day in the morning, and we were late because of the delay from the upset. Hill wanted us all to drink then we had a splendid breakfast and put him to bed in the sleigh.

From the *Rocky Mountain Husbandman* for November 21, 1878, we learn about:

Montana Herds, Flocks, Farms and Mines, 1878

Silver City is at the junction of the road leading from Helena to the Belmont,

Whippoorwill, and Penobscot mines with the Fort Benton Road. Since the development of these mines the town has assumed a fresh look, and advanced somewhat in improvements. It now has one pretty good store, blacksmith shop, and a hotel. Gredel & Wilborn [Wilburn], the proprietors of the hotel have recently completed a large bar room and added materially to the comforts and capacity of the house, and appear to be doing a thriving business.

Gredel and Wilburn are both listed as "hotel keepers" at Silver Creek for the 1880 census. Gredel was born in 1822, in Germany, while W. F. Wilburn was born in 1834 in Kentucky. Wilburn's wife Susan was also living at the hotel along with three miners, two laborers, a stage driver by the name of J. E. Taylor and a Chinese cook, Ah Ling.

The valley of the Little Prickly Pear, above the canyon, seems to have made but little advance within the past two years. There are about the same number of farmers, and their places, except that of August Greaser, show but little improvement. Mr. Greaser is one of the leading dairymen and stock raisers. The product of his dairy always finds ready buyers in the markets.

The old Clark ranch is still the home of James Fergus. The traveler at this house receives good treatment and is well entertained. The best country library I have seen for many a day is at this place. Mr. Fergus is one of the substantial stockmen and farmers. His herds of horses and cattle number several hundred. In his stables some good young stallions may be seen. Of these I may name Don A., a colt by Mambrino Chief, that has good action, and will doubtless come into the ring with the fast trotters when of age; Babe, one of Anvils, get, a very large, well-formed animal; and a young Diamond, handsome enough to be admired by everyone.

The Prickly Pear Canyon Road is in better condition than usual. Mr. Wegner, who has it under supervision, appears to be doing his whole duty, and is deserving of a kind remembrance for it.

Charles Wegner, according to the 1880 census, was living in Little Prickly Pear Valley with his wife, Eliza Jane, three sons and two daughters. Charles was born in Germany in 1846, and by 1880 was listed as a "laborer."

At and below Wolf Creek it has been much improved. The station and hotel at this place also shows a marked improvement. The house has been enlarged, and excellent barns built. The little fifteen acre field by the way is being used to good advantage. Its yields are enormous, furnishing good supplies for the tables, which Wm. Kisselpaugh, the proprietor, sets in good style.

William Kisselpaugh was Canadian born in 1838. The 1880 census shows him with the occupation of "farmer." Within a year he had taken on, as controlling partner, J. M. Carter from Nova Scotia. Carter was born in 1848, and by that same census was living with his wife, Laticia, three sons and a daughter. Kisselpaugh was also living in Carter's home. A notice in the *Helena Independent* of June 10, 1876, reminded the traveling public: "This old stand at the lower end of the canyon, thirty-four miles from Helena, has been re-established, made a stage station and kept in first class style by Mr. Wm. Kisselpaugh. Mrs. Schultz presides in the dining room. The table and bill are furnished with the best in the market, and travelers to and from Benton, ladies and gentlemen, will find this a very desirable place to stop. Give him a call."

W. S. Moore and Bros. is another good stopping place. These gentlemen are engaged pretty extensively in farming and stock raising. In their herds are to be found some high class Short Horns. Their farm lies along the flat below the road, and I am told produces exceedingly well. Next year they will enlarge it materially, and probably locate another place.

Four or five miles east of the Moore Bros. the Missouri emerges from the Grand Canyon, turns from its northward course to the east and the Great Falls. Near here the high mountains on the southside stand back forming a semicircle, having a grassy valley of several hundred acres between their base and the river. This romantic little spot has been by some person named "Paradise Valley." It is the property of F. Wegner and Stickney, who have fine herds grazing upon its luxuriant pasturage.

On the Dearborn there are a number of fine herds and flocks, the principle among which are the large cattle herds belonging to S. S. Harvey & Son of Clancy. D. Orchard, Cottrell and Densdon of Dearborn. The flocks are owned by Gillette & Weston, Ralph Wells, Ben Porter and D. Holbrook. Gillette and Weston are located about two miles above the crossing where they have a good range and accommodations for their large flock, a considerable number of which are thoroughbred and grade Merinos. The other flocks named are located near the Missouri River, and I am told have some good grade sheep among them.

From the *Helena Weekly Herald* of August 28, 1879, is a note from their "Traveling Correspondent."

A Trip to Fort Benton and Through Sun River Valley in 1879

The trip to Fort Benton in the month of August is a most unpleasant experience. The heat is unusually intense, the dust is suffocating and the alkali water is rather conducive to profanity, so that aside from the physical discomfort experienced, the effect on man's moral nature is very bad indeed.

But we are off. The ponies are in fine spirits and spin long the road at a lively rate. The Prickly Pear Valley, with its guardian hills tinted blue and green; are soon left behind. Arriving at Silver City we stop for a time, and from the contemplation of nature devote our attention to contemplating the more substantial pleasures of the supper table.

Once more on the way; the sun is just sinking behind the mountain and as with a parting benediction has tinged the skies with crimson glory. Scarcely has the last ray of light died in the west ere the golden rim of the moon appears in the east. At once a thousand sleeping shadows are aroused; they creep out from among the crags and ravines, they flit from point to point, grow bolder and advance.

They steal in long lines far out upon the prairie, join each other like phantom rivulets, and though sometimes wavering, surely advance. All nature assumes a weird, unnatural appearance. Each knoll and butte contributes to the spectral array which now in full force is marshaled on mountain and on plain.

At length the mouth of the canyon is reached. A tinkling bell and the bray of a weary mule tell why that cloud is slowly creeping towards us. Soon the lumbering vehicles appear, creaking, and groaning like spirits in

George Steele

torment. The loud crack of the whip and the hoarse shout of the teamster blend well with the discord. A rough, hard life they lead, these mariners of the plains, and rough, hard men they are, but beneath the rude exterior are warm, true hearts, where kindness and generosity go hand in hand together. Once fairly in the canyon the light of the moon is left behind, shut out by the big, precipitous walls on either side. The road stretches away before us a dim, dusty uncertainty. Occasionally over the walls, broken by a crevice or ravine, a flood of golden light is tossed across the path, but a turn or curve is reached and once more we plunge into the darkness. We dash along at a rapid rate, and in these gloomy places put our trust in the ponies, keep a sharp eye out and a foot on the brake. The stream rattles along noisily, gathering here and there a stray gleam of light which it flings back to the darkness. We emerge from the canyon and away ahead discover a long, low whitewashed building, which, beneath the brilliant light of the moon, reminds us of a marble tomb built for some Titan hero. A bright light flashes out of a window, which suggests the thought that the Titan's spirit may have lighted a candle in order to study the columns of the *HERALD* and learn the events of the day. This is Fergus' Station, and the venerable gentleman for whom the place is named receives us kindly and cares for our wants. We had looked forward to a good bed at this place, in order to make up for the wear and tear of the day's work, but disappointment awaits us, for the fame of his this house has gone abroad in the land and the beds are full. We therefore unfurl our blankets, and on the soft side of a plank floor find that rest which a clear conscience and a little exercise in the fresh air so surely bring.

Leaving Fergus' the road at once dives into the canyon, and for ten miles the changing views of rocky grandeur awaken thoughts and emotions calculated to raise one above the selfish hopes and fears of every day life and inspire higher incentives to thought and action. Possibly this is an arrangement of nature for bracing up man's moral condition preparatory to the heat and alkali water which await him beyond, but it is a deep problem and we won't attempt to solve it. The road soon reaches Dead Man's Coulee, where a new store building has been erected this spring by Mr. Geo. Steell. He also has a sawmill in operation on Wolf Creek, ten miles away, and here the lumber is piled preparatory to shipment. The place is in charge of C. H. Drew, who manipulates the scales and always gives the right change back.

According to Robert Vaughn, Dead Man's Coulee was named for the final resting place for Mr. Lowe who was murdered at that spot by Blackfeet Indians.

George Steele is listed in the 1880 census as living in Sun River Valley in the house of his brother John R. Steele. Both were merchants in the area and both were from Scotland. Also living there were George's wife, Anna, and their daughter. George was born in 1836, while his brother was born in 1841.

Surrounded by clouds of dust we arrive at Dearborn and pull up at the house of E. J. Thomas. This is a pretty place. The mountains have been left behind, only a stray spur or peak being visible. About are many buttes of strange and varied shape, crowned with rocky edges, which in some places resemble crumbling castles or ruined fortifications. The clear, rapid stream flows over a mosaic of varicolored pebbles, and clatters away at a lively rate. Stately trees are scattered along the

bank and opposite the house collect in a pretty grove. A fourth of a mile above, on a little knoll overlooking the stream, a neat white fence surrounding a small enclosure, attracts the eye. Here rest the remains of John Wareham and Gus Cottle, who last summer were killed, by Indians, a few miles above.

According to the *Helena Daily Independent* of July 11, 1878, Augustus L. Cottle and his friend, John Wareham, were murdered by Indians during the first week of July of that same year. Apparently, Cottle had been at Sun River with Wareham and had just returned to Cottle's Ranch on the Dearborn when they were surprised by a group supposed to be Nez Perces who had entered the house. Cottle was struck in the head three times with an axe after being shot. They simply shot Wareham and then dumped both bodies in a nearby creek. Cottle's Ranch was located about twelve miles from that of Evan Thomas, inn keeper on the Benton Road.

The first man to discover the atrocity found the door of the house broken in, the provisions gone along with Cottle's Henry rifle, needle gun and ammunition. There was blood on the floor and a pool of blood eight feet from the door. The Indians who were thought to have committed the murders were seen leaving Sun River along the Cadott trail on their way to Missoula or Idaho.

The next morning is Sunday. We had calculated on lying late in bed this morning but again are disappointed for breakfast waits for no one, and in this busy household a dead man could scarcely rest. So we are off again. It had been our intention to lay by this day, but the flies are out in battle array, and to remain and fight them would probably generate in our breast thoughts and feelings that would do us no good. It is a day of many ups and downs so far as the road is concerned, and hot in the extreme, but, in due time, the town of Sun River Crossing is reached.

F. N. WILSON

The *Helena Independent* for December 17, 1881, covered a part of a trip over part of the Benton Road, from Bird Tail Divide to today's Sieben Ranch.

The Benton Road, 1881

The year is very near to a close, and so we will take a look over about forty miles of the

Benton Road to notice the substantial improvements made.

James Lee, who owns the Bird Tail Ranch on the west side of the Bird Tail Divide, has built a large and commodious house for the accommodation of the traveling public. He also keeps a stock of merchandise and does some dairy business.

Next we arrive at the Keystone House, at the Dearborn River, owned by E. J. Thomas, who is all enterprise, and who has this year built a good store house, with stack of merchandise and good liquors. He has also built a large barn 30 x 50, so that man and beast can live on the top shelf at his place. After the freshet of last February he also rebuilt the bridge across the Dearborn River. It is now a toll bridge, but ought, by all means, be made a free bridge for the benefit of the traveling public.

On the south side of the Dearborn River, H. A. Milot keeps the Dearborn House, post office and a good stock of general merchandise.

Henry Milot had prior to that time been a saloon keeper at Philipsburg, Montana according to the 1880 census. There he lived with his wife Anna, four daughters and two sons.

At Rock Creek is the stage station kept by H. B. McDonald [Henry McDonald]. In connection with the place is a post office, called Power [of which McDonald was the Postmaster]; also the United States telegraph office, half way between Helena and Fort Shaw, operated by the genial and obliging Chas. L. Herzog.

The prior year, Herzog (or Hercog) was a private in Company C of the 18th Infantry, located at Fort Assinnboine in Choteau County.

McDonald listed his ranch and stage stop for sale in the *Helena Independent* of 1882. "Desiring to change my business, I offer for sale my ranch at Rock Creek, on Fort Benton Road, consisting of seven hundred and sixty acres of land with government title, under good fence. The house has ten rooms with all the convenient out buildings, such as a good stable, root house, tool house, chicken house, ice house, milk house, wagon sheds, granary, etc. This is a good hotel and stage stand, and is contiguous to a good range, being very desirable for either horse or cattle raising. Has ample water privileges."

KRUEGER'S HOTEL.

The undersigned would respectfully call the attention of all travelers on the

BENTON ROAD

to his new and

Elegantly Furnished Hotel

Which has just been completed and fitted up regardless of expense.

TWO PARLORS,

Handsomely carpeted and expensively furnished, with

Four Neat and Airy Bed-Rooms,

A SPACIOUS DINING ROOM AND TABLE PROVIDED WITH EVERY OBTAINABLE LUXURY.

The Bar will be furnished with the choicest brands of

Wines, Liquors and Cigars.

Fine Stables and Corral

With Plenty of Hay and Oats.

Thanking the traveling public for liberal patronage of the Half-Way House, during the past two years, I respectfully solicit a share o custom for my new Hotel.

may1tf   AUGUST KREUGER

Krueger Hotel Ad in Independent

About two miles from Rock Creek is the Krueger Ranch, which was lately sold to Mr. B. T. Townsend, of Prickly Pear Valley.

The Krueger Ranch was probably owned by Augustus Krueger who in 1877 decided to build a first class hotel at Spring Creek just one mile north of the entrance to the Lower Little Prickly Pear Canyon.

The *Helena Independent* of May 4, 1877, stated that the hotel would, "Become a favorite resort for parties wishing to retire for a while from the cares of business to enjoy a season of repose or to engage in rural sports." Located at the beginning of today's Recreation Road, it would seem that Mr. Krueger was blessed with foresight. Krueger must have died before the census of 1880 as only his wife, Elizabeth, and son are listed in that tally.

Benjamin Townsend is listed in the 1880 census as living on Little Prickly Pear with his wife Lotta and three sons. Townsend was born in 1838, in Pennsylvania. His listed occupation was "laborer."

Rock Creek School District, No. 13, will build a school house next season. The district is now in a flourishing condition, and may keep a five months' school next summer.

On August 31, 1880, the *Helena Independent* reported that: "At the annual meeting of Rock Creek School District, No. 13, held at the school room, Kruger's Ranch, Benton Road, August 28th, 1880, the following officers were elected for the ensuing year: Trustees: Henry B. McDonald, William S. Moore. and Wm. Kisselpaugh; Charles Wegner, Clerk."

Chas. Wegner, supervisor of the Canyon Road District, has built a new house, stables and corral adjoining the Rock Creek place.

At Wolf creek, near the lower end of the big canyon, is the Wolf Creek House, kept and owned by Kisselpaugh & Carter, who keep a stock of merchandise, liquors, etc. They also keep the Carterville Post Office. Carter is there, but the "ville" has not made its appearance yet.

Carterville was the former name of the town of Wolf Creek. Kisselpaugh is buried in the Carterville cemetery located near Wolf Creek.

R. S. Ells, at his saw mill on Lyons Creek about three miles west off the road, is making preparations for a big run of lumber, shingles and lath next season.

Martin Mitchell, who has bought the old Fergus Ranch, has lately built an addition to his house, and furnished one of the finest hat-rooms on the road. He also improved his barn lately. Mart. knows how to accommodate the weary traveler.

We understand that Messrs. Rowe & Co. will run their tour horse coaches during the winter, which will greatly benefit the traveling public, and also furnish better express and mail facilities.

R. S.

A JAUNT NORTHWARD, 1885

[John McCafferty's Notes of a Stage Trip from Helena to Benton as recorded in the *Helena Weekly Herald* for May 28, 1885.]

Fort Benton, May 23, 1885—At 7 a.m. on the 14th I mounted to a seat above the driver, alongside of whom sat Mr. Wm Rowe, a former proprietor of the line, on one of the elegant coaches of the Helena, and Benton Stage Company, 'en route for this old town, founded by the American Fur Company at the head of Missouri River navigation. It was a charming morning, and, as we skipped away to the north, the Metropolis of the Territory [Helena], with all its angularities, loomed out in bold relief. It looked emblematical of the character of the men and women who, in those early days replete with innumerable obstacles, grappled with the golden coulee and fashion it with the form and condition of the ornamental and useful beehive. They are, by the right of God, the noblemen and Spartan women of the city and should be held in lofty esteem.

Reaching the Seven Mile House in fifty minutes the horses were watered, while the other animals exhilarated in the sun shine of the interesting landlady. It is headquarters of a good horse range, and necessarily proves an agreeable halting place.

The Seven Mile House was located seven miles south of Silver City. Prior to October, 1883, it was run by Charles E. Colbert. Colbert was from Norway, where he was born in 1844.

Colbert moved his family out of the Seven Mile House on what is now Birdseye Road. as the result of a hideous experience that his family underwent at that location. The *Helena Independent* for March 14, 1882, reported the event.

SELF MURDER

Details of the Suicide which Occurred at Seven Mile House Sunday Night

Between ten and eleven o'clock Sunday night Charles Colbert, keeper of the Seven Mile House on the Benton Road, accompanied by his family, reached Helena bringing the news that, John Burke had committed suicide at their house about nine o'clock that evening. Coroner Steele, accompanied by two or three others, as soon as arrangements could be made for teams, etc., went out to Colbert's house, and finding Burke dead, brought his body to town.

At the inquest held at 10 o'clock yesterday morning the circumstances of the tragedy were, from the evidence, found to be about as follows: Burke, whose one third interest in a mine recently sold to Hauser & Holler, of this city, placed $5,000 cash in his hands, returned to Helena from a trip east a few weeks ago. Since returning he has drank too much for his own good, and in one instance had delirium tremens, for which he was treated at the hospital by Dr. Morris.

Last Wednesday he started in the coach for Benton, where one of his old partners in the mine sold to Hauser & Holler is now lying ill. The coach being an open one, Burke concluded to stop at the Seven Mile House and wait for the closed coach the next day. He did not take the coach the following day, but came to Helena. In the time intervening between this and Sunday night, he visited Helena two or three times. Saturday night he asked that a bed be made down for him on the bar room floor at Colbert's, as there was no fire up stairs in the room in which he had previously slept. His request was complied with and Sunday night a bed was again made for him in the bar room.

Colbert had not allowed Burke to drink anything at all Sunday afternoon, as he thought from Burke's manner that liquor would do him more harm than good. To guard against Burke getting to the liquor Colbert moved it all into the kitchen and locked it up.

After Burke went to bed, Colbert went into the bar room to see that everything was right for the night. Stepping behind the bar he noticed that Burke's pistol, which had been left behind the bar, was gone. He told Burke there was no use for him to sleep with his pistol under his head, as there was no danger of his being molested. Burk replied that it was not under his head, but was lying by his side. Colbert then tried to get Burke to give him the pistol, but was unsuccessful. He then went into the next room and told his wife to go and ask Burke for his pistol, saying: "Maybe he will give it to you." Mrs. Colbert was just on the point of doing so, when Burke was heard to say: "Here's good-bye to you, Burke," and then came the loud report of the pistol. The concussion put out the light in the bar room, and Colbert, seizing another lamp, hurried in. Burke's face was covered with blood, and seeing that the man had shot himself, Colbert with all haste hitched up his horse and,

accompanied by his family, brought the news to town.

The body was brought to Helena at about half-past three o'clock yesterday morning, The shot took effect above the right temple, tearing a terrible hole, and the dead man's head and shoulders were bathed in blood. After hearing the testimony, which was substantially as above detailed, the coroners jury brought in the following verdict:

An inquisition holden in the city of Helena, county of Lewis and Clark, and Territory of Montana, on the 13th day of March A. D. 1882, before Dr. W. L. Steele, coroner of said county, upon the body of John Burke there lying dead, by the jurors whose names are hereunto subscribed, the same jurors upon their oath do say that the said John Burke came to his death by a pistol, shot from his own hand while in a state of temporary insanity.

(Signed)
George Bashaw, Frank P. Sterling, Milton Witten, Isaac Young, J. W. Thom, Edward Coulston.

By 1900, Colbert was living in Helena with his wife, Bertha J., a son and two daughters. According to the *Helena City Directory* for 1889–1891 his occupations were respectively, proprietor, saloon keeper and billiard hall manager.

In February, 1884, a partnership between the new owners, Nick Baatz and Charles A. Baker, of the Seven Mile House had dissolved. Charles A. Baker was now he sole proprietor.

The mail pouch was exchanged three miles beyond; then on to Silver City, the original shire town of Edgerton (now Lewis and Clark) county. It is only a little village, situated at the crossing of Silver Creek thirteen miles from Helena. There is quite a stretch of farming land along the creek. Being "all set" we again trotted northward. From my elevated perch I got a very desirable view of the country, and from the driver I received all necessary information. As far as the eye could reach the valley seemed better adapted for cattle and horses than farming. But as we drew near [Little] Prickly Pear Creek, the agricultural belt opened out, stretching away to the mountains with a north and south trending. At 12:45 p.m. we reached Mitchell's station, where we stopped for dinner. It is situated on the [Little] Prickly Pear Creek and is twenty-seven miles from the Capital. The proprietor has several hundred acres of farming and hay land fenced in, for which he holds per fee title from the N. P. R. R. [Northern Pacific Rail Road] Mr. Mitchell owns quite a band of horses and also a small herd of cattle.

According to the *Helena Independent*, Mitchell purchased the ranch previously belonging to James Fergus in April of 1880, for $2,700. Martin Mitchell was described as "a young man with a business skill that would do honor to a much older head." In the census for 1870, he was living with his parents Irvin and Hanna Mitchell, working as a farm laborer in Iowa. Martin at that time had seven younger siblings.

The census for 1880 lists him as a single, twenty-five year old farmer, born in Iowa and living at Sun River, Lewis and Clark County, Montana. By 1881, he was married to Elizabeth, blessed with their first child and proud of the fine home in which they lived. The year 1884, found them still living on the Benton Road.

Mitchell pursued mining for most of the rest of his life, opening several new mines in the Marysville area. He died January 23, 1924, in Spokane, Washington.

> The [Little] Prickly Pear Valley could be made to support at least 1,000 families. There are many worthy immigrants rushed to other sections of the northwest who would do much better on and along the many mountain streams flowing into the Missouri, including the [Little] Prickly Pear.

> After partaking of a very substantial dinner, enlivened with a spirited discussion of the question of women's rights, which the "grizzly horrids" finally tabled, we cantered into [Little] Prickly Pear Canyon. I have seen a great variety of mountain scenery, but nothing in its line ever pleased me more than the picturesque and ever-varying panorama of this canyon. Tourists visiting this section of Montana should ever arrange to take it in. It is certainly one of nature's delightfully wanton freaks. Arriving at Ellis' lumber yard, we traded mail pouches; thence on to Cartersville, where we again swapped U.S. bags. Cartersville [now known as Wolf Creek] is a neat little village, situated in the vortex of Wolf Creek and [Little] Prickly Pear.

The lumber yard and saw mill were owned by Robert S. Ells whose name was frequently given as Ellis. Both were located about three miles west of the confluence of Lyons Creek and the Little Prickly Pear. Apparently, the stage would, on occasion, deliver mail to Ells' by traveling down Lyons Creek Road.

Ells was a transplant from the state of Maine. In 1860, he was listed at age twenty-four, living with his parents Joshua and Lois Ells at Pembroke in Washington County, Maine. By 1870, he was located at Bozeman, Montana Territory, where he operated a saw mill.

In August of 1881, some careless cattle drovers left their camp fire burning and set eight miles square of forest on fire west of the Benton Road. Ells suffered the loss of 200,000 feet of saw logs and nearly lost his sawmill as well. The *Helena Independent* of August 17, 1881, noted: "Unless there is rain very soon, there is no telling what damage will be done, as the fire is now in the best timber of Lewis and Clark County."

John McCafferty continues his story:

> There is quite a range of good farming land along both streams. Rolling into Rock Creek Station we received a relay; thence on to Dearborn, where mail, express and some freight were left. The village is located at the crossing of the Dearborn River, and will surely develop into a business centre, as it is backed up by an extensive farming and stock growing belt. Crossing the Dearborn, we were soon at Flat Creek Station, where we had supper. The station may be regarded as headquarters for an extensive horse range. This being the season or a general round-up of all kinds of stock, the horses and cattle on the range are being driven to a common centre.

Flat Creek was the home of George Warner, a Probate Judge from Jefferson City. At Flat Creek he was a farmer but still went by the title of Judge.

The stage station keeper there was most likely Thomas Wheeler although C. H. Ellis was also listed as one who "keeps hotel" at that location. Ellis was the father of Fisk Ellis, author of the story of his trip to the Blackfoot Agency in 1876. Also listed with Wheeler were his wife Elisabeth, William Smith, "cook," I. A. Burton, "laborer," and

Henry Bramen, "clerk in drug store." Wheeler was from England where he was born in 1845.

With fresh horses we pulled out on the night drive over the Bird Tail Mountain. It is more or less dangerous, owing to the many slidings, and perhaps, the most trying piece of stage road in northwestern Montana during the winter season, as the snow-drifts frequently obliterate all traces of it for miles; therefore the Helena and Benton stage company deserve the generous consideration of both the government and the people for the uniform regularity with which the mails have been delivered. Doubtless this is the natural result of the able management of the company's General Superintendent, J. M. Powers. However, about midnight, we reached Eagle Rock Station, having made the trip across the mountain without accident. Receiving another relay we dozed the time away until Fort Shaw was reached, where four companies of infantry are stationed. Mail bags being duly exchanged, we cantered on to Sun River Village. It is situated on the southwest bank of the river, and its population may be rated at 300. It is the trade centre for the valley, where there are still thousands of acres of good farming land unoccupied. In fact, there is still room for a thousand additional families. After an exchange of bags, we trotted on to the Leaving Station, where we had breakfast. Mr. Remicke not only runs this station, but he is also the owner of a herd of cattle and a band of horses, and has several hundred acres of hay land fenced in.

Edward Remicke was listed as a "tavern keeper" at Sun River Valley in the census of 1880. Apparently, the hotel there was home to men with a wide variety of occupations. There were wool growers, stone masons, farmers, laborers and carpenters living under that roof. In addition, Ida Remicke, his wife, kept house for the crowd. Edward and Ida had one daughter, Ida J., living with them.

After the enjoyment of a superb meal, we pulled out from the Leavings of Sun River, and on reaching Big Lake were furnished with another relay, when we trotted off to Twenty-Eight Mile Station. Here we had dinner—such a table I never saw spread for stage passengers before, and I have staged it in all parts of the world. Well, we all looked at that layout, and

then paid the "old liner" 75 cents each. Where there is a daily stage, no excuse should condone for such nauseous "provender." With a feeling of disgust we bolted on to Bull's Head, where we received a final relay, and thence on to the city of extravagant brick buildings, where we arrived a 3 p.m. the 17th.

I am delighted with the location of Benton, on the northern bank and at the head of navigation of the Missouri River Still, I must here say, the depression prevailing over this once renowned center of northwestern trade, seems to cast a chilling atmosphere around the meeting of even old comrades-in-arms. But in this age of sudden and gigantic changes, where is he who dares to presage the future of the grandly historic old Fort Benton? I at least shall leave its solution to time; therefore I have now only to thank the old timers for the generous hospitality extended in my behalf, with a hope that their wishes may be fully realized.

May G. Flanagan, in an unpublished manuscript dated 1952, paints a touching picture of travel on a stage coach from Fort Benton to Helena to visit her Uncle, T. C. Power and Aunt Mollie. She was only eleven at the time and saw the whole process through the eyes of a little, but very grown up, girl.

STAGECOACH TRIP AND VISIT TO HELENA FROM FORT BENTON, M. T. in 1886

It was summer vacation time and my sisters, Grace (age 9), Virginia (age 7) and I (age 11) were invited to visit our aunt, Mrs. T. C. Power, in Helena.

T. C. Power & Bro. was still operating the stage route between Fort Benton and Helena so our transportation was furnished us. [In fact, the Power Brothers had discontinued their association with the stage line some eight years earlier and it was now owned by Jacob Powers.] It was thrilling to think of going by ourselves on the long coach trip to Helena, the center of our wonder world. In those days we thought of going to Helena as people today think of going to New York or London.

Getting ready for the trip put everything in a flurry. It was difficult to get wardrobes for three young girls. The Fort Benton stores, with new materials and patterns arriving once a year on the steamboats, were very lacking in up-to-date apparel. The stock was meager and some of it very weird. It seemed planned for an Indian trading post or a mining camp. As I remember, only one of the dresses I took was at all like what the girls in Helena were wearing.

A nice linen [dress] I had shrunk at the first washing and I could not get into it, so I was minus one number in my wardrobe. Hats were even more of an undertaking. Only two of the hats originated by the local milliner passed "muster" in Helena - a brown soft straw faced with red crepe in a square tufted design and a white crepe bonnet with little flowers. But finally we were as ready as we could be.

On a bright warm August day, at seven o'clock in the morning, we climbed into the coach waiting at the Post Office door. With the grinding release of the big brake, the creak of the harness, the proverbial crack of the driver's whip, we swung around the corner of the I. G. Baker store, drove up Main Street and were soon pulling up the steep Helena Hill, leaving the Fort Benton Valley. Mother was going as far as the Sun River Leavings with us, to go home on the coach coming from Helena.

There was one other passenger leaving Benton, Mr. Griffith, a civil engineer originally from Ohio. Mother had lived the first part of her life in Philadelphia and as they were both good talkers we listened to an interesting exchange of experiences about their native states of Ohio and Pennsylvania, and to their views on life in Montana versus life in the eastern part of the United States.

Mr. Griffith told, us of an uncle who liked to tell long tales but who would stop every few minutes and say, "Are you listening? Are you interested?" Finally Mr. Griffith said, "Yes, I am interested, why do you stop and ask me that?" The old gentleman replied, "Well, I notice you don't say 'yes,' I like my listeners to look at me and say 'yes' every little while and then I know that I have their attention." We thought this must be an example of eastern good manners so when we got to Helena we practiced saying "yes, yes" when anyone was telling a story, until finally the family wondered where we had picked up the annoying habit of interrupting them with our "yes, yes."

Once on top of the hill we could look over the prairie for miles in every direction. On the south side of the river the Highwoods and the Little Belts appeared to be made of shining light blue glass in the heat waves of the summer day.

In the far southwest we could see the dim outline of the Rockies. Uncut buffalo grass covered the prairie and waved its small brushes in the air. Some hardy little red flowers and pink honeysuckle nestled close to the ground, nothing on the horizon and not a fence in sight!

The first stop was at Eight Mile Springs, a permanent spring in a spread coulee beside the road. (it is now the Great Northern Reservoir at Tunis.) The horses were unhitched, watered and then put back in their harness. It was hot and dry, the summer of 1886 just proceeding the terrible winter of 1886–87. From the springs, the horses trotted and galloped across the prairie to Twenty-Eight Miles Springs. We had a good noon dinner and stretched our backs and legs, stiff from the long ride in the swaying coach bumping over ruts and hollows of the worn dirt road. As the warm drowsy afternoon wore on we made one stop at a lone unpainted board store. The driver said it was Johnstown. It was on the west side of the river from what is now Great Falls but at that time there was no sign whatever of any town ever coming into existence at that place.

The coach pushed on to Sun River Leavings where Mother was leaving us and returning to Fort Benton on the down coach. We always said, "going up" to Helena because it was up the Missouri River and up in the mountains, although really south of us. At Sun River we saw the very large stone barn where-in lived an enormous and magnificent gray stallion. He was tied to his stall and no one dared to go near him. After a bounteous supper, cooked by Mrs. Remike we tearfully said good-bye to our dear Mother who put us in charge of our friend, Mr. Griffith and the driver. We drove off toward Fort Shaw, watching Mother as long as we could see her as she stood waiting for the Benton stage to be on its way.

At Fort Shaw a very unpleasant surprise awaited us. The front of the Post Office was black with men all determined to get on the coach. Five men got inside and. two of them sat on the jump seats but we kept our places on the big seat. The men were going to the mines and, would not wait another day. There was no more room so the driver and helper began to boost the fourteen extras, with their bedrolls and rucksacks to the top of the coach. There were no seats there, only a rail about eight inches above the top. The driver got a

Changing Horses at Sun River Leaving

rope and tied a piece around each man and then to the rail and other parts of the coach to give the men something secure to hold. Mr. Joe McKnight and Mr. George Heldt, friends of Father, were in charge of the Post Office and trading store and they saw that we were comfortably settled for the night.

Away we went through the dusk that soon became black night, up and up the grade into the mountains, bumping, lurching, and swaying through the darkness, with the men on top coming down with a thud on the roof after every rough spot in the road. It began to get cold as we started our long hard climb to the Bird Tail Divide. The coach swayed and plunged down the banks of small streams and, nearly stood on end as the horses endeavored to pull it up the other side. All the time the men on top slid from one end of the coach to the other. They groaned and swore when there was a hard jolt. We huddled up in our corner, wrapped in shawls, and, wished we were with Mother.

The side curtains were pulled shut during the night. When it got stuffy and close, one of the men would open the upper half of a door to let in some fresh air and a cold breeze. I could not sleep but my sisters went off to sleep and slept soundly until morning. The men talked mining, stock business, and smoked. They were worried that we might turn over with that top heavy load. Once or twice, one of the men passed a flask to his neighbors to have them take a swallow to warm up. I was scared that someone would take too much. I had seen drunks on the streets of Fort Benton and to me they were terrifying. But I know now that the men were most moderate in their libations and that they were following a custom of the frontier. I am sure they thought we were all asleep.

At midnight we pulled into the station at Bird Tail Divide, it was very cold. The top riders were untied and allowed to flex their muscles. I stood beside the coach to get a breath of air. In the shadow of the big Bird Tail it was a weird and spooky scene. A stock tender came out with a candle lantern to help the driver change horses it was a gloomy station, no light, no welcome, no cheer. The station was bare and uninviting. We watched the lanterns moving through the barns and corral as the men brought out the fresh horses. It was so dark and lonely that I felt very far from home. The fourteen "toppers" climbed up again, were tied on, and we started down grade.

I caught a few fitful naps near dawn, and the next I remember was the sudden stopping of the coach at Wolf Creek. I had a hard time waking my sisters. It must have been about seven in the morning, the sun was shining and Wolf Greek, a beautiful clear stream was rippling along toward its junction, with the Missouri. The fir trees were green on the mountain sides, the station was clean and cheery and it was a beautiful sight after the horrors of the night.

The poor battered men on the top were glad to walk around, even to lie stretched out on the ground. The men made a rush for the usual tin basin and roller towel at the kitchen door to wash up before eating. We girls wandered down to the stream with our little bag and washed our faces and combed our hair as well as we could. When the housekeeper had asked if we wished to wash I said, "No thank you, we have our own 'conveyances'," and then I was most embarrassed realizing that a "conveyance" was a wagon or buggy and that I had meant to say "conveniences." We had a fine breakfast of ham, eggs and hot cakes. We sat beside Mr. Griffith, who was still looking out for us. Everyone talked of the experiences and fears of the night. After a good rest, we all took our places in the coach, the men were raised to the top again, and we entered the small, but beautiful Wolf Creek Canyon.

By this time the continual bumping of the men on top had broken the laths of the coach and we did not know whether or not we could reach Helena before the men came toppling down on our heads. All day we watched the lining of the top tear a little farther and a little farther.

This day's ride was one of delight and wonderment as we followed the ever twisting canyon road up and down, now hugging the mountain side, now taking a level stretch at a gallop, now crossing and re-crossing the Prickly Pear. We drank from a spring gushing from the mountain side; we reveled in the organ rocks, the rock castles, the peaks and the countless Christmas trees. In those days there were few trees and almost no flowers in Fort Benton so the purple fall asters, the golden rod and the syringa bushes were magnificent to us.

After leaving the canyon and having dinner at Mitchell (now Sieben) mid—afternoon we came to Silver City. (The old stage barn can still be seen there.) Uncle Tom drove up in his light buggy, on his way to Fort Benton. He asked the driver, "Have you any little girls belonging to me?" The driver said, "Yes, they are here safe and sound." I imagine we must have been a weary dusty looking sight after two days and a night driving over the rough and dusty roads. Uncle told the driver where to deliver us in Helena, then on his way. After a change of horses we drove across the valley,

around a mountain, and there lay Helena on the slope of Mt. Helena, a dream city to me then, and for many and many a year after. I always pretended that I was a princess awakening from a sleep and coming home to my kingdom.

We put the fourteen miners (they had not come through the roof after all) off at the stage office. The stage drove up to the gate of the Power cottage on Benton Avenue where Aunt Mollie stood waiting to welcome us. It was a funny little cottage with a cupola on one corner. It is still there and I often think of that summer and all the people we met. Uncle Tom had sold the big house where we had visited six or seven years before. Our cousin, Charlie, was in college and aunt and uncle had spent much of the winter in the east. This little cottage was the only vacant home they could get for the summer and if Uncle Tom had been home there would not have been room for us.

There was a fine dinner waiting for us, served by the Chinese cook, but as we had absorbed the motion of the stagecoach our chairs seemed to sway back-wards, forward and sideways. The knives and forks were not clear in outline and all that evening we walked with an unsteady motion, reaching for a chair to cling to. After a few exchanges of family news we went to bed early. By the next morning we had recovered our equilibrium and were ready for the gayeties of Helena.

Charlie was in his junior year at Georgetown University in Washington, D. C. He had learned some stenography and was often away with his Father but when he was there we had a gay time. He was an exalted personage, a college man. He could sing the popular songs from the stage shows of the day. He had all kinds of funny stories to tell of college boys and their prank, and if he could manage a practical joke on us, that was his delight. We were the unsophisticated little greenhorns from the trading post at Fort Benton. He had lived there himself until he was ten years old but now, of course, he knew about Washington, Chicago and New York.

We spent long sunny days playing with Francis and Addie Murphy in their big yard filled with trees and flowers. Addie had a Charter Oak cook stove, child's size. We could make a real fire in it and attempted to cook potatoes, which never got thoroughly done while the small fire lasted. Mrs. Murphy had a studio in the back of the house where she and Aunt Mollie and other friends painted landscapes. Later they painted china which Mrs. Murphy fired in her own kiln.

We went to a party at Mrs. W. B. Raleigh's, given for her daughters, Sue and Madge. We had such a good time because the girls played a romping game of "Bear" in and out the carriage house with us. (Many homes had a carriage house on the back of the property.) The house is now in the mounds of St. Johns Hospital.

Many evenings we walked up Benton Avenue, past Dr. Brooks' stone house, turned the next corner and went up the hill to Mrs. Martin Maginnis' home. It was a homey brick cottage with a lovely grassy yard sloping down from the long porch outside the dining room. Major Maginnis was then Montana's Delegate in Congress. Mrs. Maginnis was a charming, gracious and brilliant woman with a power of caustic wit which would have qualified her to preside over a "salon" in any capital; she was a traveler and an omnivorous reader. Her sitting room walls were covered with good copies and some originals of European masters. While we were there she gave a birthday party for my sister, Grace. Governor Hauser was just building his new home on Madison. It was the first of the new houses on the west side. The barn and carriage house had just been completed. As we drove past one evening and the adults were admiring the new house arising on the site, Virginia wanted to know why the man was going to have a church of his own (the new carriage house).

The most thrilling event of the visit was attending a circus. (Buffalo Bill put on the stagecoach hold-up by Indians.) We drove out in a cab to the circus down in the valley, beyond the Northern Pacific Station. Three young girls were too much for one lady, so Aunt Mollie enlisted the services of her friends. Mrs. Maginnis took charge of me, Miss Maggie Carroll had Grace by the hand and Aunt held on to Virginia. I think the ladies were far more nervous over the performance than we were. Virginia claimed the attention of the audience near us by looking with disapproval at the plank seats, turned to her Aunt and said, "Aunt Mollie, I told you this was no place to wear a good dress." The dress was a simple white muslin (but Virginia's best). She was

finally persuaded to take the risk of sitting down and all of Aunt Mollie's friends sitting near were highly amused. In those days cabs were called "hacks." On our return to Fort Benton, Virginia astonished our friends by announcing that in Helena we went to the circus in a "hearse."

At that time we all liked to recite poems and "pieces," thanks to a "Literary" started by Mr. Downing, the principal of our school. My taste ran to tragedy like the Clansman's Revenge, "My child, my child, with sobs and tears she shrieked, up his callous ears." In Helena I had recited Whittier's "Witch's Daughter." Aunt Mollie said, "My, why don't you learn something from the good poets?" She collapsed with feigned humility when I said, "Well that is Whittier, Aunt Mollie." I suppose he was still accepted as a poet in those days but I must have been quite a prig in my self-satisfied attitude.

The Cosmopolitan and Bristol of the mining days were still in use as the hostelries of the town. The Helena and the Grandon had not been built. Raleigh's and Sands were the two leading dry goods stores. They were on south Main Street. Beyond them at the extreme southern end of Main was Chinatown, a sizable settlement of restaurants, noodle parlors, and stores, a few Chinese residences. The stores had good stocks of fine china, brass, and embroideries. One morning we attempted to walk down over the hills from Mrs. Maginnis' house to Chinatown. In the scramble I lost a five dollar bill with which I was going to buy some presents to take home so my purchases were eliminated.

We were delighted with the good times in Helena but still were intolerantly loyal to Fort Benton. No store in Helena compared in our eyes to Power's or I. G. Baker. Mt. Helena was not as big as the butte below Fort Benton, etc.

When we were leaving aunt told us we had been good girls and we could come back when we were young ladies. But, she made the admission to Mother, three at a time, of our ages, was more than she could manage!

On our return we made the trip as far as Fort Shaw under the chaperonage of Mrs. George Heldt, who with her two young daughters, Mousie and Birdie, had been visiting in Helena. The girls were very lively and had no inhibitions. They thought up, or were inspired with, a great many pranks, very amusing to us who joined in, but very annoying to some of the passengers - such as unbuckling the strap of the middle seat which caused the men in the seat to fall backwards as the coach went over a bump in the road. Mrs. Heldt, who said it made her ill to ride inside the coach, rode in the choice seat beside the driver. Although the driver had to admonish us several times to behave she contented her-self with saying, "Girls, be good," but would bother her head no more about it and settle herself in her nice seat. Mother, who met us at Sun River, was much displeased with us when we reported what a fine time we had had on the coach.

Mother had brought our little brother, Frank (age 5) with her. He was excited about his visit to the Sunnyside Ranch Stage Station where there was a big stone barn and an enormous gray stallion. All boys then dreamed of horses, saddles, bridles, and spurs as boys today study airplanes and long to fly them. The stone barn, the stone building, which was part store and part house, and the long avenue of cottonwoods are still there, but all in a dilapidated condition. G. B. Power sold the place to Heffelfinger of Minneapolis, the famous Yale fullback, but this was just before the drought years of 1917-22 and the place never paid, it is now in the hands of one of the Mormon farmers who have settled in the Sun River Valley and is used as a dairy farm.

During the homeward drive in the afternoon I was very sleepy. At one of the stops Mother allowed me to climb up in the space below the driver's seat with a buffalo robe and take a nap. On the coach was an Italian Jesuit Priest, Father Jena, on. his way to Fort Benton. With his European ideas of the proper guarding of girls he was much troubled by missing me from the family group. At the next stop he got out, looked around and not seeing me he ran to Mother and said, "The girl, the girl, she is not there, she is not there." Then Mother showed him where I was, fast asleep, but he did not think it very proper for me to be up there by myself so as soon as I awakened I was brought inside the coach.

We reached Fort Benton at dusk and as we came down the Helena Hill the low log adobe cabins, many of them belonging to Indian and half-breed families in the upper end of town, made the town look awfully dingy and flat and not the bright place of our remembrance in fact our own house was a six room low adobe, weather-boarded to look like a frame. But our trip on the Stagecoach and our traveled state gave us a certain distinction among our schoolmates, on which we capitalized to the full.

Reminiscences of the Stagecoaches

The daily arrival of the stagecoach at the Fort Benton, M. T. Post Office (near our house) was the exiting moment of the day. There was a rush of people from the stores and homes, hoping there would be mail for them that day. Our friends stopped in at our house to visit while waiting for the mail to be distributed. Often a friend of the family came on the stage or a noted traveler to continue his journey on an awaiting steamboat or several well-dressed ladies would get off the stage to wait in Fort Benton for a down river boat. In summer, when there was a large consignment of strawberries arriving by coach express there was great excitement for that meant some church would have a strawberry festival. All the neighbors of different faiths rallied to help pick the hulls from the berries. At Christmas time there were large packages of beautiful Christmas gifts. So to us, the stage was the bringer of gifts, and joy - a regular Cinderella coach.

There was the other side of the picture when the coach was late because of rain or blizzards and the life of the driver, as well as the safety of the mail was at stake. Father, as Postmaster, knew all the stage drivers. He knew which were the best drivers, the most good natured and the most dependable. The drivers were hardy, ingenious men. They were responsible for their horses, the safety of the passengers and often thousands of dollars worth of gold dust. Their faces were tanned and lined from the ceaseless winds, they often had frozen feet or fingers when they were lost in a blizzard. I remember one little man, Casey, who had his feet badly frozen. My sister, Virginia, (not knowing the facts of life) always thought he was the stage driver who had brought her to the family.

William Rowe was one of the well known drivers and later on was in charge of the whole crew, directing the runs of each driver.

In summer the drivers wore Stetsons and western clothing but in the winter they wore fur caps, felt boots inside their overshoes, buffalo overcoats with shawls wrapped round and round. As I travel the road today, I wonder how they ever managed to keep the road through a blizzard with so few landmarks -a butte -a mountain -a rock -a corral -a lonely ranch house. There were no fences, just open prairie with the mountains off in the distance.

My uncle, T. C. Power, [at one time] owned the coaches. He told me that he once bought a lot of thermometers and put one on each coach. Mr. Rowe, in charge of the drivers, came along, saw the thermometers and said angrily, "What fool put those things on the coaches?" Uncle said, "I did. I thought the boys would like to know how cold. it is." Mr. Rowe replied, "If you leave those thermometers there you won't have a driver left!" Off came the thermometers.

There were two types of stagecoaches, the big Concord, which seemed to bounce and sway on its enormous springs, and the small coach, or Jerky, which was a spring wagon with a canvas coach top. The Jerky had just two seats inside and was used on the shorter runs or in case of an emergency when the big coach could not get through. The Concord had a large curved pouch, called the boot, in front and below the driver's seat. Under the driver's seat was a recessed space where a passenger or the driver could curl up and take a nap, protected from the wind. At the rear was a large storage or baggage space with a canvas curtain to be strapped down over the baggage. Inside were two large leather upholstered seats facing each other. Between the two main seats, one at each end of the coach, a jump seat with a very wide leather strap was not very comfortable for a long ride but three large men could ride comfortably in the end seats.

When I saw two or three stagecoaches in an exposition building in San Francisco they did not look nearly as sturdy nor as cumbersome as those I remember on the Helena mail route. They were painted a shining dark red and were quite decorated and compact, in fact they were very "dapper" in appearance. Ours never were. They were big and strong and tough. Maybe it was that I looked at the Wells Fargo coaches with the eyes of an adult and at our coaches with the eyes of a child.

Silver City Stage Station about 1918

Rock Creek Stage Station

Carter and Kisselpaugh's Station at Wolf Creek 1891

Carter and Kisselpaugh's Stage Stop at Wolf Creek

Wolf Creek Saloon

Wolf Creek Saloon Interior

Dearborn Crossing 1879

Milot House at Dearborn Crossing 1883

Eagle Rock Station

Montana Hotel and Saloon-Henry Milot-Sun River Crossing

Bull House at Sun River

Store and Eating Place at Sun River Leaving

Twenty-Eight Mile Spring

Steel Store at Sun River Crossing

The Stage Driver by Charlie Russell–Pen and Ink 1901

Lyons Hill from Little Prickly Pear Canyon

May Flooding on the Little Prickly Pear

Rock Siding on the Little Prickly Pear Toll Road

Chapter VIII

Perils on the Road

Although Indians and outlaws were not a huge problem to travelers on the Benton Road (and if they became one they were dealt with in summary fashion) other hazards seem to plague the travelers and freighters year after year. Road conditions, due to poor maintenance, high water or snow depth and the temperament of the beasts of burden seemed to confound the most experienced wayfarer. Even a smallpox epidemic was carried on the road.

Upsetting the Coach

Accidents, particularly with stage coaches rushing to stay on schedule, occurred frequently. Synchronizing four or six horses was no easy task. The slightest disturbance could throw the whole system out of order.

Not many people died from such occurrences, but some were injured. The *Montana Post* of March 19, 1869, reported one such event involving a prominent pioneer.

Accident—We regret to learn that an accident occurred to the Benton coach on Monday morning, near the toll gate, some miles from town. One of the horses was taken with a fit while going around a point on the bank of the Missouri River [sic- Little Prickly Pear Creek], and its rude contortions upset the coach and hurled it over the precipice down the mountain side. The driver was badly bruised, had his arm broken and his shoulder dislocated and sustained other injuries. Messrs. C. A. Broadwater and L. E. Trask, who were passengers, each were severely injured, and Mr. Broadwater narrowly escaped death. The driver was left at a house nearby, and Mr. Broadwater, in spite of his injuries, drove to the next station [possibly Malcolm Clark's]. Drs.

Glick and Washburne [Glick was a doctor from Helena while Washburne was an express agent there] were sent for and dressed the wounds, bruises, etc. of the driver, and left him in a comfortable condition. We are glad it was no worse, and we congratulate Mr. Trask for coming off so well, and Broadwater for being spared another season of freighting delights in the Diamond "R" outfit.

Another accident occurred in May 1876, again in the Little Prickly Pear Canyon. It was reported on June 3, 1876, by the *Helena Independent*.

The Benton Coach Swamped in the Little Prickly Pear

Horses Drowned and Mail Sacks and Treasure Box Lost.

The Driver Makes a Narrow Escape From Drowning.

From Mr. Al. Fisher, who arrived here yesterday from the canyon, has obtained the information that on last Thursday the Benton coach was carried away by the current of the Prickly Pear, near Kisselpaugh's, the horses drowned and the stage coach wrecked. Mr. Corbin, Division Agent, had taken the precaution to drive his two horse buggy in advance of the coach, but the buggy was also swept away. The horses, however, were saved. Capt. D. W. Buck was the only passenger, and he saved himself by jumping off.

In an interview with Captain Buck, who arrived later in the evening, the reporter learns that the immediate cause of the accident was a caving bank. The current is rapid and the stream high, but not to an extent that would have precluded the safe passage of the coach. But to ascertain with certainty, Mr. Corbin preceded the coach in his buggy. The rapid current swept it away and the coach pressing on in attempting to ascend the opposite bank was hurled back into the stream by cave in the soil, and the horses thrown back overturned the coach, which, with the struggling animals, were whirled out into the stream, the driver became entangled in his seat, and with extreme difficulty extricated himself, barely escaping with his life. As previously stated, the horses were drowned, and the mail sacks and treasure box washed out of the coach and lost. Subsequently, the coach was got out of the river, but up to the time of Capt. Buck leaving the search for the mail sacks and treasure box had not been successful.

Under the circumstances it is surprising that both Mr. Corbin and the driver were not drowned. Altogether it was a remarkable and thrilling adventure.

The *Helena Independent* for October 29, 1875, claimed that "William Orant, who was hurt by the overturning of the Benton coach about a week ago, has been taken to the Sister's Hospital. His hip was dislocated and he was badly bruised. Dr. Ingersoll attends him."

In the summer of 1878, there were two instances of coaches upsetting coming down the Bird Tail Divide. On August 30, 1878, the *Helena Independent* noted that a coach of the Benton line was upset at that point and that all had escaped injury except Mr. Steimitz, and his wife, and child. Fortunately, they only received scratches and bruises. A week earlier, a coach belonging to Gilmer and Salisbury had upset in the same locality. By October 6, of that year the *Helena Independent* editor suggested that "Two things have become epidemic in Montana—marriages and coach upsets."

It was noted, again in the *Helena Independent*, on January 20, 1881, that the Benton coach, due in the day before, was detained by an upset in the Little Prickly Pear Canyon. Fortunately, no one was injured seriously. Less than a year later, the *Helena Independent* was commenting: "This thing of turning stage coaches over to see how they look on the underside is becoming quite too entirely fashionable to please the traveling public."

On November 3, 1883, the *Helena Independent* stated that "The Benton coach, Helena-bound, while approaching the Bird Tail Divide before daylight Thursday morning, ran off a bridge and upset, a San Francisco insurance agent named Strickland, receiving considerable shaking up. No other damage of any extent was done. Strickland was brought to Cartersville by mail contractor Power[s] and a messenger was sent to Helena for Dr. Steele, who started out at two o'clock yesterday morning. Mr. Strickland was brought to Helena last night. His injuries are not regarded as serious."

Passengers did not always forgive the stage lines for their injuries due to turned over coaches. On May 30, 1883, the *Helena Independent* reported that Dick Kennon, who had his leg broken while riding on a Gilmer and Salisbury coach, was awarded a $21,500 settlement. The next February, Chet Higley was rewarded, in a second trial ordered by the Montana Supreme Court, a $10,000 settlement from Gilmer and Salisbury for receiving a broken leg in a stage coach accident that occurred in 1875.

Sometimes, as in the case of Higley, the driver was at least partially to blame having been intoxicated when the accident occurred. Apparently, it was not unusual for drivers to drink on the job especially when the trips were overnight.

Too Much Rain

Next to the possibility of having the coach flip over, the second most pressing issue was the condition of the road. Any road that followed or crossed over a creek or river was susceptible to flooding problems. When the road through Little Prickly Pear Canyon was first conceived, the designers saw a potential for over twenty bridges in the span of less than ten miles.

The *Helena Independent* of March 24, 1876, gave ample warning to the public that trouble laid ahead: "It is believed that the large accumulations of snow in the mountains will make the largest spring freshet we have had in years."

It seems that the month of May was and is the worst time for flooding as a warm rain can melt the snow pack and cause tremendous runoffs from the mountains. In 1876, May was such a month and it just about drove the population of Helena crazy. The *Helena Independent* ran a series of articles in May and June, describing the problem and how it was addressed.

May 21, 1876
FLOODED STREAMS

Bridges Swept Away on the Benton Road.

The recent rains have so flooded the streams in the Prickly Pear Canyon that five bridges have been swept away and the road left in an almost impassable condition. It behooves the County Commissioners to take immediate steps to have them repaired. Freights are on the way from Benton to Helena and delay in their arrival will be seriously inconvenient to both merchants and citizens. Besides it is a serious obstruction to travel, which at this juncture it is necessary should be open and free of obstructions. It has been suggested that a called session, of the County Commissioners Court, to take steps to have these bridges replaced, would meet the hearty approval or the public.

THE LATE STORM

Condition or the Prickly Pear Canyon Road.

The Benton couch arrived last evening, and the passengers report several bridges gone in the Lower Canyon. The three upper bridges are standing, and travel takes the old Mullen Road from that vicinity. The coach took the Mullan Road at Wolf Creek, and traveled it for seven miles. An immense volume of water is flowing thro' the canyon and many grades are reported washed away. In some of the bottoms there is water enough to float a steamboat. The river is falling rapidly, it fell thirteen inches yesterday. Mr. Fergus is employing a number of men and will set to work repairing at once. It will be some time before freight can be hauled through the canyon, and it is reported almost impossible for loaded teams to go over the old Mullan Road. There are three boats at Benton, and times are very lively, one hundred recruits arrived on one of the boats.

The *Helena Independent* summed up the severity of the situation in its May 30, 1876, edition.

EVERY possible effort should be made to send forward our quartz. The boats coming to Benton will have to go back without tonnage unless this is done. This condition will occasion a higher price in freight and may soon diminish our freighting facilities on the

river, inasmuch as the boats cannot afford to come to Benton unless they have return cargoes. The break in the Prickly Pear Canyon, which the *Herald* does not want repaired, has already damaged the freighting interests of the territory thousands of dollars.

June 10, 1876
FREIGHTS DELAYED

The Inspection of the Canyon by Prominent Citizens.

Condition of the Benton Road.

The reporter of the *Independent* interviewed Gov. Potts, C. A. Broadwater, J. T. Murphy, John Kinna, D. C. Corbin, and H. M. Paichen; who returned late last Thursday night from trip of inspection to the Prickly Pear Canyon, and their statements confirm in every particular the account published in yesterday's *INDEPENDENT*. The summing up of the information gleaned from them is that it will be impossible for freight to arrive here from Benton earlier than three or four weeks from this date. Mr. E. Beach, County Commissioner, is on the ground with a force of hands, and is endeavoring to expedite the repairs in the canyon, but at present it is not possible to accomplish much work on account of the great freshet.

It will be seen from an interview with some of our prominent citizens, just returned from the Prickly Pear Canyon, that it will be three, if not four, weeks before freights can get through it. The bridges have been swept away and the grade in many places has been washed away. Under these circumstances it seems to us that some extraordinary exertions should he made to guard against a recurrence of such a condition in the future. Inasmuch as the chief freights of the territory pass through it, and the business community is largely dependent on this road, it ought to be made a public highway and kept up at the expense of the territory. Already freights have been delayed three weeks, and it will be fully three weeks more before it is repaired to a degree that will allow heavily loaded wagons to get over it.

Prickly Pear Canyon

The road up as far a Kisselpaugh's, Wolf Creek Station, was very good except at the point where the stage went over. This was to be fixed at once. Above the station and just below Steele & Adams' saw mill the flat was muddy and water from two to five feet deep over the road. Took my baggage around over the point; arrived, at fifth bridge below Fergus', the water up to top of bridge, and in getting to it through the mud and water, got my horse down, and had to take him out and haul the wagon out by hand; had to ford water three feet deep on the grade above the bridge; got to the fourth bridge, and found it dropped on the upper side two feet and the water running over it with several logs lodged on it. The bank on the lower end sluiced out from three to four feet and a rapid channel running round the upper end. Crossed on foot and prospected with a pole, but not considering it safe, carried out baggage around above the third bridge, took buggy apart and carried it up the mountain to where the horse could draw it; then drove zigzag until we got to top of mountain; then along the ridge to where it was no longer safe; then took out the horse, locked wheels and backed down the steep mountain side to the road, and got to Fergus' station at six o'clock. Apprehending trouble, I brought a pilgrim, Mr. James Dorman, through with me, and had it not been for his assistance I could not have got my team through. The water was running over the third bridge and heavy channels on both sides.

The stream was still high Wednesday morning and freights, mail-stages and all are blockaded until the waters abate. Commissioner Beach has twenty men at work but can do nothing more than make grade and get out timber while the water is up. Should the water go down and the fifth, fourth, and third bridges, or even the third remain, the road can be made passable by repairing the grade on the Mullan Road, on the right rising from Medicine Creek. But before the road thru' the canyon can be repaired so teams can go through on the old route, the stream will have to fall to fording stage, as many of the grades are washed out and deep channels and holes cut in the road bed where it ran through valley or flat.

Friday morning the Prickly Pear had not yet fallen; third and fourth bridges gone. Silver Creek was higher at noon than ever before known.

June 15, 1876
The Benton Road

Messrs. Fergus and Beach were in town yesterday, the former direct from the canyon. No teams can go through it yet and all travel is over Lyon's Hill. About forty men are at work, and by next week sixty hands will be employed. The water is falling slowly.

June 25, 1876
The Roads and the Flood

The Benton coach which arrived here last evening, came through the Prickly Pear Canyon. The delayed trains there were going through all day yesterday morning.

The *Helena Weekly Herald* of July 16, 1876, summed up the situation.

PRICKLY PEAR CANYON

Action of the County Commissioners.

The County Commissioners Met on the 11th and 12th of this month.

The principle business before them was auditing the accounts for work done on the Prickly Pear Road. From the proceedings, we learn that the amount of orders, allowed for work, tools, and material furnished for repairs on the road in Prickly Pear Canyon to date is $3,682.54. Of this amount orders were given for work done before the freshet amounting to $182.54, leaving about $3,500 allowed so far chargeable to the extraordinary high water. There are probably bills to the amount of $150 remaining to audit, and the county has tools to that value left from the work, leaving the net outlay about $3,500. About $100 is still needed to complete two of the bridges when the water gets lower. There are four bridges gone where the river has to be forded, and two now standing are very rotten. To obviate the necessity of building these bridges, and repairing and keeping in order the road through the soft bottoms, the Commissioners have let a contract for building three grades. The first commences at the third bridge, (counting down stream) and keeping on the right hand side of the river to the fourth bridge, thereby doing away with both. The second commences at the fifth bridge and keeps on the right side of the creek to the sixth, or ford. The third grade commences about half a mile below this, and goes over the foothills one mile and a

Old Mud Wagon on the Benton Road

quarter to the hill above on this side of the ninth bridge, doing away with the necessity of rebuilding the seventh and eighth. R. S. Ells has the contract for all three grades at $3,509 cash, and is now at work on them with a force of men, the county furnishing tools. By this arrangement there will be but five bridges, where formerly there were eleven, and two of these five are above high water mark, while the remaining three are considered safe in any reasonable freshet, but would have been better built and more secure had the water been lower and more time expended upon them.

This road, as is well known to all old settlers, was formerly a toll road, owned by King & Gillette. Their charter expired winter before last. As it is not in any organized road district, it has been under the immediate charge of the County Commissioners since it became a county road. At the expiration of King & Gillette's charter it was found to be in a very bad condition.

An expenditure of about $1,200 was found necessary last summer to keep it in traveling condition, and men were at work on it the present summer when the high water stopped the travel. This is a very difficult and costly piece of road, and ought really to be a territorial charge, and will never be considered perfectly safe from high water until it is graded on the foothills through the entire length of the canyon, which the Commissioners are essaying to do as rapidly as possible. When the present contract is finished, about 7 miles of the upper end of the canyon will be secure, leaving only about four miles additional to grade. There will then be but three bridges where there were originally thirteen.

The "all clear" was sounded by the *Independent* on June 30, 1876.

The Benton Road through the Prickly Pear Canyon is reported by freighters to be in a better condition than before the rainstorms washed away the bridges. It is hardly necessary to say that it was not a very attractive piece of road at any time, and several years neglect by the road supervisors had not tended to improve it. Now, however, the grade has been mended and the shackling bridges replaced by sound ones, it does very well, and will probably serve for travel until superseded by the air line railroad, which the citizens are so industriously engaged in projecting.

The spring of 1877, was another rain filled season. On May 24, of that year the *Helena Independent* carried a short article on the condition of the Benton Road.

The Roads

On the down trip the roads, though not the best, were not in bad condition. The repairs made in Prickly Pear Canyon embrace several grades, made to avoid so many crossings as were on the old road. One of the new grades is rather steep, but taking the road altogether, it is much less likely to get out of repair than it would have been had the old track been repaired. ...

[On the return trip] leaving the station [Twenty-Eight Mile] we got along very well until within five miles of the Leaving [Leaving Sun River], when the wheels began to clog with the putty like mud, moistened by the heavy rain of the previous day, and from this point on we were three hours in making three miles. We had a good four horse team and no load notwithstanding the mud accumulated on the wheels in such proportions as to stall the team on a down grade. Every few rods we had to stop and disengage it. It beats anything I ever saw, reminding me of "Aunt Jemima's sticking plaster, which the more you tried to pull it off, the tighter it would stick the faster." There is a peculiarity about this clay that I never saw anywhere else. It resembles the finest quality of putty and might, if kneaded with oil, be made of equal value. I think of taking up a putty ranch under the Desert Land Act.

The year 1878, was not much better for travelers on the Benton Road. The *Helena Independent* of June 1, 1878, noted that "A freighter arrived from Prickly Pear Canyon last night with the news that the Bird Tail bridge was gone, and that the Dearborn bridge was somewhat damaged by water at one end, and it is not passable for heavily loaded wagons. The coach, which was due here on Thursday afternoon, is detained at Spitzley's [Eagle Rock Station]. The river is booming—running bank full—and Mr. Dunks, the freighter above mentioned, says it is not fordable, and in the low places the road is flooded. The bridges and road through the canyon are alright."

August of 1881, saw more heavy rain in the canyon. The *Helena Independent* noted: "The driver who brought in the Benton coach last evening says that the rainfall yesterday morning in the Prickly Pear Canyon was very heavy. The mountains were covered with snow."

Snow on the Road

The *Helena Independent* for June 21, 1937, reflected on a story entitled "Perils of Winter Travel in Old Days Recalled by Teacher's trip to Helena."

Except for a few days each winter when snow blocks a few passes, cold weather traveling on modern highways in heated cars is enjoyable, but winter journeys when grandma was a lass were not only uncomfortable but dangerous.

Gathered in the lobby of the Placer Hotel yesterday, a group of old-timers related the trip undertaken in 1878 by Belle Johnston who was a teacher in Chestnut Valley (near Cascade) and Cal Adams stage driver, from Fort Shaw to Helena.

Home for New Years

Miss Johnston had been unable to get home for Christmas, and decided she would get there for New Year's or know the reason why. She was the only passenger to board the Helena stage at Fort Shaw at 7 o'clock in the evening, on New Year's Eve.

The driver, Cal Adams, tried to dissuade her from making the trip, which, under the most favorable conditions required from 12 to 14 hours. Upon this occasion it was snowing and the temperature was 30 below zero. He told her that four men at Fort Shaw who had intended making the trip had backed out because of the weather and that he himself wouldn't think of tackling it if it wasn't for the mail he was carrying which had to go through.

Miss Johnston, however, insisted upon going. All of his arguments exhausted, the driver arranged her as comfortably as possible inside the coach, buttoned the curtains closely to keep out the wind mounted the box and started. It was a 25-mile drive from Fort Shaw to the old town of Chestnut (now Cascade). After passing Eagle Rock about 10:30 the driver stopped a short distance beyond, and he told her they were off the road. He had to get off and hunt it on foot.

Lost Road in Storm

The girl climbed out of the stage and the driver turned the horses' tails to the wind. Miss Johnston climbed to the box in Adams' place and held the lines while he went off in the storm with a bobbing lantern in his hand in an effort to locate the trail. She watched the light until it disappeared from view. The horses were restless and she had trouble holding them. A half hour passed before she heard a whistle from the driver. She answered with a shrill whoop that frightened the four horses and they broke into a run.

The snow was so deep, however, that they were unable to gallop more than a few steps and she succeeded in bringing them to a halt.

Just as she succeeded in stopping them, Adams appeared out of the darkness with the lantern and said be had found the road. The girl was again tucked away inside the coach under a pile of blankets, and Adams, remarking that they soon would be at Dearborn Crossing, resumed the trip.

Adams' tramp through the snow in search of the trail had nearly exhausted him and sitting on the box in the wind afterwards he came near freezing to death. The girl slept comfortably inside, unaware of the agony Adams was suffering on the driver's seat.

Makes Crossing

Arriving at Dearborn Crossing, he tumbled from the seat, but could not gain his feet he crawled to the stage station, managed to open the door, and crawled inside only to fall unconscious on the floor. Sitting in front of the fireplace in the station were six wood haulers who had arrived only a short time before and who were waiting for food to be prepared for them. They had come from up the Dearborn River, and the cook was at work fixing them a meal.

They sprang to the aid of the driver, whom they all knew, and in the confusion which attended getting him into the room and out of his heavy clothing no one gave any thought of the stage outside. The horses continued to pull the stage a couple of miles beyond the station when they stopped with a jolt which awakened Miss Johnston inside the, coach.

"What's the matter now, Cal" she called.

Receiving no answer, she called again. and then, alarmed, scrambled out from under her blankets unbuttoned the curtains and looked out.

All she could see was swirling snow. She could feel the bite of the cold.

"Cal where are we?" she called.

Still no answer.

She clambered out of the stage and was horrified to find the driver's seat empty.

Frantic, she started to run forward past the team calling for Cal. The wind choked her cries. The horses, totally exhausted paid no attention to her screams.

She fell down.

As she scrambled to her feet she calmed herself with an effort.

Cal, she thought, undoubtedly had been overcome by the cold and either had fallen or had been jolted front the seat and was lying back along the trail somewhere.

He would freeze to death. She must get help.

She remembered hearing Cal say that they soon would be at Dearborn Crossing. She tried to get the lines together, and found they had become entangled about the hind legs of the off the wheeler. She pulled them loose. Snow was drifting about the wheels of the stage.

Takes Wheel

From the interior of the coach she dragged a couple of the blankets under which she had been sleeping and clambered to the driver's seat. She wrapped herself up as well us she could and urged the horses onward. She did not know of course, that they had already passed Dearborn Crossing, and with all her stamina she drove forward in the hope of getting help to find Cal Adams.

There was no trace of a road visible. She just kept going, the only thing she could do. It finally seemed that her efforts were of no avail. The horses were fagged, she was off the road, where, she did not know. She had just decided the best thing to do was to unhitch the horses and turn them loose, then crawl into the stage coach, cover herself with blankets and wait until the night and the storm were over.

Just then she saw a light in the distance, and hope flamed again in her heart. She drove towards it. About 100 yards from the light, which she now could see came from a house, she encountered a fence. The horses stopped. She dropped the reins, clambered down from the box, managed in some way to get trough the fence and walked to the cabin.

Without the formality of knocking, she opened the door and entered the room where Adams had fallen exhausted and partly unconscious nearly two hours before. It was 2 o'clock in the morning. The six woodsmen were still before the fire after having cared for Cal and eaten their meal.

They leaped to their feet and assisted her into the room, removed her wraps. When she told them Adams had fallen from the driver's box and must be lying long the trail some place, they told her that he was in the next room with his hands and feet frozen. She rushed in to see him blaming herself for his misfortune. Cal, who to this time had not spoken, roused sufficiently to tell Miss Johnston that what had happened to him was "nobody's fault." In the meantime the woodcutters unhitched and stabled the horses. At daybreak the trip was resumed with another driver. Two of the woodcutters went to Chestnut on the stage and Miss Johnston went to Helena, which she reached without further incident.

The next week Adams was removed to Helena and placed in a hospital where the toes of one of his feet were amputated.

When he recovered be returned to the stage line. Miss Johnston afterwards taught school in Butte for several years. Adams, years later, went to Boise, Idaho, and engaged in fruit raising.

Large accumulations of mountain snow and the potential for sudden runoffs posed the greatest threats to the road. Occasionally, heavy snow occurred on the road itself and that could be troublesome as well. On February 17, 1882, the *Helena Independent* reported:

The Benton coach arrived last evening at 7 o'clock. Shortly after leaving Benton, the passengers noticed the cattle gathering by hundreds, and the old-timers on the coach knew that a fierce storm was brewing. On Bird Tail Divide, about midnight, the passengers got out and walked up the hill. One of them, Nathan, came near freezing his hands. About 11 o'clock yesterday morning, when near Mitchell's, the storm in all its fierceness struck them. The snow scudded along in blinding clouds, and the cold was intense. At Silver City the passengers endeavored to have the coach lay over, but the driver refused. He had weathered many a storm on the Benton Road,

and was satisfied that he could make Helena all right; and he did it "in style," too.

By October of the following year it was noted that there was already three feet of snow in Prickly Pear Canyon.

Smallpox

Robert Vaughn in his book *Then and Now* related that in the winter and spring of 1870, many Indians and some whites died of smallpox. Two stage coach drivers who covered the route from Helena to the Sun River Leaving, where he was living at the time, died as well and Vaughn figured that was why he contracted the disease. Fortunately his was a mild case and he was only sick for two weeks.

Although the years 1882–1883, saw small outbreaks of smallpox in the towns of Butte, Miles City and Missoula; Montana as a whole did not experience the major epidemics that occurred in eastern cities such as Chicago, Illinois and Lexington, Kentucky. Concern for the possibility of such an epidemic ran throughout the territory and that portion served by the Benton Road was no exception.

The *Helena Independent* for August 25, 1882, carried the following article.

Smallpox at Silver City

We understand that the County Commissioners have declined to quarantine the house at Silver City in which smallpox exists. A man took dinner in the house yesterday and then came on into Helena. This should be stopped at once. In all other localities, we understand, where smallpox exists, the house is quarantined and parties forbidden to enter it. This should be done at Silver City. An officer should be immediately deputized, if necessary, to prevent ingress to the premises, except of nurses, physicians, etc. We trust that the county fathers will take the necessary steps in the matter to have the house in question quarantined, and it should not be disregarded.

By October 18, the same newspaper stated:

A telegram received at the United States land office in this city from Mr. Ben. Townsend conveys the intelligence that there is a case of smallpox at his place on the Benton Road, and a case in the land office set for hearing today has been postponed in consequence of the inability of the parties to attend.

On October 19, 1882, the *Helena Independent* reported that: "The driver of the Benton coach which came in last evening, and also the passengers, say that there is no sign of smallpox at any point along the Benton Road, and that everybody at Townsend's is well. It seems that it has been all scare and no smallpox."

In sharp contrast, the same paper noted on June 12, 1883: "Dr. Steele has caused to be burned down the house occupied by Mr. Gibson, the stage driver, at the time he was sick and died of smallpox last fall. It was at the mouth of Prickly Pear Canyon."

Thirty year old Eli Gibson had been residing with two other stage drivers, Peter Mitchell and Charles Thompson, in Helena for the 1880 census. Apparently he was isolated at the old toll house at the entrance to Lower Little Prickly Pear Canyon after contracting the disease.

The Benton Road, one hundred forty miles in length, presented many challenges to both passengers and drivers. Nevertheless, its existence was a step forward in the development of Montana.

Some traveled by stage, some rode horseback, some walked and some even rode in their own carriages or wagons. A few of the latter left us their views on the trip.

The Road Through Little Prickly Pear Canyon

A Road too Close to Little Prickly Pear Creek

Bridge Construction on the Little Prickly Pear

Rutted Road Through the Canyon

The Beginning of Fall at Wolf Creek

Mountain Goats near Wolf Creek

White Tail Deer at Wolf Creek

Sunset on the Benton Road

Chapter IX

Impressions Along the Road

Traveling the Benton Road during the early days was an adventure beyond the imagination of present day voyagers. The hardships encountered and the resolve necessary to get from one point to another warranted a detailed write up, and fortunately for us, some chose to document their experiences. Some of the most interesting were written by those who rejected public transportation, selecting instead vehicles of their own choosing.

One of the most detailed and fascinating accounts of traveling the Benton Road comes not from a freighter, stage driver or passenger, but instead from the family of a little boy who passed that way in 1876. Fisk G. Ellis was only six months old when his family and two other family groups undertook travel from Helena to the Blackfeet Agency on the Teton River, in the dead of winter. The article appeared as a Montana News Association Insert, courtesy of the *Judith Basin Star*, on June 17 and 24, 1935. Their mode of transportation was by covered wagons and the resulting adventure is amazing to the traveler of this age.

"Tell me about going to the agency when I was little." I pleaded, leaning against mother's knee one lonely summer afternoon in the early [eighteen] eighties. What a saga the story of that journey was to my youthful mind. To me its men and women were heroic adventurers of the first water. No matter how many times retold, I never tired of hearing it again and was continually begging mother or one of my brothers to recount its tales. Although fifty years have passed since I last heard it told, my interest has not waned. In truth, it is still so great that now I am gathering the fragments left after fifty years of forgetting and stringing them

like vari-colored beads of different sizes on a thread of imagination into a retold tale of what a handful of pioneers once did in frontier days to carry on.

It was a risky venture as I see it now, to attempt a midwinter wagon journey with women and children from Helena to the Teton and the old Blackfeet Indian Agency near the site of the present town of Choteau. However, it was not only attempted but actually done in the winter of 1874. It was no quick dash such as the automobile would make today but a matter of fortitude and raw patient toil. Its participants trusted not to speed to get there before a storm struck, as we would do now, but to their ability to endure and survive if a blizzard did strike and to fight their way through weather and over roads that would bring disaster under modern modes of travel.

Less than six months old at the time, I took no part in the activities of the journey except in a sort of musical way. I was simply along, a care, a hindrance, and an annoyance. To hear my immediate family tell it in after years, I was a sort of a miniature siren going strong most of the time. For convenience in telling this story, I shall call myself the Siren.

The antecedents from which this story grew were dealings between the Blackfeet Indians and the whites. The Blackfeet were fighters and had been fighters for generations back. Beset from the east by the Sioux, from the south by the Crows, they had repelled these raiders of their hunting valiantly for many years. Indeed, it appears they were as often the attackers as the attacked and stole as many horses from the Sioux and the Crows as these two tribes stole from them and, withal, took their fair share of scalps.

The truth is that horse stealing was made a sort of intertribal sport, from which all tribes derived as much zest as did our ancestors from their tournaments and probably with no more fatalities. Between buffalo hunting and two frontiers to defend, the weaklings of the Blackfeet were eliminated and only a body of hardy vicious warriors remained.

It had been a bitter resistance waged by the Blackfeet against the invasion of their domain by the white man. Ever since the time of Lewis and Clark they had been imbued with a special fondness for white scalps. They were willing that white traders should build trading posts on their frontiers, where they might exchange furs and robes for guns, blankets, knives, and ammunition, but demanded that the whites leave unmolested their buffalo and beavers, and also reserved for themselves the special privilege of scalping any white man caught far enough away from the stockade.

The white men, then as today, regarded themselves as beings of special privilege and insisted on killing buffaloes and trapping beavers wherever they chose. Many a man lost his scalp in so doing. They seem to have regarded it right for them to kill the Indians' buffaloes, but as depredations and atrocities [increased] any retaliatory acts on the part of the Indians [were frowned upon]. The whites encroached, the Indians defended and retaliated. Such, was the situation up to 1870.

The killing of Malcolm Clark, August of 1869 brought a crisis. White settlers in outlying localities seemed no longer safe. Emphatic representations were made to authorities at Washington. At last orders arrived at Fort Shaw, military headquarters for Montana, to subdue the Blackfeet.

Baker marched. A Blackfeet village was encamped on the Marias. At daylight the troops were in position, unsuspected by the sleeping Indians. Under rifle fire that swept their campground, bucks, squaws, and papooses, old and young fell. It is called the "battle of the Marias." The fight on the Little Big Horn was called "the Custer Massacre." It is all in how you look at it. The Blackfeet were utterly crushed and never afterward made any special trouble.

The four years following this fight seem to have been a period of difficulty at the agency.

No agent seemed successful. M. M. McCauley, appointed in 1870, was removed in 1871. His successor, Jesse Armitage, was suspended in 1872. William E. Ensign was next, and resigned after less than a year's service. In 1873, William F. May was appointed, and he was suspended in 1874. It was during the winter of this last incumbency, that our trip to the agency was made.

Origin of these frequent changes probably centered more at Helena than at the agency itself. A certain group in the little town in Last Chance Gulch felt, if I remember the story correctly, that the military authorities were treating the Indians with undue harshness. This group was brimful of sentimental sympathy for the broken tribe, though it seems to me I heard something about this sympathy being fanned more or less among the members of the group by a desire for jobs for themselves. They were certain the surly Blackfeet could be controlled better by love than by force, and finally were given the opportunity to practice their theories, which was good for the theorists but hard on the Blackfeet, as we shall see later.

My father was one of the group, but I imagine not a very strong partisan. At least, I never knew him to be a strong partisan in anything, except being a Republican all his life, and he weakened in that during his later years. However, he was appointed agency carpenter.

He and mother braved the Montana winter in a wagon trip to the new job with their five children, two half-grown boys, two girls in their teens and the Siren. Eight inches of drifted snow lay on the ground. One hundred twenty-five miles of frozen wagon road over mountains, through canyons and across prairies was to be traveled. It meant not less than four or five days of exposure at least, but in company with two other families, they started.

Their outfit was well adapted to the work before them. It consisted of three six-horse teams. The horses were typical mountain animals of the time, weighing from 900 to 1,100 pounds each. They were in shaggy winter coats, well fed and strong, and shod all around with heavy, sharp-calked iron work shoes for service on icy roads, Each wagon, with its dingy canvas cover stretched tightly over strong ash bows, was bedecked with camp tools and equipment. On one side hung tent poles, nosebags and halters; on the other, in rawhide holsters, were axes, saws, and shovels. A projecting rack at the rear held a tent, the driver's bed roll and a box of miscellaneous small tools, nails, bolts, and screws as well as frying pans and coffee pots. Coils of extra rope swung from the sides of the box. Two heavy rough lock chains were looped across its front. All In all, each wagon was a unit unto itself ready for any emergency.

Interiors of the wagon were fitted to give as much protection against cold as possible. Boxes were lined with heavy canvas to keep out the wind. Buffalo robes covered the floors. Set in boxes of sand, small stoves, whose pipes protruded through iron guards in the wagon covers, furnished heat, but never enough to make the travelers really comfortable. Without them, however, the trip would have been almost unendurable for women and children.

The front of our wagon, under the driver's seat, was loaded with a tier of sacked oats for the horses. With these for a back rest and father's tool chest on the wagon bottom for a seat, the whole covered with a buffalo robe, mother had a fairly comfortable place in which to ride, facing the little stove and holding the Siren in her arms. Other members of the family sat on bedding rolls elsewhere in the wagon and found what comfort they could as the wagon jolted over the rough, frozen road.

In early morning of a midwinter day the start was made. The little town in Last Chance Gulch was scarcely awake when the teams assembled in front of Lehman's Grocery, which opened by one lamp light during the short winter days. Buffeted by keen blasts that swept down from nearby mountains, a few early birds scurried along the streets, half-blinded by fine snow dashed in their faces by the eddying gusts, and wondered how the women and children in the wagons would keep from freezing.

While sunrise was yet a roseate glow in the east, the drivers climbed to their seats. They were clad in buffalo over coats, 10-inch leather belts, felt boots and overshoe, heavy wool shawls over their shoulders, doubled across their chests; silk handkerchiefs over their ears and two pairs of loose fitting gloves on their hands. Inner gloves were of lisle thread, the outer of heavy buckskin.

The full force of the wind was felt as the teams passed from the shelter of Last Chance Gulch to the level stretches of Prickly Pear Valley. From beneath low purplish-gray wind clouds clinging to the continental divide, cold air swept down the valleys of Ten Mile and Seven Mile [creeks] in wild fury laden with fine snow particles whirled from the ground and carried on by the gusts. Entering through cracks and crannies, the fine snow sifted onto the occupants of the wagons arid added a chill the little stoves and the sunshine on the wagon covers could not dispel.

Progress was slow. The cold, brittle snow drifted in the road and hindered like so much dry sand. Cutting into it deeply, the wheels carried the fine loose particles up to where they were caught by the wind and, after whirling a moment in the lee of the wagons, went scooting off across the valley like dust. The horses had no footing and slipped and slid continually. Two and a half to three miles an hour was all they were able to travel under such conditions.

In a sheltered spot among the willows on Silver Creek a noon halt was made. The horses were watered, fed and allowed a long rest. Coffee and a hearty lunch served in the sunshine by a hot campfire in a spot not reached by the wind put every one in good spirits. Even the "Siren" forgot for a time his self-appointed task of making life miserable for others, and stopped crying.

To work off stored up energy and limber their legs after the morning's ride, the Siren's brothers climbed a bank across the road to the sagebrush flat above. They were scarcely on top when 40 or 50 sage hens burst from the snow and roared into the air. The noise of an adult sage hen taking off at one's feet almost, rivals that of a small plane. The startled boys first thought their end had come. Returning to the road a hundred yards or more above camp, through a patch of buckbrush, they flushed a flock of willow, or sharp tailed, grouse. These sailed cackling over the camp and lit a few hundred yards down the creek in the edge of the willows.

The sight of the prairie chickens, as the sharptails were called, roused the two hunters of the party to activity and they were not long in getting out their double-barreled, muzzle-loading shotguns and following the flock. Out of meat, not sport. It mattered little to them whether they killed the birds on the ground or in the air. They were like the half breed who, when asked if he shot his birds on the wing, replied:

"Yes, shoot 'em on the wing, shoot 'em on the tail, shoot 'em anywhere." In a short time seven or eight birds were killed. Swinging onto the hills on returning to camp, the hunters found the flock of sage hens and bagged several.

The two boys were much interested when the birds were being dressed to find that, while the prairie chickens had gizzards, the sage hens were provided with capacious stomachs, similar to rabbits. Some writers believe that if this largest American member of the grouse family were provided with a gizzard instead of a stomach, it might be far more palatable. The afternoon's journey lay up Silver Creek across sagebrush flats past Silver City to Billy John's Ranch and into upper Prickly Pear Canyon. Traveling was little different from that of the morning except that the sky was cloudy and the air colder. An hour before supper, the teams turned off the road at a sheltered spot and stopped for the night. The place selected was a little flat extending back into the circle of a steep timbered hill, a sort of amphitheater, with a heavy growth of young firs on the encircling slopes down to the level ground. At one point an almost perpendicular ledge rose 10 or 12 feet from the flat and then dipped back under the hill. Camp was pitched in front of this ledge.

Making camp for the night was no small task. Everyone except the Siren and his mother tumbled out in the snow and worked. First a roaring fire was started 15 or 20 feet from the per-pendicular ledge. The boys, with shovels cleared most of the snow away between the fire and the cliff. In a little while heat reflected by the rocks melted the remaining snow and dried away the moisture so the area between the fire and the ledge was comparatively comfortable. In it the women and children gathered and were joined there by the Siren and his mother. The Siren blinked his eyes, and took a big whiff of campfire smoke. It was his first outing.

While the teamsters cared for the horses, the other men dragged in wood, set up tents and laid bough beds. The snow was first swept off where the tents were set and the boughs laid on frozen ground. While this work was going on, the women prepared supper. Hot biscuits had been called for, so the big Dutch oven was brought out. It was a round, flat-bottomed, kettle-like affair, perhaps 18 inches in diameter, and six inches deep, of heavy cast iron, with a cast iron top, and stood on three legs about five inches long. A Dutch oven was always part of the equipment of any up to date freight outfit and, though crude, was a highly efficient baking arrangement. A pile of glowing coals was raked to one side of the fire and the oven set over them. Then several shovels full of coals were piled on the cover and around the sides of the oven. After giving time for heating, the cover was removed, the oven greased and the biscuits put in. The cover was then replaced and more embers piled on top and around the sides. When uncovered some 25 minutes later the contents were just that shade of brown a housewife loves to see on biscuits.

A tired group gathered in the fire light for supper. There was little talk to drown the rattle of wood handled knives and forks on tin plates. Biscuits, fried grouse, boiled beans and dried apple sauce, with tea and coffee, made the bill of fare. Lack of variety was more than offset by keenness of appetites. When the meal was over the cooks had no complaint of their cooking not being appreciated

Everyone was in bed early. A full moon rose above the eastern mountains and, shining on the snow, flooded the canyon with light almost equal to that of day. The campfire of big logs sent a drifting column of blue smoke toward the stars. Though the wind was scarcely felt in the sheltered camp. It could be easily heard sweeping the mountain tops and was manifest in the fleecy scurrying clouds that hurried overhead from west to east.

The Siren was quiet part of the night. He was a bottle baby. As long as there was plenty of warm milk in his bottle when be wanted it and everything else was to his liking, he was fairly quiet. But everything else was not to his liking all of the night, if late reports are to be credited. Toward morning, when the whole camp was the sleepiest, the Siren started. Nothing his father and mother did suited him. For hours he exercised his lungs with lusty squalling. Not until too late for the grownups to sleep anymore, if they were to travel that morning, did he subside, apparently satisfied in his mother's arms, and slept sweetly.

Long before daylight the men turned out. The moon had set. The dark blue vault of night was ablaze with myriads of twinkling stars toward which shot streams of sparks as logs were thrown on the bed of coals left from the fire of the previous night. In the blazing firelight the horses were watered and fed, breakfast prepared and eaten, tents taken down and bedding packed. At daylight the day's travel began.

At the time of which I write the canyon or the Little Canyon, as it was called, was comparatively new. It had been built in 1872, by Nicholas Hilger and William Johns. Its purpose was to avoid long steep hills of the original Mullan Survey, which extended from near Silver City northeast up a long gulch past Diamond Springs over the crown of a range of high hills and then down another gulch in the Malcolm Clark Ranch on [Little] Prickly Pear. The new road was probably no shorter than the old, but it followed the water grade, and save for a few deep natural grades where the mountains came down to the creek was an excellent mountain road for that period.

Half a mile, perhaps, from the camp of the previous night the leading team stopped. As the other teams drew up behind, its driver pointed to a ridge ahead where, in silhouette against the sky, stood 25 or 30 mountain sheep looking down at the teams lined on the road. The two hunters climbed from the rear wagon and moved carefully up a little draw leading to the ridge, at a point above the band.

The occupants of the wagons raised the wagon covers and watched the animals with as much interest as the bighorns watched the wagons. The Siren's two brothers, in the lead wagon, had their eyes fastened on the big ram bringing up the rear. If the men could only get him! Their eyes popped with excitement.

Presently the two men were on a level with their quarry. They moved to a ledge between them and the herd. The boys saw the little Henry rifles shoved over the top of the ledge as the hunters aimed. They saw the bursts of gray smoke from the guns and heard the reports of the rifles reverberating from the canyon wall to canyon wall. But the big fellow was not down. Instead he bounded over the ridge unharmed, though four fat young ewes were stretched in the snow.

To say the boys were broken hearted is putting it mildly. They were little appeased when told what poor eating the old ram would have been and insisted they could have eaten him if the others couldn't.

When dressed, the four sheep were dragged down to the road and swung along the sides of the wagon boxes, where they soon froze stiff.

The old Malcolm Clark Ranch between the two canyons of the [Little] Prickly Pear was reached nearly an hour before noon. The buildings were on the gravelly bench about a hundred yards above the present highway, almost directly across the stream from the present railroad station of Siben and less than a quarter mile from the Big Prickly Pear Canyon.

It was here where Malcolm Clark, White Lodge Pole, as the Blackfeet first called him, and later changed to Four Bears, settled in 1864, with his Indian wife, a Blackfeet chief's daughter and their half-breed children.

The son of an army officer, trained for a while at West Point, Clark came west in early life, mingled with the Blackfeet and become a man of some prominence in Montana territory. He was a member of the first Board of County Commissioners at Edgerton now Lewis and Clark County. As mentioned before, his death in 1869, at the hands of the Blackfeet was the culminating event of the series of atrocities that led to the Marias fight. It would seem not unfitting if the site of the old buildings were to be marked by at least a properly inscribed boulder in memory of a romantic pioneer family.

As usual at any halt, the company sought a sheltered spot in the willow during the noon hour to escape the wind. The horses were fed hay and oats and given a long rest. Again, the Dutch oven was brought into action and brought forth another batch of biscuits, which went the same way as those of the night before.

During the afternoon, the lower canyon of the Prickly Pear, or the Big Canyon, as it was called, was traversed. It was an eventful afternoon for the Siren's brothers. The teams had gone but a little distance into the canyon when they encountered the mail wagon from Fort Benton on a high, rocky grade, where there was no room to pass. The mail, of course, had precedent but there was nothing the drivers of the wagons could do. The final solution was to unharness the team from the mail wagon and back the vehicle by hand to a point where it could be lifted to one side of the road for our wagons to pass.

Farther along, a band of mule deer or black tail, as they were called, was found crossing the road. The deer were in easy rifle range and three big does rode into camp that night on the sides of the wagons. The boys were again disappointed when the big buck bringing up the rear of the band was allowed to bound off unharmed.

Toward evening, squatting on the ledges of a rocky point perched in the nearby trees, hundreds of blue grouse were seen. The hunters, with their shotguns, killed a dozen or more, which the boys collected gleefully.

Men and horses were tired when the mouth of Wolf Creek was reached that evening. The day's journey had been 18 miles over rough, frozen ruts covered with snow. Going down many of the hills rough locks had been required to keep the wagons from sliding onto the horses.

The rough lock was the forerunner of the automobile chain. It was simply a heavy chain wrapped several times around the felloe of the rear wheel and hooked securely. The other end was fastened to some solid part of the wagon with just enough slack for the wheel to roll up onto the chain, stop, and ride there. The links of the chain, with the wagon's weight on them, dug into the ice and snow on the ground. Sometimes even rough locks on both rear wheels did not hold a wagon on a very steep and icy hill. To guard against a bad mix-up in such cases, the lead and swing teams were usually taken off and the wagons taken down with the wheel teams only.

The road through this canyon was built originally by King & Gillette, who operated it for a number of years as a toll road. Like the road thorough the upper canyon, it was constructed to avoid the high, precipitous hills of the Mullan Road laid out in 1850–1862. Undoubtedly, Lieutenant Mullan would have followed the canyons in the beginning if he had been furnished enough men and equipment to get the job done in the time allotted him. As it was, he selected a hill route over which it was possible to haul wagons if weather conditions were favorable and enough horses or oxen

used. We must bear in mind that from 1860 to 1865, the government was too busy with matters in the east to spare any soldiers for road building in Montana.

That night at Wolf Creek the Siren was noisy. Traveling did not suit him, nothing suited him. He wanted the whole world to know he was not suited and did his best in broadcasting the fact.

One of his brothers afterwards said a pregnant coyote howling on a nearby hill gave up the contest and slunk off toward the Missouri in disgust. Late in the evening the Siren seemed to remember something. If he was to wake the camp an hour before getting up time the next morning, he must have rest, so he subsided and slept in his mother's arms like a little angel. An hour before waking time for the grownups, however, he awoke and howled for an hour or more like a little imp.

The start for the third day's travel was at daylight as usual. Sheltered under the mountainside at the mouth of Wolf Creek, the party scarcely felt the wind during the night. It was heard however, roaring on the ridges and the trees were seen to be swaying and bending in the gusts on nearby mountain tops. The teamsters knew what was ahead and one of them remarked "It will be tough out on the open hills."

About an eighth of a mile from the night's campground the road led away from the stream up what was known as the Black Grade, named because of the color of the decomposed rock through which it had been dug. As the teams ascended this grade and turned toward the Krueger Ranch on Rock Creek, they found themselves in a furious gale laden with clouds of fine drifting snow. The wind was from the rear and whirled the snow in the lee of the wagons, casing the drivers and wheel horses in white.

Traveling was hard and slow, for the road was drifted deeply. On the east side of one hill the men all turned out with shovels and opened a way through a deep drift for the floundering horses and creaking wagons. One coulee was drifted full and the roadway had to be cleared before the drivers could see the bridge on which to cross. No stop was made at noon except for a cold lunch, with hot coffee made by shivering women on the little stoves in the wagons. The teamsters were pulling straight through to the Dearborn and shelter, a distance of 17 miles, where they arrived late in the afternoon.

Camp that night was in a cottonwood grove on the river bottom. As evening came on the wind died down and the sky became overcast with haze.

The situation for a comfortable camp was not good. However, a big cottonwood was felled and then another dropped on top and lengthwise of it. Willow brush was leaned against these and snow piled against it to hold it in place. With this for a reflector and a big fire of dry logs in front of it, the space between was fairly warm. In it the usual evening meal was prepared and eaten.

Everyone was asleep early, toward morning a cold northeast wind rattled the frozen tops of the cottonwoods. When daylight came a storm was on. Snow was falling and drifting along the ridge of the road.

All the forenoon the horses toiled through drifts against the storm. Interiors of the wagons were cold and the men often got out and walked to keep warm. Toward noon a halt was made on a little stream coming down from the Bird Tail Divide to Flat Creek at the old Wareham place. Horses were watered and fed and again coffee was made on the little stoves in the wagons. Everyone got out for a few minutes to limber up, but there was comfort for none.

The afternoon's drive was colder than that of the morning. The road led up Flat Creek and around Bird Tail Mountains across Benton Flats to Bird Tail Creek and Eagle Rock Stage Station. The Bird Tail Divide cutoff was well known and much used at the time but, because of ice on its northern slope, the teamsters decided on the longer and more exposed route. The storm had a clear sweep on the prairie and the occupants of the wagons suffered much with cold, though wrapped with blankets and buffalo robes.

In the shelter of a sandstone ledge in Bird Tail Creek, the night's camp was made. Cottonwood logs brought from the Dearborn furnished fuel for a campfire by which everyone tried to get warm. Sandstone slabs were heated to put in the beds. There is nothing much more comforting of a cold night in bed in a tent on the prairie than a hot rock—unless it is two of them.

In the morning the storm was over, but it was cold—bitter cold. The Bird Tail Mountains, Bird Tail Rock, Crown Butte, and Square Butte stood in bold relief against a clear blue sky. In the bright sunlight the air truly sparkled with glinting frost crystals borne on the forth wind down over Crown Butte and is adjacent hills.

Little time was spent by the morning fire. The big stones used in the beds the night before were reheated, wrapped in empty sacks and placed in the wagons, where the travelers felt they would do the most good. The younger of the Siren's two brothers sat on his. The Siren's brothers also tied empty sacks around their legs and feet as did such of the men as were not extra well clothed.

How the wheels sang as they crunched through the cold snow. Young folks today who have never heard steel tires singing in frosty snow have missed something. I wonder if it was the day, of which I write, when I first learned to like the music of winter wheels.

As the teams toiled along drifted roads the drivers wished they had not attempted the trip. Walking beside their horses and clapping their hands for warmth, it seemed that the sun, with a sundog on either side, over Square Butte only made the air colder. They had aggravating visions of warm rooms and comfortable chairs left behind.

Presently, on a windswept ridge above the road, a band of pronghorn antelope was sighted watching the wagons. The two hunters dropped from the wagons and made their way up a ravine to within rifle range of the herd. Smoke from the rifles could barely be seen against the background of frost and snow, but the reports cracked sharply through the cold, cold wind. The animals bounded over the hilltop in headlong flight except three, which lay stretched in the snow. These were dressed hastily, dragged to the wagons and slung alongside with the deer and sheep. One of the men remarked that all that was needed to complete the assortment was an elk and a buffalo.

Disaster came to the Siren about the middle of the forenoon. His father put the young man's bottle of milk in hot water to warm and the bottle cracked. It was the only bottle in the outfit for this was a band of teetotalers, who regarded any bottle with suspicion. The Siren was hungry. The teams were out seven miles from Fort Shaw, which meant nearly a three hours drive before another bottle could be had. A long drawn, soulful blast expressed the Siren's disappointment when his dinner was not forthcoming. He refused warm milk from a cup or a spoon and cried while his mother rocked him in her arms, crooning a cradle song and wondering why on earth she ever came on such a trip with a six month old baby. At last, worn out with crying he fell asleep.

As the teams drew near the fort the Siren awoke, rested but hungrier than ever. When passing the barracks, his mother said in after years, his cries brought the soldiers out to see if the Sioux were attacking. In front of McKnight's Store the wagons stopped. Bottles were more or less taboo even around the frontier fort but at last a sweet oil bottle was found and cleaned so it was usable. When it was filled with warm milk and the Siren had the nipple in his mouth, he gave his mother a look that seemed to say, "See what persistence does."

"It's 20 degrees below zero right now by the government thermometer," said the Siren's father as he crawled into the wagon and the teams started on. A mile or more from the fort, in the shelter of a cottonwood grove and a patch of willows, the halt for the night was made. The keen north wind was still blowing but, in the scant shelter of the leafless trees and brush, it seemed a little less severe than on the open prairie.

The hour was late and preparations for the night were hurried. A fire soon blazed a little distance from a big down cottonwood. Brush was leaned over the log to make a wind break and around the fire in its lee the women and children collected to get warm while the men cared for the horses, set up tents and gathered more firewood. Supper was a cold meal, even with hot biscuits, coffee and fried grouse. All were shivering and stood by the fire, turning first one side and then the other to its warmth as they ate. The Siren seemed comfortable for a little while. He appeared to be listening to the mournful howl of a gray wolf greeting the rising moon from the benches north of the river. Then a Canada lynx, searching for cottontail rabbits along the river, uttered a few screeches. This was too much. The Siren's little heart leaped with envy. He pitched in and for hours made everyone miserable with his crying.

There was no comfort for anyone that evening or that night. The fire was so big and hot no one could get near enough to be warm.

The Indians say:

"White man heap damn fool, makes big fire, get long way off, cold; Indian make little fire, get close, heap warm."

There is much truth in this and had several smaller fires been used perhaps less suffering would have resulted.

The night was little better than the evening. Even with hot rocks in beds, no one was warm and several of the older ones lay awake nearly all night and shivered.

When morning came the cold had increased and the north wind still prevailed. The teamsters deemed it too risky to attempt crossing the treeless benches between Sun River and the Teton under such conditions and insisted on staying where fuel was plentiful until warmer weather.

Preparations were made for a day or two's stay in camp. One man went to a ranch two miles away and bought a load of hay, which the rancher delivered on a homemade sled. Others added more brush to the windbreak and extended it farther around the fire on either side. Hay was spread on the frozen snow between the windbreak and the fire. On this the party lounged in partial comfort. Tents were piled deep with hay and beds made on it instead of on cold snow as the night before. Horses stood in the lee of the willows, ate and rested. That night everyone was warm and slept soundly.

The following day was milder. The north wind died away and light air currents drifted from the southwest. The a.m. sank in a roseate glow behind the mountain range at the head of the Dearborn. The cold spell was broken. Half an hour before sunrise the next morning the teams crossed the bridge at Sun River Crossing and turned northwest toward the agency.

It was a wonderful winter day, with not a cloud in the sky. Across the western horizon lay the mountains, a great jagged white wall. Steamboat Mountain on the Dearborn and Cut Rock on Sun River loomed in silent majesty as they do today. Scapegoat, back farther in the main range, rose white above its base wall of perpendicular cliffs. At the head of the south fork of Sun River, at the edge of the prairie, squatted Haystack Butte, a volcanic invader among the limestone, its lava cone black against the white background of the mountains.

As morning advanced to noon and the sun was in the south, the air was so warm occupants of the wagons raised covers on the sides toward the sun and enjoyed its warmth. For the first time since leaving Helena they were all really warm. The Siren, warm and comfortable, slept most of the day in preparation for his usual nightly concert.

A long winding drifting ridge in the snow marked the road over the bench lands. Theirs were the first wagon, over it, since the storm and the drivers found easier traveling beside the road than in the heavy drift of the road itself.

At noon the horses were fed and given a long rest. A hot lunch was prepared on stoves in the wagons. Most of the party ate standing in the snow beside the wagons.

With the approach of evening, light clouds formed above the mountains. Wind driven snow could be seen whirling across the distant ridges and hanging mist-like clouds in the lees of the peaks. In the sunset light, clouds turned to crimson; the drifting snow glowed like smoke above many fires; a deep roseate light bathed the prairie on all sides. Then the color faded and the mountains lay in shadowy outline against a steely blue afterglow.

That night, in the gloaming before moonrise, camp fires and columns of smoke along the Teton to the right of the road told the travelers the location of the Blackfeet lodges. Farther along the square, the dark mass of the agency stockade loomed in the dusk. As the teams approached it, lights appeared in the windows of the block house nearest them. Gates opened for the three wagons to pass to the shelter of the stockade, where the new arrivals received the warm welcome of friends who preceded them earlier in the season.

Stockades were simple, but highly efficient fortifications much used by early day traders in the Indian country a well as by the military. They were usually about 200 feet square, built of logs set side by side endwise in the ground and projecting 12 to 14 feet in the air. Around the interior of the walls, several feet below the top, a. firing platform was built. From this, in

case of attack, the defenders might fire on an approaching enemy through loopholes cut for the purpose.

At two corners, diagonally opposite each other, projecting, overhanging blockhouses were built. Loopholes in the two commanded the four sides of the stockade so the entire exterior of the structure could be swept by the rifle fire of the garrison. A comparatively small force could defend a stockade against attacks of greatly superior numbers armed only with rifles of pioneer days. Against artillery or modern high power rifles, they would have had little value.

The situation at the agency was serious. When the Indians should have been killing buffaloes, and drying meat the fall before, the kind hearted agent issued them rations. Then, instead of hunting and laying by a winter supply of food of their own, they lay in camp and ate that provided by the government. Then winter came, there were scarcely enough rations left for the whites, to say nothing of the red men, and the Indians were left to shift for themselves. Even then they would perhaps have not been so bad off had not the buffaloes for some unknown reason crossed the Missouri onto the Musselshell to winter instead of staying on the Marias and Teton as usual.

Issuing of rations was a blunder on the part of the agent. It showed his little knowledge of Indian character to think they would provide food for themselves when plenty was already being given them. His intended kindness came near finishing the tribe.

Such were conditions when our party entered the stockade. With a tribe of desperately hungry Indians outside and none too much food inside, the agency force was uneasy. Riflemen in the new party were a welcome addition to the defensive force. Little less welcome were the deer, sheep, antelopes and other food the party brought with them.

That night the wagons were unloaded and at daylight the next morning were started on the return journey to Helena.

One may properly ask why the government did not send in supplies for the hungry Indians. The answer is simple. Ample supplies had been furnished the fall before had they been judiciously used. No additional supplies could be brought by river until early summer.

The mountain road from Corinne, 600 miles away on the Union Pacific Railroad in Utah was well impassable, so additional supplies were virtually an impossibility.

How the Indians got through the winter, I do not know. Many died from hunger and disease. Spring came, the buffaloes returned, the Indians had food in abundance, forgot their winter suffering and were more friendly. The whites ceased worrying. Contentment reigned on the Teton.

In the spring and summer that followed, the Siren became much of a ladies' man. Some of the Indian girls were admitted to the stockade from time to time. Frequently they came to mother and asked:

"Where papoose?"

With "papoose" in their possession, they would play for hours inside the stockade, or until he remembered his bottle. They were never, however, allowed to take him outside the stockade.

On his return from these little excursions with the dusky maidens the Siren's mother always undressed him and shook his clothes over a paper spread on the floor as a precaution.

Many incidents occurred that were of great interest to the Siren's brothers. An old skunk contrived to establish her home under a building inside and near the stockade wall. Here she brought forth her family and lived for months. At last, when her six were half-grown, she led them proudly forth onto the parade ground in the center of the stockade in the dusk of a summer evening.

This was most unfortunate for the skunks as well as for everyone else. Two young, inexperienced dogs saw them and dashed with much barking, in great glee, to defeat. As the two dogs retired in disgust, rubbing and rolling on the ground, two others from the other side of the stockade rushed at the seven skunks which had formed a circle, heads out. The skunks had their fighting blood up by this time and the second pair of dogs retired in greater chagrin than the first.

Men, women, and children, hearing the melee, gathered from all parts of the stockade. The dogs whined and rubbed against their master's clothing. At last, one of the men, remarking, "It can't be any worse," got his shotgun and killed the skunks. Then, with a pitchfork, he carried the seven little bodies outside the stockade. The next day an old squaw found them, and feasting followed in a tepee on the river bank. It was many moons before the inhabitants of the stockade forgot the incident.

Two of the men were rival fishermen. They vied with each other as to which could get the largest trout. Sometimes one was ahead, sometimes the other. At last one came in carrying a five and a half pound cutthroat trout and gloated over his rival unmercifully.

The unfortunate one examined the fish for a while, admiring its beautiful rosy sides and then said, "If you can catch such a fish as that, it must be easy," and trudged off with his fishing tackle.

An hour later he came back with another fish which could not be told in size or color from the first. In those days there were real fish in the Missouri and its tributaries.

Boy Chief and Heavy Runner were rival chiefs, each with his group of followers. Time hung heavily on their hands, for they were no longer permitted to raid the Sioux or the Crows. They could not even go on a horse stealing expedition against the whites, so to relieve the tedium, they staged a fight of their own. Heavy Runner was killed and buried just outside the stockade, and his three wives mourned on his grave. Each tried to evince more grief than the other two together. Wailing mournfully, they dug up the fresh mound of earth in the efforts to uncover the body. Now and then, as a more complete expression of sorrow, a finger was whacked off or they gashed their bodies with knives. It was a gruesome sight, and with the boys and girls who witnessed it, it still remains as a sort of nightmare.

Stockade life was neither very pleasant nor very profitable, at best, so when summer had passed into autumn and the Indians were killing buffaloes and drying meat and the great white wedges of swans were sweeping over from the north, the Siren's parents loaded their five into a wagon and returned to Last Chance Gulch. A new agent was in. Perhaps that had something to do with their return, I do not know.

Glowing accounts of the Little Prickly Pear Canyon abound in books, brochures and newspaper articles. One occurred in the July 15, 1881, *Helena Independent*.

DOWN THE BENTON ROAD

Lovely Scenery—Bears, Berries and Rattlesnakes.

The Finest Drive in the Mountains.

The drive from Helena to Mitchell's (Fergus' Ranch) is one of the most delightful in the mountains. The road is smooth and level, and the scenery varied and pleasing. A. couple of miles or so this side of Mitchell's clusters of ripe currants and gooseberries dot the roadside, and the canyon narrows in; the steep, craggy, slate cliffs throwing their cool shadows across the road and over the willow-fringed banks of the swift-flowing [Little] Prickly Pear. Suddenly, the canyon widens and a perfect little gem of a valley spreads out to view. It is Mart Mitchell's Ranch and Station at the mouth of [Little] Prickly Pear Canyon. Waving fields of grass and grain, and vegetables of all descriptions, and even apple trees surround the house. It is one of the very best locations in the territory, and Mr. Mitchell is one of the best of landlords. The accommodations are good and travelers generally make a hard drive to reach Mitchell's for the night. A short distance down the canyon, a quarter of a mile, or so, the roadside is literally red with raspberries, the vines drooping down with their load of rich, red berries. Ripe gooseberries and currants are also plentiful in the vicinity. Mr. Mitchell states that he never saw the berries so plentiful as they are the present season. The drive through the canyon from Mitchell's to Kisselpaugh's is, perhaps, the grandest in the mountains, the slate cliffs rising hundreds of feet, almost perpendicular, on either side of the road. At Kisselpaugh's we started up Wolf Creek for a fish and a ramble over the mountains.

A party of about eighty Pen d'Orielle Indians had camped on the creek several days, and had only left the day before our arrival, and they succeeded pretty well in thinning out the large trout- for an Indian.

The Montana News Association Insert for November 9, 1925, carried an article concerning travel on the Benton Road from a woman's perspective.

"This is the story of the experiences of one pioneer Montana family on a trip from Helena to old Fort Benton before the days of the railroad, as told by Mrs. Gus Senieur. In these days of grievous road conditions in Montana, it is at least consoling to herein learn that the pioneers experienced conditions much worse than do present day travelers."

INSTEAD of taking this trip from Helena to Fort Benton in the regular coaches, which left the former place every day, making connections at the old trading post town with the boats bound for Bismark and the "states," we decided that it would be much easier to travel by private conveyance although the trip in this manner consumed much more time. We cooked our own meals and camped at the end of each day, thus losing much of the traveling time gained by the coaches through the accommodations of the stage stations along the route.

Through the Canyon

In the party besides myself and child were an old lady and her husband and a daughter 18 years of age, a young man and our driver. The distance to be covered between the two points was about 150 miles and we were six days completing the trip.

The first day out, we drove about 35 Miles and made the best time of our journey. We passed through a long canyon in which was a small stream, winding in and out so many times that it was necessary to cross it on different bridges. The night after we traversed this canyon there was a terrific rainstorm, which washed out every one of those bridges, and if our trip had been delayed, another day we would have been compelled to travel over the mountain, which would have made the trip much longer, and would have been much harder traveling.

Reach Sun River Crossing

The second day it rained continuously and the traveling was heavy. It was still raining when we made camp that night. The women slept in the wagons and the men wrapped themselves in their blankets and bunked under the wagons, as, best they could until the rain became so heavy that they were forced to shelter under the wagon tarpaulins. This camp was at Sun River Crossing where there were then about six houses and a stage station. I finally decided to take my baby and go to the hotel where we could get a good night's rest. The next morning the weather was still threatening, and travel was very slow. We could not build a fire to cook lunch, so were forced to be content with a cold meal. After permitting the horses to rest for a few hours, we proceeded, and after dragging slowly through deep mire, we reached the Big Muddy. It was still cloudy and had the appearance of more rain, so our driver selected a low place the driver feeling that we would be more protected there if it did rain.

I was still so wet that we could not cook our supper, other than to make some coffee with some dry wood that the driver had placed in one of the wagons. It started to rain early in the evening, and we were compelled to remain up all night, using our blankets to hang around the inside of the covered wagon to keep out some of the rain. During the night it became necessary to hitch the horses to the wagon and pull the wagons out of the hollow or we would have been washed away.

By morning we were a sorry looking lot. However, the sun was bright and warm, and we had a good hot breakfast. We remained in camp all that day, drying out our clothing and blankets by spreading them on the sagebrush. We were miles from any houses, the nearest being at Sun River. Finding an abundance of wild greens growing close by, we secured enough for a welcome addition to our lunch.

Across Big Muddy Flats

The Big Muddy is named for a fairly large lake, which was once at that point, where it was always muddy, and through which the wagon road then passed. It was necessary to shovel the mud from the wheels continuously to make travel at all possible over this stretch. There was a thin crust dried on top of this mud and we women were able to walk over it by walking fast. If we stood still for one moment, our feet would break through. It was impossible to stop for rest, and being very tired, from carrying my baby, I put her on my back papoose fashion and found it helped very much.

We finally reached more solid ground, and made camp for the night. At this point the stage passed us, but was hardly recognizable as it was completely coated with mud. We passed freight at many points along the road, where freighting outfits had dropped it off to lighten their loads. At one place a lone woman was sitting on some boxes that had been left. The stages were so crowded in those days that often whole families would make the trip with the, freighting outfits. This woman told us, that she was afraid the boxes might he picked up so she had remained with them. If she had known, the country as well as we, she would have remained with the freight wagons regardless. She was one of the many tenderfeet to make the trip in those days to Fort Benton on route to civilization.

Fort, Benton–a Rough City

We were then on the last lap of the arduous trip. We had passed the worst of the roads, and our next stop was at Twenty-Eight Mile Springs Stage Station, where passengers were fed and stage horses changed for fresh ones. We camped at this station for the night and got an early start in the morning. This was the last day on the road, and we reached Fort Benton. Here we found that the boat which was to take us down the river had not arrived, so we went to a hotel where we waited almost a week. Fort Benton in those days was quite a rough and ready place, its principle population being Indians, half-breeds, [and] squaw men It. was an interesting sight to see some of these squaw men, dressed up in eastern clothes and accompanied by a squaw with her blanket and a papoose tied to her back. All in all, the trip was one of the great events of my life, and quite a contrast to the method now available for making the same distance over the same territory.

Despite the beautiful scenery to behold and the wonderful people to visit along the way, the citizens of Helena, Fort Benton and all the places in between knew there had to be a better way to travel or ship freight between the river port, the capitol and the mining districts. A railroad was the obvious answer and Montanans were not slow to pick up on the idea.

Morrow Family Traveling from Fort Benton to Helena with Personal Vehicles

Tunnel on the Montana Central near Lyons Creek

Giant Spring at Great Falls

Lyons Hill from the Tracks of the Montana Central

Chapter X

Mr. Hill's Railroad

After trudging for twelve years over the rough, flooded, frozen, snow-bound and sometimes impassable Benton Road, the citizens of Helena figured out that a rail line from Fort Benton to their fair city would make life easier, safer, and more profitable for everyone.

Other schemes had been proposed for getting freight and passengers over this 140 mile stretch of one of the most beautiful portions of Montana. The *Helena Independent* for June 6, 1878, suggested the following:

NAVIGATION ABOVE THE FALLS

Passengers from Benton report the road lined with freight teams loaded for Helena, and many of them laying by unable to move on account of the heavy condition of the roads, caused by the late storms. Of the freight landed by the first two boats at Benton, now nearly a month ago, but very little of it has yet reached Helena, and none, we believe, has been received of the cargoes of the six or eight boats that have since discharged at that port. If this season were exceptional in this respect the difficulty would not be so grievous. But it is not. For three or four years past matters have been no better than they are this season, and under the most favorable circumstances it is usually midsummer or later before the bulk of the spring shipments of goods, made by the merchants of this place, reach their destination. Teams loaded at Benton twenty days ago are still out and in all probability will not reach here for ten days to come. These facts prove conclusively the necessity of a more certain and speedy method of transportation between this place and the head of navigation on the Missouri River. It was these necessities which gave birth to the

scheme of a Helena and Benton railroad, and which at one time seemed likely to result in the construction of a narrow gauge road between those points.

That enterprise, however, has fallen through, mainly for the want of some energetic person to take hold of it and push it through to complete success. A narrow gauge road between the points named is hardly within the means of our citizens, even with such assistance as could be given it by the counties most directly interested in its construction, and outside capital would probably have to be obtained before the road would be an assured fact.

There is another enterprise; however which is entirely within the means of our merchants, and which would greatly expedite if it would not cheapen the delivery of freights from Benton, and that is a steamboat above the Falls. Every person at all acquainted with steamboat navigation who has had occasion to examine it has pronounced the river to be entirely navigable from the Falls up to the mouth of the Prickly Pear at all seasons, and navigable much higher up during high water. Mr. Thos. P. Roberts in August, 1872, at the instance of the Northern Pacific Railroad Company, made a very careful reconnaissance of the river from the Three Forks to the Falls. He made soundings, took measurements, and calculated the velocity of the current on rapids, and after the most careful study pronounced the river entirely navigable and between the points above mentioned, viz.: the Falls and the mouth of the Prickly Pear, a good piece of water with the exception of one, rapid, which he found to be short and no worse than any of the several rapids encountered between the foot of Cow Island and Benton. In short, it can safely be asserted that the Missouri River, for 120 miles above the Great Falls, is a better piece of water for navigation than it is the same distance below Fort Benton. With this fine piece of water, right where it is so badly needed, it seems a shame that it is not utilized. With a boat above the Falls, a wagon road could be cheaply constructed on good hard ground from there to Benton, and thus the long, hard pulls over the Sun River Valley. the Bird Tail Divide, and through Prickly Pear Canyon would be saved. Added to this, goods would be laid down at the Helena landing within five days after they were unloaded at Benton. Would the enterprise pay? Could it help paying?

With this route open it is safe to say that every pound of freight discharged at Benton from the forty or fifty boats, which will unload there this season and destined for this quarter of the territory would come over it and not only this, but by the opening of this route business on the river would be increased. If Virginia and Bozeman and Bannack could have their heavy spring shipments laid down at Gallatin City they would gladly avail themselves of the low rates of freight offered by the river.

We would say then to our merchants and business men, incorporate a company at once and subscribe a sufficient amount of stock to build a good staunch boat for the upper river trade, and put a good wagon road from the head of the Falls to Benton. Have this ready to meet the increased requirements of next year's trade, and it will be found sufficient, we have no doubt, to meet our necessities until the increased wealth and business of this section of the territory will make the building of a railroad a matter of easy accomplishment.

Someone was listening to the editor, as the first company to incorporate for the purpose of attempting navigation on the Upper Missouri River came into existence in September of 1878. An article from the *Helena Independent* entitled "The Montana Steam Navigation Company" was published on September 19, 1878.

MONTANA STEAM NAVIGATION Co.

INCORPORATED AUG. 10, 1878

Capital Stock $100,000 divided 2,000 SHARES OF $50 EACH

The Stock Subscription Books of this Company will he found at the Drug Store of Messrs. H. S. Hale Co., Main Street, Helena where subscriptions to the Capital Stock of Company will be received. As soon as the subscriptions reach 50,000 DOLLARS, there will be an election of permanent officers, by the Stockholders.

JOHN T. MURPHY, President.
M. Parchen, Secretary.

The Montana Steam Navigation Company

We call attention to the advertisement in another column of the Montana Steam Navigation Company. This company was organized by filing a certificate of incorporation in the office of the Secretary of the Territory and a duplicate in the office of the County Recorder of Lewis and Clark County on the 10th day of August last. The company, however, before proceeding beyond a mere temporary organization thought it prudent to send out a party, accompanied by competent and experienced steamboat men, to more carefully examine the river both above and below the Great Falls to Fort Benton. This party having reported the project feasible and practical in every way, the company now invites subscriptions to their capital stock, and persons wishing to subscribe thereto will find the books at the drug store of R. S. Hale & Co., where their subscriptions will be received. Something over forty thousand dollars of the stock has been already subscribed, and as soon as the subscriptions reach fifty thousand dollars it is the purpose of the company to proceed to a permanent organization by the election of officers and at once take steps to procure one or more steamboats for the navigation of the river. The navigation of the Upper Missouri River has long been a favorite project with the *INDEPENDENT*, and we have more than once urged the wisdom, nay, the almost absolute necessity of utilizing the advantages presented to us by the river for transporting our heavy freights from Fort Benton. We are glad to see this matter taken hold in earnest by our business men, and the tact that such substantial men as A. M. Holter, John Kinna, Abram Sands, John T. Murphy, Henry Klein, R. S. Hale, Isaac Greenhood, Charles and Frederick Lehman, and numerous others of our leading business men are engaged in promoting this enterprise, is a sufficient guarantee of its complete success. They will not, however, have the entire field to themselves, as we understand that Col. Woolfolk, Messrs. Kleinschmidt Bros., James M. Ryan and others are now engaged in organizing and will shortly incorporate another company for the same purpose.

On October 29, 1878, the *Independent* included a note showing interest on the part of the Northern Pacific Railroad in the Upper Missouri River navigation project.

N. P. R. R. Aid

At a recent meeting of the directors of the Northern Pacific Railroad Company, it was determined to grant $15,000 to the Montana Navigation Company in aid of the improvements above the Falls.

By January, 1879, another company was formed to utilize the upper Missouri River for transporting freight from Fort Benton to Helena. The *Helena Independent* of March 13, 1879, notes:

A company was formed in Jan. 1879, called the Missouri River Navigation Company, the object of which was to complete the navigation of the river to a point near Helena, by building boats to run above and below the falls, and a portage around this obstruction. The directors were: A. Kleinschmidt, A. M. Holter, A. Sands, J. M. Ryan, Henry Klein, John T. Murphy, T. C. Power, C. Keuck, M. Parchen; J. T. Murphy, president, A. Kleinschmidt, vice-president, E. W. Knight, treasurer. The N. P. R. R. [Northern Pacific], it was understood, would aid the enterprise. Congress was asked for appropriations, and did appropriate $25,000 for the improvement of the river below the falls, $20,000 to improve it above the falls, $15,000 to survey the Yellowstone, and $25,000 for its improvement.

At that time the Northern Pacific had not yet appeared in Helena. That would not happen until September, 1883.

Another railroad, run by Brigham Young of Utah was also interested in the route from Helena to Fort Benton. In 1881, a team of their surveyors was searching for the best route along the Missouri River. From the *Independent*:

Captain Robert J. Hilton, in charge of the Utah & Northern surveying party running the line from the mouth of Little Prickly Pear to Benton, arrived in the city last night. The Captain's party are now about twelve miles below the mouth of the Little Prickly Pear and are making good progress, their chief difficulty being to get through the brush growing on the Missouri River bottom. This line follows the Missouri River as closely as practicable.

On a more humorous note, the *Independent* for May 3, 1882, announced a problem on the Benton Road some ten miles north of Sun River.

THE SPREADING WATERS

The Lakes on the Benton Road Gradually Increasing in Size.

Gentlemen connected with the Benton Stage Line that arrived in Helena yesterday, state that the lakes, some ten miles beyond Sun River, are bubbling up and spreading over the country to an alarming extent. A few years ago the lakes were seemingly only small stagnant pools, growing smaller and smaller as the rays of the summers sun beat steadily down upon the flats. Some years ago a well was stink near the lakes, and ashen water was struck it filled the well so rapidly that the roan had barely time to escape, and on reaching its surface fled in terror from the gushing spring Ids pick had opened. Since the day that well was sunk, the lakes have gradually spread over the country, and now, it is asserted, that they are five miles wide; and ten miles long with the waters steadily creeping along and expanding on all sides. This increase in size is attributed to the well, which is supposed to pour a steady stream into the lake. If the lake keeps increasing Sun River may yet be the head of navigation—at least the head of the lake navigation, and finally solve the mixed question of the portage around the falls of the Missouri.

Helena got its first railroad in September, 1883. It did not come from Fort Benton, but rather from St. Paul, Minnesota and was called the Northern Pacific. At first the citizenry was delighted, but soon they found that the freight rates were not as low as they had expected. Of course, this was a private company, holding a monopoly position on the population of Montana, especially the businesses of Helena. Little wonder that they would prefer a more public spirited railroad over which they would have some control, especially where shipping rates were concerned.

By early 1884 the railroad issue was getting serious attention. The *Helena Independent* for March 2, 1884 reported on the important meeting of the previous evening.

HELENA AND BENTON RAILROAD

The Meeting Last Evening and Suggestions
In Regard to the Enterprise.

The meeting last evening was a move in
the right direction.

For years the people of Helena have yearned for a closer connection with the head of navigation, and at no time has the necessity been more apparent than now. Cities are not built by accident, but usually by far seeing enterprise. For some time it has been apparent that something was needed to make Helena a commercial centre and that something is

CHEAPER FREIGHTS.

The merchant at Miles City secures a lower rate of freight from the east than Helena, and the Bozeman merchant as cheap. We are on the line of the Northern Pacific and so is the population of those cities. There is no reason at present for giving us a better rate of freight than they receive.

They are nearer the eastern depots of supply than we. The railroad in supplying them has a less distance to transport, and hence can effort to give a lower freight rate than we receive.

As the case stands at present Helena must rely for her importance upon her surrounding mines, her concentrated capital and her central position. To become a commercial centre she wants something more, and that something is free and untrammeled communication with the head of navigation. This would make her independent of railroad dictation, and command lower freights. We want a railroad to Benton, but we want that road to be controlled in the interest of

OUR OWN PEOPLE.

As, however, the stock of corporations is liable to be transferred and fall into wrong hands, it is necessary in the charter, if one be granted, that the rates of freight be definitely fixed by the legislature. They should be reasonable, and it is fair to say the more reasonable the greater business the road would

do and the greater profits would result from the enterprise. Such restrictions could not be imposed until the meeting of the legislature.

But in the meantime there is no occasion for

THE ENTERPRISE TO LAG.

The road should be surveyed and located. Col. Bousenwein is sanguine that a much better road could be surveyed than any yet projected, and we have no doubt he is correct. The money should at least be raised for the experiment. It is supposed that it would run by way of Silver City, from which a branch could easily be extended to Marysville. The road to Marysville, like that to Wickes would pay from the start. The home incorporators would have a good thing as far as it went. Such a road could be graded and tied for a comparatively small amount, say $100,000, and a mortgage of the road bed would secure the track and rolling stock. It is fair to say that if a company should advance the necessary amount, the investment would pay a good interest besides slightly reducing the mortgage every year.

When the road bed reached this point, say in the autumn, it is probable that then

A SUBSIDY

might be asked of the counties of Lewis and Clark and Choteau to extend it on to Benton. Then would be the time for the legislature to fix the freight rates and let the subsidy be voted on with these rates definitely settled, as the condition upon which it should be granted and accepted.

Of course, if a home company undertakes the enterprise they need ask no restrictions. They build the road for profit and are entitled to make out of it all they legitimately can. The same is true if the Northern Pacific builds it. The people, in either case would rejoice to see it built, and bid it God speed. But if a subsidy is asked of the people, then the restrictions are proper and necessary, for in such case the enterprise is subsidized not for speculation, but purely for the good to be derived from it, the enterprise is fruitful of suggestions and is

FULL OF PROMISE.

It would tap the best coal lands in Montana. It would pass by rich mining regions. It would penetrate the finest grazing fields, and some of the most fertile valleys in the territory. More than all, it would strike the Upper Missouri somewhere near the mouth of the Prickly Pear, and the Upper Missouri is navigable for small steamers for nearly three hundred miles. All the fertile valleys along the upper river, abounding in stock and agricultural productions, would thus become tributary to this railroad. Its commerce would be borne to the point where the railroad tapped the river, and from thence transported to either Helena or Benton.

IN CONCLUSION,

we believe that the road should be built and built now. Such opportunities as this, fix the destinies of cities. We have the opportunity to occupy the most commanding position on the line between St. Paul and Portland, to become the virtual head of river navigation in Montana. With such advantages we can become a great commercial center, without them, it is not probable.

Within ten days, a full report written under the auspices of Chairman E. W. Toole was carried in the *Independent*.

HELENA AND BENTON RAILROAD

The Report of the Committee Appointed to Investigate its Feasibility

The above committee, through its chairman, Hon. E. W. Toole, made the following report to the railroad meeting last evening:

MR. PRESIDENT: Your committee appointed to investigate the feasibility of constructing a railroad from Helena City to Fort Benton, to ascertain the opportunities of securing a right of way over the most practicable route, and to draft a certificate of incorporation, suitable and proper for the organization of a company for such purpose, has had the matters submitted under advisement, and after giving them such consideration and investigation as time and facilities at our command afforded, would most respectfully report:

That the benefits and advantages to be derived from the construction of the proposed road to the head of navigation on the Missouri River, is fraught with more significance and importance to the city of Helena and surrounding country than any enterprise that can be presented for consideration. Our

prosperous and growing city, situated as it is, on the main line of the Northern Pacific Railroad, requires other facilities for transportation, which its locality so fortunately possesses. No other city within the territory is so favorably located to secure the advantages of cheap and adequate transportation and become a commercial center of so large a scope of country, comprising to so great an extent all the elements of wealth and prosperity. With her present surroundings she has through the intrepid spirit of her enterprising citizens, attained a position first of importance of any city between St. Paul and Portland without other material advantages, from a commercial standpoint over rival cities along its entire line.

The construction of this road, owned, and operated by a home company, which is now within our grasp, will not only secure to us permanency in wealth and population, but inaugurate an era of prosperity not otherwise to be obtained.

It will develop the immense and inexhaustible coal mines along its line, unequalled in extent and quality it is believed by any within our reach, and thereby furnish abundance of business for the road, cheap fuel for the city, insure the erection of works for the reduction of our ores, and the construction of factories, foundries and machine shops, to utilize the other productions from the vast and varied resources of the country. It will secure direct communications by river and rail from Helena to the mouth of the Mississippi. It will become a check upon all other roads, and cheaper transportation, by water, by securing a supply of freight in exports and imports to and from the head of navigation. It will open up a vast region of country rich in minerals and fertile in soil, contribute to our trade and increase our population. It will enhance the values of real property, impart new life to every department of business, and stimulate every enterprise and industry. It will invite capital and secure its investments. It will inspire confidence and insure success. It will dissipate all apprehensions of the removal of the capital, and eventually result in the erection of public buildings suitable for such a metropolis. It will give us advantages, in the transportation of passengers and shipment of freight, which will establish here that populous city, which it is conceded now will somewhere be built along this great transcontinental line. It will disburse the moneys invested in constructing, maintaining and operating this road, among our people at home, instead of paying it over to foreign capitalists and contractors.

For the foregoing reasons, which your committee does not believe transcends the results reasonably to be expected from the consummation of this enterprise, under the auspices of a home company, we are of opinion that its construction is entirely feasible.

As to the opportunity of securing the most practicable route between the point designated, we are of opinion that no such rights have attached to any company as will interfere therewith, and that the same is open for the selection of any that may prove the most available. Upon this question, however, we suggest that a more thorough investigation be had with respect to any prior rights that may have attached on account of certificates of incorporation filed with the Secretary of the Territory. Corporations organized under our statutes for this purpose, are required to commence operations on the line of its road within two years after filing its certificate and thereafter grade at least ten miles each year, and prosecute the same to completion within five years. Provision is also made for the forfeiture of its charter and all right and privileges secured to it, upon a failure to comply with any of the above requirements. This could easily be secured, upon an application by the District Attorney to the Court for such purpose. So far as we are advised, no such right of way has accrued in the first instance, nor has the work required been commenced and prosecuted so as to perpetuate and maintain the same, had any such theretofore attached. Besides this, no exclusive right of way is granted to any company, under the laws of Congress or the Territory, through canyons or defiles, which would be the only obstacle that could materially interfere in selecting the most favorable route. In all such cases, even where prior rights have attached, the privilege of constructing other roads and the use of the track of the road is secured upon just and equitable terms. The right and franchises usually conferred upon such corporations are amply secured by the act in locating and selecting the line of the road, with 100 feet on each side of the center of the track, grounds for the erection of station buildings, work shops, depots, machine shops, switches, side-tracks,

turntables, and water stations, as well as the condemnation of private property necessary for such purpose upon just compensation to the owner, except when the same may fall upon the public domain, when these rights are granted without cost. Your committee are therefore of opinion that no material obstacles are to be encountered in selecting the most practicable and available route.

In preparing certificates of incorporation we have thought it advisable to include within this contemplated enterprise a branch line from Silver City to Marysville, which bids fair to become at an early day one of the richest and most productive mining districts in the Rocky Mountains. This will open up direct communication with the already famous Drum Lummon Mine, whose fabulous wealth and inexhaustible resources in the production of ore is almost without a parallel, with the immense wealth and output of the Gloster, and many other mines of less renown, which will make a valuable contribution to our commerce and a source of great profit to the road.

Viewing this enterprise with great favor, we herewith present the certificates of incorporation as requested, leaving blanks for the names of the directors and title of the company, to be filled at your pleasure.

In conclusion your committee would most respectfully recommend the organization of a company, the subscription and collection of sufficient money to complete the survey and location of the road and estimate the probable cost of a narrow gauge and a standard gauge road and report the same to the officers of such company at the earliest practicable period for their further action in the premises.

All of which is most respectfully submitted,

E. W. TOOLE, Chairman

Barely a month later, on April 6, 1884, the editor of the *Independent* struck on the reason why a north-south line would be of such importance to the folks of Fort Benton and Helena.

There is one advantage to be derived from the building of the Helens and Benton Railroad that has been but partially developed. If built at an early day, it would doubtless place Helena and Benton on the great north and south line of this longitude.

The earlier roads were built on the east and west lines of migrations and the Star of Empire. The next systems run north and south and connect the tropics with the frozen regions, giving every climate all the products of all climates. The first class is roads of necessities and the last class, roads of luxuries. As a civilized people, we are compelled to have the manufactures of the east, and as a luxurious people we need the fruits and other products of the south, and the furs and ivory of the north.

Helena has within the last year been placed on the grandest and best of all the east and west transcontinental lines of the world, which places us in easy communication with all the peoples and products of our latitude. The building of the Helena and Benton Road would put us on the north and south line that will then be complete from Benton to the City of Mexico and Guaymas, the best port on the Pacific south of the Golden Gate. There is now but one small gap, that from Wickes to Butte, between Helena and the City of Mexico.

When the road is finished from Wickes to Butte we shall have almost an air line road all the way to the City of Mexico. The only divergence is from Mormon Fort on Grand River to Las Lunas on the Rio Grande, which is now filled by a detour through Colorado; but will soon be filled by a direct line, between those two points.

The building of the railroad from Winnipeg to Fort Churchill is already secured, and then to make our line complete from Mexico or the Gulf of California, or the Gulf of Mexico to Hudson's Bay, we shall only have to extend our road from Benton to the Canadian Pacific. This will place Helena on the two most important transcontinental lines of North America, the one from Puget Sound to Long Island Sound, or from the mouth of the Columbia to the mouth of the Hudson, and the other from the Gulf of California to Hudson's Bay.

Such a position secured for our young city, added to its other great advantages, cannot fail to make it the Queen City of the mountain (north and south) line; and the building of the Helena and Benton Road will beyond all doubt secure that position. But a road from Benton to some other point on the Northern Pacific would deprive us of that position and all its great advantages. It was by a prompt securing of such advantages that Chicago, and Denver

James J. Hill

and Kansas City have made themselves the great emporiums of the regions surrounding them and made all tributary. Helena had better advantages than either of them had and all they now have above what we have, they made for themselves.

The argument was now in place and all the idea needed was a competent quarterback to head up the operation. Such a man was just waiting in the wings. By the 15th of April, the *Independent* copied an article from the *River Press*.

J. J. Hill Coming

C. E. Conrad, of Fort Benton, has just received a letter from W. G. Conrad, who states that he met Mr. J. J. Hill in New York City and had a conversation with him in reference to the proposed Helena and Fort Benton Road, finding Mr. Hill favorably inclined toward the enterprise. Mr. Hill stated that he expected to start for Montana in a few days from the time of the interview, and would pay Fort Benton a visit. According to this the arrival of the railroad king of the northwest may be daily expected, after which the Helena & Fort Enterprise will begin to take definite shape— *River Press.*

On April 22, 1884, the *Independent* quoted another article form the *River Press* concerning the rail line between the two cities.

The Railroad to Benton.

The Fort Benton *River Press* expresses itself as follows relative to the proposed railroad between Helena and the head of navigation. The position taken at their last meeting by the Helena incorporators of the company organized for the purpose of building a railroad from the capital to this city, viz.: to make it a home enterprise, a railroad built by the people of Helena and Fort Benton and intervening points, and controlled by them, is the correct one, if it is possible to accomplish that result, provided the means to carry out the enterprise can be obtained. It is particularly important to citizens of Helena that this road should be entirely independent of the Northern Pacific so that the great transportation advantages offered by the Missouri River cannot be offset by high freight tariffs from the head of navigation to Helena. Such a road would give the capital city an advantage over any other town in the territory (except Fort Benton) and would insure its commercial supremacy. A narrow gauge road between Helena and Fort Benton would serve every possible purpose, and because of the greatly reduced cost of construction and of operation would be a paying institution from the day of its completion. A narrow gauge road connecting these two cities could be run at a less expense than the Helena & Benton Stage Line and would be certain to make money. If the other schemes that have been talked about are not brought to a focus very quickly the enterprising citizens of Helena, Fort Benton and intermediate points should take the work upon their own shoulders and carry it through. For every dollar they put in it they will get back, directly and in directly, ten dollars, and will not have long to wait for the returns.

Another article from the *River Press* followed in June and it too was carried by the *Independent* on June 14, 1884.

JIM HILL'S RAILROAD

What the Great Northwestern Railroad Builder says about the Helena-Benton Route.

Benton *River Press*, June 14.

The visit of Mr. J. J. Hill to northern Montana is fraught with importance to Fort Benton and the surrounding country. It insures us a railroad at least a year sooner than it would have been built otherwise, as the preliminary step, the definite location of the line, are to be under taken at once, just as soon as Mr. Hill can return to St. Paul and organize his force of engineers. He has seen Montana and is more than satisfied with it. In all respects it has surpassed his expectations. The resources of the country are greater than he had dreamed of. He is satisfied that it is a rich field for railroads, more particularly the northern portion of the territory, and he is willing to invest his money here.

He said to the reporter:

"You can say that I think very favorably of the proposed road from Helena to Fort Benton. Col. Dodge, who visited this section a few days ago, came in my interest and has made his report. I am well satisfied with the outlook. In a few weeks I will have a force of engineers in the field, and as soon as practical the route will be determined upon. But what this section of Montana wants is cheap transportation, and that is best secured by direct railroad communication, rather than that which is circuitous. By information I have gleaned from various sources I know there is a country of great resources and capabilities east of us, the region north of the Missouri in Montana and Dakota, and that is the direction whence your most important railroads will come. By that route northern Montana can ship her grain and ore and cattle at a profit, when it might not be possible to do so by any other. I am very much interested in that country and will watch with as much interest as any of your citizens the action of Congress in regard to the reduction of the immense northern reservation [Blackfeet]."

With reference to the particular route that would be selected for the Helena-Benton Road, he was not prepared to answer, stating that it would depend entirely upon the report of the engineer in charge. The several proposed routes will be examined, and that which, all things considered, is the most practicable, will be adopted. While he did not make the statement directly, all his conversation on the subject indicated that the work of construction will begin as soon as the route is approved. His purpose is clearly to build from Butte to Helena, thence to Great Falls and on to Fort Benton, this section, in fact, to be a link of his coming transcontinental line north of the Missouri. His scheme is a grand one, and there are not many men in the land more competent to carry it through.

It did not take long to accomplish the dream once J. J. Hill entered the scene. On Friday afternoon, November 18, 1887, the job was done and the Montana Central entered Helena, but not without one final delay. The *Great Falls Tribune* for November 18, 1887, reported the incident under the banner headline:

Enters Helena

Helena, November 18, 10 a.m. The track will be completed to the city in the afternoon. It is reported that the Northern Pacific will try to prevent the Manitoba from crossing their tracks here.

3 p.m. The Northern Pacific still refuses to allow the Manitoba to cross its roadbed on its way to the center of the city. The people are indignant at this shabby conduct. Colonel Broadwater has made inquiry by telegraph regarding the St. Paul through train, which will pass through Great Falls on its way to Helena. He is desirous to have Great Falls well represented at the celebration.

4 p.m. The Montana Central is crossing the Rimini track of the Northern Pacific. A crowd of people threatened to throw the Northern Pacific train off the track.

The Montana Central is at Helena. This completes another link in that system of allied lines which begins in St. Paul, whence it will extend to Butte and perhaps to the Pacific Coast. The Montana Central might claim to be the parent of the Montana extension (Minot to Great Falls) although the latter was finished first. In 1885, Colonel Broadwater, who has close connections with James J. Hill induced him in engaging this important enterprise. He pointed out to the sagacious railroad magnate the broad field which central and northern Montana presented for railroad enterprise. Mr. Hill whose lines had been gradually extended westward in the path of immigration and sometimes in advance of it, entered readily into the project which was initiated quietly. Colonel Broadwater secured the services of

THE
Montana Central Railway,

THE SCENIC ROUTE OF THE NORTHWEST.

PASSING THROUGH

The Prickly Pear and the Missouri River Canyons

AND NEAR

THE GREAT FALLS OF THE MISSOURI,

WHERE IT CONNECTS WITH

THE
MANITOBA
RAILWAY,

FORMING A

THROUGH LINE

BETWEEN

Helena and St. Paul,

AND

ALL POINTS IN THE EAST.

Apply for Information, 15 North Main Street,

HELENA,   -   MONTANA.

P. P. SHELBY, General Manager.

Ad in the **Montana Gazetteer** *for 1888–89*

Colonel Dodge, an eminent engineer who had been constructed with the construction of the Northern Pacific Railway and had a thorough knowledge of Montana topography.

Colonel Dodge went over the ground in the winter of 1885–86, and in the spring it was announced that the Montana Central Railroad would build lines from Great Falls to Helena and from Helena to Rimini, where Mr. Hill, Colonel Broadwater and their associates had acquired extensive mining property. This announcement caused great surprise in railroad circles, and gave a great shock to the Northern Pacific people, who had laid claim to the northern route and had placed on their maps a projected line from Helena to Benton, as a warning to invaders.

The route of the new railroad was largely determined by the interest, which Mr. Hill had acquired in this region through the zealous efforts of Paris Gibson, who had induced him and his associates to assist in founding here a city on a comprehensive scale, in order to develop the immense power of the falls, and other resources of this richly endowed mineral and agricultural region.

The first survey for the new railroad was begun in January 1886, by Mr. Watson, who had become associated with Colonel Dodge in other important surveys. Mr. Beckel and Mr. Bryan were also engaged in the surveys, which were promptly completed. Contracts were let for grading. The roadbed on the Rimini branch was completed by June of that year It was the intention of the company to begin track laying the following summer, but the Northern Pacific was so insanely jealous of the new enterprise that it demanded $35 per ton for hauling the steel rails from St. Paul to Helena. Mr. Hill came promptly to the aid of the young enterprise and declared that he would build westward and carry his own track rather than submit to such extortion. Accordingly he let the contract for the Montana extension, a railroad of 550 miles which, as the world knows, was completed in the interval from April to October, a feat unprecedented in the record of railroad construction.

All of this success was not without cost in human lives as the *Helena Independent* reported on August 9, 1886.

On the Montana Central Railway in Prickly Pear Canyon

INDEPENDENT REPORTERS ON THE SCENE.

LIST OF THE KILLED AND INJURED.

SUNDAY, August 8, 8 p.m.

Early this morning a most startling report reached Helena that some 30 men had been killed by a cave-in at Green's Tunnel on the Montana Central in Prickly Pear Canyon. Dr. Steele was called to attend the wants of the wounded and Dr. Brown to inquire into the circumstances connected with the deaths, immediately left for the scene, of the accident and an *INDEPENDENT* reporter soon followed.

Happily the first report was, grossly exaggerated. The dead are only three and two were injured to an extent that may prove fatal and is certainly serious.

The accident occurred shortly after 12 o'clock last night in the north end workings of Green's Tunnel. The formation in that part of the tunnel is composed of heavy strata, lying loosely and easily broken when jarred. The tunnel is partially timbered as work proceeds wherever the formation seems to demand it. Just where the accident occurred the timber, seems to have been weak and a heavy slab of rock, probably jarred down by the blasting broke the timber and fell amid an accompanying mass of fragments of rock upon the devoted workmen underneath

The killed were: Henry Klantz, J. A. Smith, and a man unknown. The wounded were: Gus Erickson and a man unknown but sometimes called Joe Bush. The two unknown men had but just gone to work and the reporter could not ascertain their names. Dr. Brown held an inquest this afternoon, the result of which is not now known.

In view of the wildly exaggerated accounts that have reached Helena. The *INDEPENDENT* has thought it well to give this early though brief account of the occurrence.

Nevertheless, the job was done and the railroad ran from Fort Benton to Helena. A traveler one year later paints a detailed portrait of what he saw en route from Helena to Great Falls. The article appeared as a Montana News Association Insert from the *Judith Basin County Press* on August 9, 1937.

TRIP TO GREAT FALLS IN 1888

OLD MONTANA CENTRAL HELD ONE OF THE MOST SCENIC ROUTES IN U. S.

"Dr. A. H. Hershey, one of the best descriptive writers in the west," says the introductory to an article that appeared in the *Helena Record* of April 15, 1888, has written for this paper a description of his trip to Great Falls over the Montana Central Railway. In the doctor's opinion the Montana Central was one of the outstanding scenic routes in the United States. His article, which deals with the scenery between Helena and Great Falls, reads in part as follows:

The sleeping valley with its winding, willow-fringed streams, its yellow fields and meadows, and its nestling cottage homes, as it lies bathed in the radiant sunlight of a perfect April day, makes a lovely and peaceful picture in its frame of azure, snow-tipped mountains, but this soon gives way to a wide expanse of broken hills through which the road follows a sinuous course to the entrance to the upper Prickly Pear Canyon.

Blending of Weird

The title of "The Scenic Route" could most justly be assumed by the Montana Central Railroad. Nowhere among the mountain lands of the earth is there so magnificent a blending of the weird, the grand and the picturesque as is presented in this panorama of changing landscape through which it has wrought its iron path, and the most vivid descriptive portrayal can shadow forth but dimly the majestic and beauty which entrance the traveler from the beginning to the end of his journey over the country in this mountain-climbing, chasm-leaping railroad line.

Its rugged entrance from the wide valley and fertile plateau of the Missouri, through the mighty gorge at the head of which stands the cloud-swept portals of the Gate of the Mountains, and the deep cleft canyon of the Prickly Pear, is the most fitting one to the territory whose purple domes and snowy peaks are among the grandest in the world; and, should the tourist extend his wayfaring no farther, he has witnessed a series of mountain views such as none other of the deep recesses of the continent can reveal. ...

... Lewis and Clark accomplished the marvelous passage on their memorable voyage to the Pacific.

Here some of the gods have labored on the talismanic chiseling of the rocks. In their fantastic fashioning the shadowy wraiths of every architectural device in which man has sought to voice his story through the ages can be dimly traced; domes, pyramids, pillars and monoliths pierce the sky, monuments of spectral ruins. Beneath the sculptured cliff and obelisk a ghostly face appears, or, in colossal dimension: suddenly stands forth the dim outlines of a mailed warrior; one is reminder of the accounts given by travelers of the storied Tyrian and Babylonia carvings of Phoenicia and the Euphrates, which are as crude as and scarcely less mysterious than these weird tracings of the elements.

Out from between the giant obelisks, which mark the extreme outposts of the mountain battlements, the Missouri becomes the tamest of streams for many miles until its forces begin again to gather for the mighty plunge of the Black Eagle and Rainbow Falls. Here may be seen all the majesty and poetry of waters.

Observer Spellbound

Not Niagara nor Yellowstone with all their immensity and power, no Minnehaha nor the Bridal Veil, with their serenity and romantic beauty, can offer more wondrous attractions than here keep the observer spellbound with the voice of the cataracts and the fairy tints of curling eddies and floating mists.

Near at hand is the Giant Spring, wonderful cauldron of bubbling waters of fabulous depth, fairly described by Lewis and Clark, and unchanged today in the ceaseless flow of its crystal stream its source as mysterious as that of the bubbling waters of the geysers of Wonderland.

The tourist who crosses the continent and looks not upon the scenery of the Montana Central has failed to see some of the richest grandeurs and beauties of the western hemisphere.

Runaway Train

A remarkable event occurred on the Montana Central Railroad in the year 1895. A single individual, through an act of extraordinary heroism, stopped eleven runaway cars and a caboose, which were hurtling down the track through Little Prickly Pear Canyon.

Having risked life and limb to preserve the rolling stock of the railroad, as well as his own life, Hugh J. Rogan asked only to be given an annual pass on the line so that he could travel at will from Helena to Great Falls. Instead he was offered one free trip to that destination. Someone convinced him that he should get more compensation, at least for his injuries suffered, so the matter went to court.

Rogan won the trial by jury and was rewarded $1,000 of the $10,000 he had asked for. The Railroad wasn't about to pay that amount without a fight, so the issue was brought before the Montana Supreme Court in 1897.

The following is Rogan's testimony in front of the Justices of the Montana Supreme Court. The tale is riveting.

I am Hugh J. Rogan, the plaintiff in this case. I am thirty-eight years old. My occupation is farming and vegetable raising, fruit gardening in Prickly Pear Valley, four or four and a half miles from Helena. I have been a resident of that locality since 1879.

When I was coming up from Craig, Montana, on the night of March 9, 1895, I was thrown violently from the seat that I was sitting on in the caboose, that I was laying on, resting or sleeping. I was right in the pilot with the conductor and the brakeman, and just about four or five miles from Silver I retired and went to sleep. I never knew anything more until I was thrown violently from that seat and lit on something on the floor. As it was real dark in there — there was no light at all — I could not tell what it was.

In fact, I got up immediately and there was something up from the seat that I struck my head against and threw me back against the other side of the car, and the car was just swaying back and forth and I couldn't keep my feet, and I fell over boxes — there was two boxes in there — and went to the side again where I had been laying on the pillow that I had procured and I yelled out what was the matter, and there was no answer whatever, and I realized then it was a runaway, that the train was running back down the canyon and I went to the door thinking it would be a good idea to jump off, and in opening the door the door flew back so rapidly that it struck me and threw me back on those boxes, and I lit with my back right on the edge of one of those boxes that was in the caboose.

I got on my feet again and made to go out on the platform, that is, the platform of the car that was going down the canyon, the Prickly Pear Canyon, and I reached along and got down on the lower step and prepared to jump, but it was passing at such a rapid speed that I [could] see death was staring me right in the face if I should ever leap, and then I made up my mind that I would go back to the car and endeavor to stop the train in some way.

I went back and closed the door and when I came in the car I see then that the stove doors were open, and the car was heaving, and the coals came out on the floor. That was the first light I had seen in there. And I opened the door towards the cars which was up the canyon, so that the wind was not striking it. I took the shovel out of the coal box and I shoveled the live coals out of the car for fear that it might take fire and that I would be burned up, and then I thought it would be a good idea to put the brake on, which I did.

I took the shovel handle and twisted the shovel handle in the break [brake] — in the break [brake] in the caboose. Then I came into the caboose and went up in what I call the pilot — I don't know whether that is the proper name — it is where the conductor and brakeman generally sit so they can see over the train. I went up in the pilot and just when I got in it the train made a curve and threw me back clear out of the pilot right down, and I struck my shoulder right against the opposite side of the car; and I went up again and it threw me again from the pilot — just threw me bodily from that pilot into the caboose.

I went up and endeavored to open the window and hold on, there is a slight window on top that a person I presume can get out of, but I could not get it open, and as the caboose was newly painted and had paint upon it, I just lunged through the window, which I presume the height of the glass is eighteen inches, and went on top of the caboose, and my breath was taken there so terrible that it took me quite a while to gain courage and strength to work on.

I placed my feet against the side and top and worked as carefully as I could to the end of the car on the top, and reached across and got hold of the brake and drew myself onto the first freight car from the caboose, and I watched back down the canyon to see where I could get a straight piece of road and where there would be a curve, and then I raised up on my feet and set the brake, for she was running at such a terrible speed that I looked every minute to be dashed to pieces.

Then I got on my hands and on my knees and as I quit [sic] crept along the foot board that passes along the top of the freight car, I had a hand on each side and a knee on each side and I walked on my hands and knees along that car to the next brake. I reached across from between the two cars right over to the other cars, and got hold of the brake and pulled myself over and set my brake. There had been a good heavy fall of snow that night, we were going up the canyon and the cars were all covered with snow. And then that was the second car I put the break on.

I continued just as the first one on my hands and knees — that was on the next car — that was the third brake — then I went on the third car on my hands and knees the same, and then she passed through a big tunnel while I was on top of the car — on top of the third freight car. And I kept on until I set six brakes just that way.

One of the brakes I remember quite well came pretty near throwing me off. I went to turn the brake and the fastening that fastens the brake to the top of the car; as I went to turn it gave way, and the brake went right out, and then I thought I was gone between the two cars, but I got set a good hand-hold and recovered myself. I set that brake as good as I could and it was in line.

When I got six brakes set I found the train beginning to slack up, and soon it could go no further, and when the train stopped I came back to the caboose and went back through the window, the pane of glass that I had broken my way out through, and went down in the caboose, and I got tremendous sick and went out to the door and went down out of the caboose, and a few steps down to the creek, and threw myself down by the creek, and threw water on my face and head.

After I did that I came back into the caboose, and there was no lights in the caboose, all was in darkness. On the outside the lamps had all gone out. I took a lantern off the caboose and lit it and for fear of another train coming up the canyon I went down the track 170 yards and built up a kind of rock pile and put this lantern on the top, so that it would be a signal to any train that would come up on that curve.

I then got back into the caboose and remained there for the train, which I think took about two hours and a half for the engine and conductor and brakeman to get back. I think the train ran twenty or twenty-five miles before I succeeded in bringing it to a stand still. Oh, my land, she ran down that canyon at a terrible rate of speed — she must have run sixty miles an hour at least.

Rogan was probably cross examined at this point. His testimony continued:

The reason the door flew back and threw me when I opened it was because of the concussion – the force threw me down. That

was in the caboose. That was the end going down the canyon, and the door flew back and struck my back with my back right on those boxes. The lights were off the caboose, there were no lights on the caboose, and all was in darkness. No one was on board those cars with me. I think there were eleven cars in all– counting the caboose and all. They were heavily loaded. I don't know where the brakeman and conductor were; they had left the train some place; I don't know when they got off or where; I was asleep.

I was sleeping when the train broke away. I didn't wake up till I was thrown off of where I was asleep. I was sleeping when the train broke away. I didn't wake up until I was thrown off on the curve. I was thrown right off the seat, on top of something that was in the caboose. I found out afterwards that it was a bucket; it was about half full of water. I struck that bucket across my chest here (pointing to chest) was thrown down, clear down the pilot twice. I was thrown right down to the floor. There were two boxes in there, cases or boxes or something I guess; they were sliding around through the car. The car was swaying back and forth. I think from the floor of the car to the floor of the pilot it must be five or six feet– probably more. A man could stand under it without his head touching; I don't know how much clear space there would be; I think about six feet is the height– maybe a little more. It would give me a fall of about six feet. When I fell I struck right against the other side of the car, a lunge; that struck me right on the shoulder. That was the first fall. The second fall I came down just about the same way struck about the same place and struck the same shoulder. When I got into the pilot it seemed that the car commenced swaying and hurled me right out. My mental sensation, I tell you, was terrible; I knew that death was staring me right in the face; at least I realized that it was one of the impossibilities for that train to go down that canyon without a wreck–without being wreaked. I consider that I was in danger of great injury. I realized that while I had worked so hard to get the train stopped that the train while I was working was libel to jump at any time.

The reason I had for believing that the train would leap the track and wreck itself was that while going up the canyon that evening I was in the pilot–as I call it the pilot– the pilot is on top of the caboose–a square place with windows in it with Lemon and Mr. Jewel, I believe, was the conductor, and I with these two parties I asked them if they had ever experienced a run away down that canyon, and they said "no," that they hoped that they never should, that it, was of no use talking, that it would be clear destruction to life and property if a runaway should ever occur down that canyon, and judging from this conversation, and thinking about it as I was going back, led me to believe that my days were numbered all right, or hours or minutes. These men I conversed with were men in charge of the train; experienced railroad men. They told me what the effect would be of such an accident. After I had stopped the train and gone down to the river I felt so sick that I could hardly see, and I thought I was going to die, I was so scared and hurt besides, but, of course my injuries I did not feel them there very much at that time. I didn't know hardly what I was doing, I was so very sick, and throwing the water upon my face and head revived me quite a good deal, and I came back to realize what was done, and the next thing was to save the property from destruction by another train coming up the canyon (interrupted). After I stopped the train I think it was about two hours and a half or three hours. before the engine with the train [from which the eleven cars had broken away] got back to me. When they got down there they hooked on to the engine and pulled the train back to the side track, this, was about the coal kilns [Gleason] and switched off one car, which two wheels had went out from under, which was the back car or rear car, as it was going down the canyon the rear car, they switched that off at the coal kiln somewhere off at the side. I could not tell you how far they switched it back from the side track; probably forty or fifty rods. I said that the train ran from twenty to twenty two miles before I stopped it. I remained in the caboose and came on up with the train. In fact I was pretty sick all the way up. I came on to Helena. I stopped the train at twelve minutes to twelve midnight. It had snowed that night and it was windy in the canyon; there was a fog resting right in the canyon I could not see but

very little. I could not see any while I was in the caboose; it was so dark in there. When I went home I went to bed. I was in bed for three or four days, and was terribly sick. The injury to my breast was the one that stood with me worse than any, and stays with me now. At that time it was black and blue– it came up about four or five inches– it was on the left side of the breast. Both of my shoulders were skinned quite a good deal; there were black spots all over my arms and shoulders where I would get struck in falling down.

There was quite a lump on my head– right on top. That was caused by, the door of the caboose throwing me on the bucket. My back was terribly sick for–yes, for two or three weeks. The small of my back had come in contact with the boxes when I fell. At night I could not sleep. I would take cramps in my limbs. I would have to get up and walk the rooms through the night; and I took porous plaster and put it on my back, and that hurt me a great deal. My other injuries I doctored them. That injury to my back stayed with me about three weeks. It was not entirely cured at the end of that time. If I would lift anything or strain myself, the injury, the hurt, would come back on me. It was painful to me. At night it was worse—that was the worst time. The injuries on my shoulders began to get well in about two or three weeks or a month. ...

Rogan won the case, again and collected his $1,000, a pittance compared to the nearly $100,000 worth of hardware he saved for the company. The Montana Central Railroad could not come up with a better idea than to have the cars switched off into the Missouri River at Craig. Yet, one heroic man made everything alright without any help and for very little compensation from the railroad.

For the next one hundred years the railroad carried the freight and passengers between Helena and Fort Benton, along the old Benton Road. It may in the future be called upon to carry sightseers, on one of the most scenic routes in North American, for generations to come.

Montana Central Locomotive at Helena

Montana Central Train in Little Prickly Pear Canyon

Montana Central Railroad Track in Little Prickly Pear Canyon

Chronology

1806–Lewis and Clark travel the Missouri River from what is now Fort Benton to the Three Forks area south of Helena.

1861–Civil War began.

1859-1862–Mullan and crew build the Military Road from Walla Walla, Washington to Fort Benton, Montana.

1862–Gold discovered in Montana.

–First emigrant use of the Mullan Road.

1864–Gold discovered in Last Chance Gulch, now Helena, Montana.

–Montana becomes a territory.

1865–Civil War ends.

1866–King and Gillette construct a toll road through Little Prickly Pear Canyon.

–C. C. Huntley granted the mail contract from Fort Benton to Helena, Montana.

–First stage coach travels from Helena to Fort Benton.

1867–C. C. Huntley sells out the Helena to Fort Benton Stage Line to Wells Fargo.

–First Toll bridge is constructed across Sun River by Largent and Healy.

–Fort Shaw established to ensure the safety of travelers on the Benton Road.

1867-1868–Problems with Blackfeet and Piegan Indians foment.

1869–Wells Fargo sells Helena to Fort Benton stage to Gilmer and Salisbury.

–Fur trader and rancher, Malcolm Clark is murdered by his Indian in-laws.

1870–Toll road built by Johns and Hilger, through Upper Little Prickly Pear Canyon, is opened.

–Diamond "R" Freight Company is purchased by Carroll, Steel, Maclay and Broadwater.

–Smallpox epidemic kills many Indians and some whites.

–Piegan Indian band wiped out on Marias River. Colonel Baker leads the attack.

1876–Spring floods destroy half the bridges in Little Prickly Pear Canyon.

1878–Nez Perce Indians attack depot and freighters at Cow Island.

–William Rowe awarded mail contract from Helena to Fort Benton.

–Alternatives to the Benton Road, such as navigation on the Missouri above Great Falls, are suggested by the citizens of Helena.

1882–Jacob Powers purchases mail contract and stage line from William Rowe.

1883–Northern Pacific Railroad tracks are completed to Helena. This is an east-west line which doesn't help when traveling from Helena to Fort Benton.

1884–Con Murphy robs Stage on Benton Road.

–Serious consideration is given to a railroad from Helena to Fort Benton.

1887–Montana Central line is completed from Great Falls to Helena.

1889–Montana gains statehood.

Art and Photo Credits

Page	Title	Photographer/Artist	Reference	Courtesy
1	The Medicine Rock	L. J. Hanchett, Jr.		
2	Approximate Route of Mullan Road North from Medicine Rock Mountain	L. J. Hanchett, Jr.		
8	Captain John Mullan			
11	Mullan Map Showing the Military Road Constructed 1859 to 1862	Unidentified	A-64	MHSRL
13	Benton Lake on the Mullan Road	L. J. Hanchett, Jr.		
13	Mullan Road Cut on Lyons Hill	L. J. Hanchett, Jr.		
14	Lyons Hill near J. P. Lyons Gravesite	L. J. Hanchett, Jr.		
14	Tough Grade North from Medicine Rock Mountain	L. J. Hanchett, Jr.		
29	Steamer 'Far West' at Cow Island, 1880	F. J. Haynes	H-317	MHSPA
30	Fort Benton 1860	George Sohon		JORCSL
30	Mackinaw Way Home to the States	W. E. Hook	Stereograph Coll.	MHSPA
31	Upper Little Prickly Pear Canyon	L. J. Hanchett, Jr.		
31	Entering the Sieben Ranch	L. J. Hanchett, Jr.		
32	The Pillars on Little Prickly Pear Canyon	L. J. Hanchett, Jr.		
32	The Old Road in Little Prickly Pear Canyon	L. J. Hanchett, Jr.		
34	Warren C. Gillette	Bundy & Traim	942-403	MHSPA
48	Nicholas Hilger	Unidentified	942-755	MHSPA
49	Sun River Toll Bridge and House	Unidentified	951-193	MHSPA
51	Missouri River Below Fort Benton	L. J. Hanchett, Jr.		
51	Missouri River from the Fort Benton Levee	L. J. Hanchett, Jr.		
52	Lime Kilns Above Last Chance Gulch	L. J. Hanchett, Jr.		
52	Miners cabin on Main Street in Helena	L. J. Hanchett, Jr.		
53	Bull Train			JORCSL

57	Matthew Carroll	Unidentified	941-519	MHSPA
57	Charles A. Broadwater	Scholten	941-375	MHSPA
60	John T. Murphy			JORCSL
64	Gus Senieur			JORCSL
68	Kirkendall Freight Train in Little Prickly Pear Canyon	W. E. Hook	Stereograph Coll.	MHSPA
69	Kirkendall Mule Train in Little Prickly Pear Canyon	Unidentified	A-Z File	MHSPA
69	Main Street in Helena–1866	Savage & Ottinger	952-949	MHSPA
70	The Wharf on Front Street, Benton, MT	W. E. Hook	Stereograph Coll.	MHSPA
70	Murphy, Neel Freight Company	Unidentified	947-075	. MHSPA
71	I. G. Baker and Company	W. E. Hook	Stereograph Coll.	MHSPA
71	T. C. Power and Brother at Fort Benton	W. E. Hook	Stereograph Coll.	MHSPA
72	I. G. Baker Train in Front of Record Building–Fort Benton	Dan Dutro	947-074	MHSPA
75	Old Malcolm Clark Cabin on Sieben Ranch	L. J. Hanchett, Jr.		
75	Malcolm Clark family Graveyard Below Medicine Rock Mountain	L. J. Hanchett, Jr.		
76	Dearborn Crossing Cemetery	L. J. Hanchett, Jr.		
76	Commanding Officers' Quarters at Fort Shaw	L. J. Hanchett, Jr.		
83	Malcolm Clark	G. W. Floyd Studio	941-761	MHSPA
86	General Alfred Sully	D. F. Barry	945-230	MHSPA
88	General John Gibbon	D. F. Barry	942-387	MHSPA
91	Lt. Colonel Eugene M. Baker and Group of Army Officers at Fort Ellis 1871	W. H. Jackson	947-248	MHSPA
91	The Infantry at Fort Shaw	C. Eugene LeMunyon	947-374	MHSPA
93	Bird Tail Butte on the Benton Road	L. J. Hanchett, Jr.		
94	Dearborn Crossing	L. J. Hanchett, Jr.		
94	Sun River Crossing	L. J. Hanchett, Jr.		
97	S. S. Huntley	Lawson	942-942	MHSPA
103	William Rowe	Unidentified	Montana- Its Story and Biog.	
105	Jacob Matthew Powers	E. H. Train	Pac 80-55	MHSPA
110	Partygoers on Stage near Helena			
111	Stage stopping at Wells Fargo Office on Bridge St. Helena	Unidentified	954-177	MHSPA
111	Sun River Stage	Unidentified	952-979	MHSPA

112	Charlie Rowe Driving the Mail Stage	Unidentified	952-950	MHSPA
112	Last Stage through Little Prickly Pear Canyon	Unidentified	952-938	MHSPA
114	Benton Road Stage Stops			
115	Entrance to Little Prickly Pear Canyon	L. J. Hanchett, Jr.		
115	Dearborn Crossing on the Benton Road	L. J. Hanchett, Jr.		
116	Bird Tail Divide on the Benton Road	L. J. Hanchett, Jr.		
116	Bird Tail Butte on the Benton Road	L. J. Hanchett, Jr.		
118	James Fergus	Unidentified	942-155	MHSPA
119	Robert Coburn	Unidentified	941-765	MHSPA
121	John Largent, Sr.	Unidentified	943-411	MHSPA
122	Ed Kelley			JORCSL
127	George Steele			JORCSL
135	Changing Horses at Sun River Leaving			JORCSL
140	Silver City Stage Station, 1918	Unidentified	951-056	MHSPA
140	Rock Creek Station			JORCSL
141	Carter and Kisselpaugh's Station at Wolf Creek	Unidentified	952-911	MHSPA
141	Carter and Kisselpaugh's Stage Stop at Wolf Creek	Unidentified		Bob Wirth
142	Wolf Creek Saloon	Unidentified		Bob Wirth
142	Wolf Creek Saloon Interior	Unidentified		Bob Wirth
143	Dearborn Crossing 1879	Ralph Wells	946-680	MHSPA
143	Milot House at Dearborn Crossing	Unidentified	946-681	MHSPA
144	Eagle Rock Station	Unidentified	952-885	MHSPA
144	Montana Hotel and Saloon-Henry Milot Sun River Crossing	Unidentified	951-203	MHSPA
145	Bull House at Sun River	C. S. Bull	951-207	MHSPA
145	Store and Eating Place at Sun River Leaving	Unidentified	952-901	MHSPA
146	Twenty-Eight Mile Spring			JORCSL
146	Steel Store at Sun River Crossing		JORCSL	
147	The Stage Driver	Charlie Russell	MHSM	
149	Lyons Hill from Little Prickly Pear Canyon	Peter Tofft		MHSM
150	May Flooding on the Little Prickly Pear	Greg Hanchett		
150	Rock Siding on Little Prickly Pear Toll Road	L. J. Hanchett, Jr.		
155	Old Mud Wagon on the Benton Road	Unidentified		JORCSL

159	The Road Through Little Prickly Pear Canyon	Ralph DeCamp	Pac 78-21.74	MHSPA
160	A Road too Close to Little Prickly Pear Creek	Ralph DeCamp	Pac 78-21.38	MHSPA
160	Bridge Construction on Little Prickly Pear Creek	Unidentified	Stereograph Coll. #23	MHSPA
161	Rutted Road Through the Canyon	Unidentified	Stereograph Coll. #32	MHSPA
163	The Beginning of Fall at Wolf Creek	L. J. Hanchett, Jr.		
163	Mountain Goats near Wolf Creek	Don Vick		
164	White Tail Deer at Wolf Creek	Kraig Bancroft		
164	Sunset on the Benton Road	Kraig Bancroft		
177	Morrow Family Traveling from Fort Benton to Helena with Personal Vehicles	S. J. Morrow	Stereograph Coll.	MHSPA
179	Tunnel on the Montana Central near Lyons Creek	L. J. Hanchett, Jr.		
180	Giant Springs at Great Falls	L. J. Hanchett, Jr.		
180	Lyons Hill from the Tracks of the Montana Central	L. J. Hanchett, Jr.		
187	James J. Hill	Riehle Studios	942-766	MHSPA
195	Montana Central Locomotive at Helena	Unidentified	GNRR Collection	MHSPA
195	Montana Central Train in Little Prickly Pear Canyon	Unidentified	GNRR Collection	MHSPA
196	Montana Central Railroad Track in Little Prickly Pear Canyon	Ralph DeCamp	Pac 95-61 Album	MHSPA

Abbreviations:

MHSPA — Montana Historical Society Photo Archives

JORCSL — Joel F. Overholser Historical Research Center-Schwinden Library and Archives

MHSM — Montana Historical Society Museum

MHSRL — Montana Historical Society Research Library

Acknowledgements

My heartfelt appreciation goes out to those who helped research and produce this book:

First, to my dedicated researchers, Clint Attebery and Karen Bjork who sacrificed many of their Saturdays to research the Benton Road for me and always presented their findings in a very professional way.

Second, to the staff of the Montana Historical Society's Research Library, Photo Archives and Museum who were tolerant of my numerous requests for scans, newspaper films and manuscripts. They never stopped searching for that missing item that would "finally" finish the book.

Next, to the staff at the Joel Overholser Research Center of Fort Benton for their assistance and encouragement.

Then to my flying neighbor, Gil Johnson, who spent a Saturday piloting me over the Benton Road so that I could photograph it from a different angle.

And, last, but far from least, to the local ranchers, Bob Wirth, Nina Baucus and Zack Wirth who took the time to show me where to look for landmarks of Montana's incredible past.

Finally, I wish to say thank you to the other people who assisted this project in many ways: Greg and Jane Hanchett, Jon Axline, Barbara Rodriguez and Kathy Springmeyer.

Bibliography

Books and Periodicals

Acts, Resolutions and Memorials of the Territory of Montana Passed by the First Legislative Assembly Convened at Bannack, December 12, 1864. Virginia City Montana: D. W. Tilton and Company, 1866.

American Biography Containing Sketches of Prominent Americans of the Present Century. New York: News Companies, 1871.

Burligame, Merrill G. *The Montana Frontier.* Bozeman, Montana: Big Sky Books, Montana State University, 1980.

Cheney, Roberta Carkeek. *Names on the Face of Montana*, Missoula, Montana: Mountain Press Publishing Company, 2003.

Dearborn Homemakers. *Dearborn Country-A History of the Dearborn, Wolf Creek and Criag Areas.* Fairfield, Montana: The Fairfield Times, 1976.

Delany, John O'Fallon. "Up the Missouri River to the Montana Mines: John O'Fallon Delany's Pocket Diary for 1862." Edited by John E. Sunder. *The Bulletin, Missouri Historical Society*, (October 1962) 3–22 and (January 1963) 127–149.

Erickson, Harvey. "Mullan's 1862 Interstate Road." *The Pacific Northwesterner* (Fall, 1974): 53–66. Spokane Corral of the Westerners/Spokane, Washington.

Ewers, John C. *The Blackfeet-Raiders on the Northwestern Plain.* Norman and London: University of Oklahoma Press, 1958.

Federal Writers' Project of the Works Projects Administration for the State of Montana, *Montana-A State Guide Book.* New York: Hastings House Publishers, 1955.

Fifer, Barbara. *Montana Battlefields 1806–1877 Native Americans and the U. S. Army at War.* Helena, Montana: The Farcountry Press 2005.

Leeson, Michael A. *History of Montana 1739–1885.* Chicago: Warner, Beers and Company, 1885.

Hamilton, James McClellan. *From Wilderness to Statehood.* Portland, Oregon: Binfords and Mort Publishers, 1957.

Huntley, Chet. *The Generous Years.* New York: Random House, 1968.

Jackson, W. Turrentine. *Wagon Roads West.* Lincoln and London: University of Nebraska Press, 1964.

——*Wells Fargo Stagecoaching in Montana Territory.* Helena, Montana: Montana Historical Society Press, 1979.

Kurtz, August V. "From Missouri to Oregon in 1860." Edited by Martin F. Schmitt, *The Pacific Northwest Quarterly*, (July, 1946): 193–230.

Lang, William L. "Corporate Point Men and the Creation of the Montana Central Railroad, 1882–87." *Great Plains Quarterly.* (Summer, 1990): 152–166. Center for Great Plains Studies, Lincoln, Nebraska.

Leahy, Ellen. "Montana Fever, Smallpox and the Montana State Board of Health." *Montana-The Magazine of Western History.* (Summer, 2003): 32–45. Montana Historical Society, Helena, Montana.

Lepley, John G. *Birthplace of Montana-A History of Fort Benton.* Missoula, Montana: Pictorial Histories Publishing Company, 1999.

——*Packets to Paradise*. Missoula, Montana: Pictorial Histories Publishing Company, 2001.

——*Blackfoot Fur trade on the Upper Missouri*. Missoula, Montana: Pictorial Histories Publishing Company, 2004.

——"Helena to Fort Benton Stagecoach" (Spring 1977) 51–54 *Montana the Magazine of the Northern Rockies*.

Miller, Joaquin, *An Illustrated History of the State of Montana*. Chicago, Illinois: The Lewis Publishing Company, 1894.

Mullan, John, *Report on the Construction of a Military Road from Fort Walla Walla to Fort Benton*. Fairfield, Washington: Ye Galleon Press, 1998.

——*Miners and Travelers Guide to Oregon, Washington, Idaho, Montana, Wyoming and Colorado via the Missouri and Columbia Rivers*. New York: The Arno Press, 1973.

Overholser, Joel. *Fort Benton World's Innermost Port*. Fort Benton, Montana: Joel Overholser Publishing, 1987.

Paladin, Vivian and Baucus, Jean. *Helena an Illustrated History*. Helena, Montana: Montana Historical Society Press, 1996.

Payette, B. C. *The Mullan Road*. Montreal, Canada: Printed privately for Payette Radio Limited, 1968.

Powers, Jacob Mathews. "Montana Episodes: Tracking Con Murphy." *Montana-The Magazine of Western History*. (Autumn, 1980) 52–56 Montana Historical Society, Helena, Montana.

Progressive Men of the State of Montana. Chicago: A. W. Bowen & Company, 1901.

Raymer, Robert George. *Montana the Land and the People*. Chicago and New York: The Lewis Publishing Company, 1930.

Richards, J. R. "Jaded Journey–1875 Stagecoach Ride." (Summer, 1954) 30–36 *Montana-The Magazine of Western History*. Montana Historical Society, Helena, Montana.

Sanders, Helen Fitzgerald. *A History of Montana*. Chicago and New York: The Lewis Publishing Company, 1913.

Schwantes, Carlos A. "The Steamboat and Stagecoach in Montana and the Northern West." (Winter, 1999) 2–15 *Montana-The Magazine of Western History*. Montana Historical Society, Helena, Montana.

Stout, Tom, Editor. *Montana Its Story and Biography*. Chicago and New York: The American Historical Society, 1921.

Stuart, Granville. *The Montana Frontier 1852–1864*. Edited by Paul C. Phillips, Lincoln and London: University of Nebraska Press, 1977.

——*Forty Years on the Frontier*. Edited by Paul C. Phillips, Lincoln and London: University of Nebraska Press, 1977.

Thompson, George A. *Throw Down the Box-Treasure Tales from Gilmer and Salisbury The Western Stagecoach King*. Salt Lake City, Utah: Dream Garden Press, 1989.

Thompson, Francis M. *A Tenderfoot in Montana-Reminiscences of the Gold Rush, the Vigilantes & the Birth of Montana Territory*. Edited by Kenneth N. Owens. Helena, Montana: Montana Historical press, 2004.

Vaughn, Robert. *Then and Now-Thirty-Six Years in the Rockies 1864–1900*. Helena, Montana: The Farcountry Press, 2001.

Walter, David. *Christmastime in Montana*. Helena, Montana: Montana Historical Society Press, 2003.

Wilson, Gary A. *Outlaw Tales of Montana*. Havre, Montana: High-Line Books, 1995.

Unpublished Documents and Manuscripts

Montana Historical Society, Research Center, Archives, Helena, Montana:

Diekhans, Anne M. *A History of Fort Shaw Montana from 1867 to 1892*. Submitted in Partial Fulfillment of "Cum Laude" Recognition to the Department of History Carroll College, 1959.

Dougherty, Mary Hilger. *In and Out of Montana*. Small Collection 602, undated.

Flanagan, May G. *Stagecoach Trip and Visit to Helena from Fort Benton, M. T.-1886.* May G. Flanagan papers, 1952. Small Collection 1236. Folder 12.

Higginbotham, Charles. *Life Lines of a Stage Driver.* Undated. Small Collection 852, Folder 1.

Hugh Kirkendall vs. The United States and the Blackfeet and Piegan Indians, 1896–1910 Small Collection 83.

Pollinger, Elijah M. *Letter to James E. Callaway, 1904.* Small Collection 655.Folder 1.

Regis De Trobriand Papers 1869–1870. Small Collection 5. Folder 2.

Rogan, Hugh J., Montana Supreme Court Case #957. Supreme Court transcript from *Hugh J. Rogan vs. Montana Central Railway Company,* June 18, 1896.

Mail Contract, 1878, and Deeds, 1878. T. C. Power Papers. Manuscript Collection 55. Box 316, Folders 13 and 14.

Vertical Files examined:

Stage Coaching, Freighting and Fort Shaw.

Lewis and Clark County Recorder's Office:

Board of Supervisors Meeting Records (Microfiche) for November 2, 1869, and February 8, 1870.

Lewis and Clark County Coroner's Office:

Coroner's Record Book Entry for William and Hattie Moore, 1886.

National Archives:

Letter from P. M. Engle to Captain John Mullan. From Fort Owen. Dated January 15, 1860. Cartographic Records, Records of the War Department, Office of the Chief of Engineers RG-77 File W76-27.

Letter from Major Blake to Colonel Cooper, Adjutant General, Washington, D. C. From Camp on the Hell Gate River. Dated August 23, 1860. Microfilm Publication M567D: 620 (1).

Newspapers

Helena Independent

Helena Daily Herald

Helena Weekly Herald

Fergus County Argus

Virginia City Tri-Weekly Post

Weekly Montana Democrat

New Northwest

Great Falls Tribune

Montana News Association (Inserts)

Montana Post

Judith Basin County Press

Judith Basin Star

Index

A

Adams 154
Adams, Cal 156–158
Adams, J. C. 82
Adams, Jack 108
Adams, Jim 58
Alden, Judge I. R. 108
Ammet, Lieutenant 121
Anderson 24
Andrews, L. 81
Angevin 41
Antoine 17
Argui, J. J. 81
Argui, O. M. 81
Atchison, Dr. 24

B

Baatz, Nick 131
Babbage, Catherine (Cullinane) 103
Babbage, John 103
Babbage, Katie Jane 103
Bailey, Sargent 19
Baird, Lieutenant 64
Baker, Charles A. 131
Baker, George A. 58, 95
Baker, Isaac G. 53, 58
Baker, Lt. Colonel/Major Eugene M. . . 84, 85, 87–89, 91,
166
Baker, W. S. 44
Baldesto, E. 81
Barker, Fred 63
Barlow, Bradley 97
Barnes, E. 81
Barris 41
Bartlett, Rev. J. F. 26
Bashaw, George 131
Bateman, Frank 56
Beach, Mr. E. 153, 154

Bears, Four 169
Beckel, Mr. 190
Bell, B. F. 81
Benson, Lieutenant 121
Berry, General 97
Biddle, Lieutenant 64
Bishop, J. W. 81
Blake, Major George A. H. 8, 10, 15, 17, 21, 78
Boblin, W. 81
Botkin, Marshal 109
Boyce, Major 55
Boyle, Lyle H. 22, 25, 26
Bradley, Edmund 63, 65
Bramen, Henry 132
Broadwater, Charles A. . 38, 40, 53, 57–60, 151, 153, 189
Brook, H. 81
Brooks, Colonel John R. 90
Brooks, Dr. 137
Brown, Catharine 124
Brown, Dr. 63, 190
Brown, John D. 90, 120, 124
Bryan, Mr. 190
Buchanan, President 35
Buck, Captain D. W. 151
Bull, Charles 121
Bull, Cornelia 121
Bullard, Massena 59
Bullard, Oscar M. 59
Bullard, Walter S. 53, 59
Bullard, William F. 59
Bullard, William L. 59
Burke, John 130
Burruss, Miss Annie F. 59
Burton, I. A. 132
Bush, David 81
Bush, Joe 190

C

Cadotte 27

Callaway, Colonel J. E. 95
Campbell, Daniel 22, 23, 25, 26, 100
Carpenter, O. H. 81
Carr 19
Carroll, Maggie 137
Carroll, Matthew 38, 53, 56, 57
Carson, Charles 77
Carson, Kit 77
Carter, J. M. 126, 130
Carter, J. R. 80
Carter, Laticia 126
Caruly, P. 81
Cary, Chas L. 81
Casey, Mr. 109, 123
Castro, L. 81
Cavanaugh, Hon. Jas. M. 86, 87
Chancelor, First Sargent 19
Chapman 29
Chase, Jos 81
Chemidlin, Mary 120
Chemidlin, Nicholas T. 120
Chestnut, Robert 58
Chief, Boy 174
Childs, E. M. 80, 117
Chowan, Mrs. O. H. 90
Chutaux, Mr. 15
Clark, Horace 67, 84, 85
Clark, Malcolm 8, 16, 17, 27, 28, 33, 34, 36, 40, 41,
. . . . 63, 67, 75, 77, 78, 83–87, 89, 99, 166, 169
Clark, Miss Ellen P. 85
Clark, P. B. 97
Clark, Senator W. A. 97
Clary, Tom 82
Clendennin, Colonel 63
Cleveland, Jack 39
Clinton, Major William 79, 80
Coburn, Robert 119
Colbert, Charles E. 130, 131
Colbert, Mrs. 131
Coleman, Mr. 101
Collins, William 79
Compton, Mac 46
Comssa, Joseph 81
Congiato, Father (Cargiatti) 17, 18
Connor, F. 80
Conrad 107, 108
Conrad, C. E. 187
Conrad, Charlie 56
Conrad, George 106, 109
Conrad, W. G. 187
Cooper 63, 64
Cooper, Dr. 17
Cooper, F. R. 81
Cooper, Mr. Charles W. 108, 109

Copeland, Mr. 40
Coppick 40
Corbin, D. C. 151, 153
Cottle, Augustus L. 128
Cottrell 126
Coulston, Edward 131
Cox, General J. D. 86
Cox, Mr. J. R. 120, 121
Crabtree, Nathaniel 81
Creighton, Mr. 10
Cris, Petit 77
Crittenden 20
Culbertson, Jack 27
Culbertson, Major Alexander 84
Culbertson, Mrs. 27
Cutter, Captain 87

D

Daraleau, Joseph 81
Davis, Mary Ann (Rowe) 101
Davis, Mr. 20
Davis, William 101
Davy, Captain 44
Dawson, Major 38
Dawson, Mr. 7, 16, 17, 19, 20, 23
De Smet, Father 22–24, 27
Dean, Anna 98
Dean, Ellen (Watson) 98
Dean, Simeon 98
DeBough, Captain Sam 95
DeLacy, Captain 18, 19
Densdon 126
DeTrobiand, General 87, 89
Detwiler, Geo 80
Devereux, J. 81
DeWitt, W. C. 109
Doane, Lieutenant 87, 88
Dodge, Colonel 189, 190
Dog, Little 26, 38, 77
Donovan, Martin 62
Dorman, Mr. James 154
Douglass 20
Douthett, J. G. 81
Downing, Mr. 137
Drew, C. H. 128
Dudley, Charles E. 108
Dunks, Mr. 156
Dunphy, E. M. 37

E

Eastman, H. H. 48

Edmondson, Henry 106–108
Ellis, C. H. 132
Ellis, Fisk G. 103, 132, 165
Ells, Joshua 132
Ells, Lois 132
Ells, Robert S. 104, 130, 132
Emerson, James 66
Emerson, Tip [William] 66
Emersons 66
Emmet, Corporal 19
Engel, P. M. 3, 8
English, H. W. 44
Erickson, Gus 190
Evert, Susana 48

F

Fall, A. 38
Farmer 63, 64
Farrond, R. 81
Fellows, B. 81
Femmisee, Chief 36
Fergus, Andrew 119
Fergus, James 85, 118, 126, 130, 153, 154
Filley, Frank 27
Filley, Mr. Giles 27
Fisher, Mr. Al. 151
Fisk, Captain James L. 37, 78, 118
Flanagan, Frank 138
Flanagan, Grace 133, 137
Flanagan, May G. 133
Flanagan, Virginia 133, 137, 138
Flinn, Patrick 81
Flinn, Thomas 81
Florence, Chas 81
Floweree, Daniel 120, 121
Fox, Billy 123
Fraisey, James 80
Freeraut, D. H. 81

G

Gallagher, Mr. 107
Galmiche, Frank 120
Galpin 27
Garido, E. A. 81
Garrett, Ed 122, 123
Garrison 53, 85
Gebeau, Moses 125
Gethard, H. 80
Gibbon, Colonel John 64
Gibbon, General John 88, 90
Gibson, Paris 39, 60, 104, 159

Gillespie, R. T. 80
Gillette, Warren C. 21, 33, 34, 41–43, 49, 127, 170
Gilmer 100
Gilpatrick, Stephen C. 106
Gipley, J. W. 81
Glass, Andrew 117
Glass, Looking 64
Godfrey, Captain 64
Goff 77
Gourley, James 38, 39
Graham, Major 25, 28
Graham, R. 80
Grant, John 25, 38
Grant, President 86, 88
Graves, C. 80
Graves, F. L. 80
Greaser, August 126
Gredel 126
Green, Chas 80
Green, Isabella 117
Green, John 117
Green, P. 81
Greenhood, Isaac 182
Griffith, Mr. 134, 136
Gulden, F. 81
Guturres, F. 81

H

Hade, S. A. 81
Hale, Captain 64
Hale, R. S. 182
Haley, Sargent 19
Hamilton 82
Hancock, General 86
Hanley, Sargent 19
Hanson, John 79
Hardin 16, 17
Harkness, James 26
Harkness, Margaret 27
Harkness, W. G. 27
Harney, General 18
Harrison, S. B. 81
Hart, A. H. 81
Hart, E. 81
Hartigan, Thomas J. 108
Harvey, S. S. 126
Haskell, A. E. 81
Haskell, Wm. 81
Haskill, Dallas 109
Hathorn, John 81
Hauley, Thomas 81
Hawkins, Miss 97

Head, Dr. 16, 17
Healy, John J. 49
Hedlebrand, L. P. 81
Heffelfinger 138
Heldt, Birdie 137
Heldt, George 120, 135
Heldt, Mousie 137
Heldt, Mrs. George 137, 138
Henry, P. 81
Hershey, Dr. A. H. 190
Herthern, L. H. 81
Herzog, Chas. L. 129
Higginbotham, Charles 124
Higgins, Dr. W. W. 59
Higley, Chet 152
Hilger, Daniel 48
Hilger, David 45, 118
Hilger, Louisa 45
Hilger, Mary Dougherty 44
Hilger, Nicholas 43, 44, 48, 49, 108, 118
Hill 125
Hill, James J. 57, 187–189
Hill, Joseph S. 100
Hilton, Captain Robert J. 183
Hoffelt, Miss Margaret 49
Hogan, Lieutenant 78
Hogan, Mr. D. J. 120
Holbrook, D. 127
Holter, A. M. 182, 183
Honeywell, Thos 81
Horgan, Corporal 19
Horr, Major 78
Hosebay, M. 81
Houck, George 125
Houken 17
Howard, Lieutenant 20
Hubbell, J. H. 79
Hunicke 77
Huntley, Charles Clarence (C. C.) 95–98
Huntley, Daniel 97
Huntley, Mr. 78
Huntley, Silas S. 96, 97

I

Ingersoll, Dr. 152
Irvin, Mr. 16, 17, 20

J

Jaccard, Eugene 27
Jacob, H. T. 81
Jacob, S. E. 81

Jake 22
Jeffrey, Alexander 62
Jeffrey, Isabella (McCardy) 62
Jena, Father 138
Jessup, General 20
Jewel, Mr. 194
Johns, Annie L. 49
Johns, David F. 49
Johns, Florence 49
Johns, Katharine 117
Johns, William (Billy) 43, 44, 49, 117, 118
Johns, William J. 49
Johnson 20
Johnson, B. F. 81
Johnson, Mr. W. W. 9
Johnston, Belle 156, 158
Johnston, Mr. 18
Jones, Captain 16, 18, 19, 29
Jones, West 102
Joseph, Chief 64, 65
Juneau 35

K

Kates, Elijah H. 108
Kautz, First Lieutenant, August V. 15
Kearney, General 97
Keating 108
Keating, M. 80
Kelly, Edward 122
Kelly, Rosa 122
Kennedy, William 99
Kennon, Dick 152
Keuck, C. 183
Key, D. M. 100
King 170
King, Elizabeth (Lunn) 41
King, James 33–35, 38, 39, 41–43, 49
King, Laura B. 43
King, Walter 41
Kinna, John 153, 182
Kinsely, Wm. 80
Kipp, Joseph 40
Kirkendall, Andrew 61
Kirkendall, Hugh 53, 61, 62, 67, 68, 85
Kirkendall, Nancy (McCreary) 61
Kirtland, Captain 63
Kisselpaugh, William 104, 126, 130, 153, 175
Klantz, Henry 190
Klein, Henry 182, 183
Kleinschmidt Bros. 183
Kleinschmidt, A. 183
Klindt, Henry 80

Knight, E. W. 183
Kohrs, Con. [Kohn] 38, 120
Kolecki, Mr. 9
Krueger, Elizabeth 129
Krueger, Augustus 129, 170

L

La Barge 39
La Barge, John 35
La Barge, Joseph 35
La Barge, Bob 26
La Barge, Madam 27
La Barge, Tom 27
Ladd, Charles D. 79
Lainleiu, M. 80
Lane 20
Larche, Emery 81
Largent, John, Sr. 49, 82, 90, 121
Law, Sargent 19
Le Baron, E. 81
Lee, Daniel H. 79
Lee, Mr. James 120, 129
Leffingwell, G. R. 81
Lehman, Charles 182
Lehman, Frederick 182
Lemon 194
Lemon, Robert 36, 37
Lenline, Martin 117
Letherage, H. 80
Levatta, Thomas 38
Lewis, Edward A. 33, 34, 40
Lider, J. L. 81
Lindwedel, Wait 117
Ling, Ah 126
Livingston, Mr. 15–17
Lowe, Mr. 128
Lynch, Mr. 25
Lynch, P. 80
Lyon, Lieutenant Hylan B. 15, 16, 18, 20, 37
Lyons, J. P. 21, 22, 25, 37

M

MaClay, Charles 59
MaClay, Ed. 125
MaClay, Edgar Gleim 53–57, 59, 60
MaClay, Edgar G., Jr. 60
MaClay, John 59
MaClay, Theodora J. 60
Maginnis, Mrs. Martin 137
Mancham, V. 81
Manderville, Mr. 22

Margue, J. 81
Mark, Mr. 20
Marley, Chas 80
Marlow, Tom 58
Martin, Dad 66
Matkins, Jim 82, 83
May, Richard F. 121, 122
Mayhew, Captain 64
McCafferty, John 130, 132
McCann, P. 80
McCleary, J. H. 80
McClure, A. K. 53
McCullaugh, Mr. 19, 20
McCullough, C. L. 57, 58
McDonald, Henry B. 129, 130
McFarland 109
McForres, T. 81
McGlees, Jas 80
McKellops, Dr. 23, 29
McKinley, President 98
McKnight, Joseph H. 120, 134
McNamara, C. J. 57
McQuail 85
Mead, A. 81
Mead, John 106
Means, John 81
MeCheny, S. D. 81
Meeker, Agent 88
Mejia, Lorenzo 80
Mendall 19
Mike, Three-Fingered 122
Miles, General 64, 65
Milot, Anna 129
Milot, Henry A. 129
Minetry, Father 44
Mitchell, Elizabeth 132
Mitchell, Hanna 132
Mitchell, Irvin 132
Mitchell, Martin 105, 106, 108, 130–132, 175
Mitchell, Peter 159
Moersch, Miss Susannah 48
Mooney, Thomas J. 79
Moore, Hattie 119
Moore, William S. 119, 126, 130
Morris, Dr. 131
Morton, Miss Elizabeth T. 61
Moss, John 81
Mountain Chief 84
Mud 25
Mullan, Captain/Lieutenant John
. . . . 3, 8, 11, 15–21, 28, 33, 42, 78, 170
Mullholld, J. 81
Mullins, Lieutenant 16, 17
Munn, George 108

Murphy, Addie M. 61, 136
Murphy, Con 106–110
Murphy, Francis D. 61, 136
Murphy, J. E. 80
Murphy, John T. 59–61, 153, 182, 183
Murphy, John T., Jr. 61
Murphy, Miss Blanche 60
Murphy, Mrs. 137
Murphy, William M. 61
Myers, Ira 60

N

Ne-tus-che-o 84
Neel, Sam 59
Nelson, Christopher (Dalager) 79
Nutter, Fred 81

O

O'Brien, Miss 38
O'Fallon Delany, John 22, 37
O'Hara, Roger 80
O'Neil, John 106–110
Orant, William 152
Orchard, Clancy. D. 126
Owen, P. 81

P

Paichen, H. M. 153
Paladino, Father 46
Parchen, M. 182, 183
Parker, Wm. A. 81
Payne, Christopher L. 36
Pepin, Simon 58
Picotte, Mr. 36
Pierce, Mr. 15
Pierreault, P. 81
Plummer, Henry 38, 39
Pole, White Lodge 169
Pollinger, E. M. 95
Ponsford, Captain J. W. 85
Pooley, J. H. 80
Pope, General 90
Pope, Nat 90
Porter, Ben 127
Potts, Governor 67, 153
Power, Aunt Mollie 133, 136, 137
Power, Charlie 136
Power, G. B. 138
Power, John W. 100
Power, Thomas C. 100, 103, 133, 136, 139, 183

Powers, Ammi 105
Powers, Francis 105
Powers, Hannibal 105
Powers, Jacob Matthew 105, 109, 133, 152
Powers, Phillip 105
Powers, Stephanie 105
Powers, Texas 105
Pyle, Marsh 25

Q

Quail, James 83

R

Raleigh, Madge 137
Raleigh, Mrs. W. B. 137
Raleigh, Sue 137
Ralston, F. 80
Raynolds, Captain 10, 16, 17
Reed, Mr. 27, 107
Reeves, General 79
Reid, G. W. 80
Remicke, Edward 133
Remicke, Ida J. 133, 134
Reynolds, Captain 15, 17
Richardson, Edmund Bradley 65
Richardson, Mr. 65
Richardson, Mrs. 65
Risely, Mr. Dave 22, 24
Roberts, Henry 101
Roberts, J. S. 80
Roberts, Mr. Thos. P. 181
Roe, John J. 53–56, 59
Roe, Lieutenant Faye 90
Roe, Mrs. 90
Rogan, Hugh J. 191, 192, 194
Romeyn, Lieutenant 64
Ross, Dad 98
Rowe, Charles 98, 103
Rowe, Harry 103
Rowe, James 101
Rowe, Julia (Williams) 101
Rowe, William 100–103, 105, 122, 123, 130, 138
Runner, Heavy 85, 174
Rush, J. R. 80
Russel, Charley 7
Russel, Wm. 81
Ryan, James M. 183

S

Salisbury 100
Sanders, Mr. B. W. 121
Sands, Abram 182, 183
Sauchy, I. 81
Schultz, Mrs. 126
Scott, Amos 79, 80
Scott, Charles R. 79, 80
Scribner, Colonel 81
Searles, Daniel 56
Senieur, Gus 63, 64
Senieur, Mrs. Gus 175
Shaw, Colonel Robert O. 79
Sheridan, General 86–88
Sherman, General 86–88
Shipley, Evan C. 66
Shipman 22, 24
Shodde, Henry A. 53
Shorty, Long 124
Sieben, Henry 119
Silverstein, H. 81
Silverstein, S. 81
Simms, Captain 95
Smart, Daniel 79
Smith, Green Clay 80, 81
Smith, J. A. 190
Smith, Lou 108
Smith, Mr. 17, 19, 22, 23
Smith, William 132
Sohon, Mr. 10
Spitzley, Steve 100
Stafford, J. L. 80
Stanger, E. M. 81
Steele, Anna 128
Steele, Dr. W. L. 130, 131, 152, 159, 190
Steele, George 38, 56, 127, 128
Steele, John R. 128
Steele, Mr. 22, 53
Steele, William 106–108
Steele 154
Steimitz, Mr. 152
Sterling, Frank P. 131
Stevens, Mr. A. J. 119
Stewart, Hank 108
Stewart, Mr. 16
Stickney 126
Strickland 152
Strob, Chas 81
Sturgeon, L. 80
Sullivan 24
Sully, General Alfred 86–89
Sutton, Mr. 23
Sweet, Dr. 65

T

Tacket, Mr. 23, 26
Taylor, J. E. 126
Taylor, Sargent 19
Taylor, Wallace 124
Thexton, George, Jr. 108, 109
Thom, J. W. 131
Thomas, Evan J. 49, 125, 128, 129
Thomas, F. H. 80
Thomas, Rachel 125
Thompson, Charles 159
Thornburg, Major 88
Thoroughman, Bob 105
Tingley, Mr. 37
Todd, Wm. H. 63
Tom, Gold 38
Toole, Bruce 106
Toole, E. W. 185, 186
Townsend, Benjamin T. 129, 158
Townsend, Lotta 129
Trask, L. E. 151
Trucho, Peter 81
Turner, Dr. 123

U

Upham 17, 19, 20

V

Vail, I. A. 37–39
Valle, Mr. 23, 24
Van Anda, Brother 56
Van Horne, Colonel J. J. 90
VanCorp, Father 46
VanGosh, T. 44
Vaughan, Colonel A. J. 6, 10, 16, 18–20
Vaughn, Major 35
Vaughn, Robert 82, 83, 120, 128, 158
Vawter, Colonel 55
Vient, G. 81
Viges, Luke 81
Vreeland 28

W

Waken, Ed. 81
Wall, Captain Nick 38, 39, 53, 54, 56, 59
Wallace 125
Wallendorf, Miss Elizabeth 49
Walter 63
Walton, M. E. 80

Wareham, John 128, 171
Warner, George 132
Watson, Mr. 190
Wegner, Charles 126, 130
Wegner, Eliza Jane 126
Weicand, Mr. 121
Weimer 63
Welch, A. C. 80
Wells, Ralph 127
Weston 127
Wheeler, Elisabeth 132
Wheeler, Marshal, William F. 85, 89
Wheeler, Thomas 132
White, Lieutenant J. L. 10, 18, 19
Wilburn, Susan 126
Wilburn, W. F. 126
Wilkens, Al H. 65, 67
Wilkins, Al 122
Williams, Captain Constant 65, 121
Williams, John 28
Williams, O. 80
Williamson, Mr. 18
Wilson, F. N. 128
Wilson, Joe 46
Wilson, W. J. 81
Witten, Milton 131
Wood, R. C. 81
Woodruff, Major J. C. 8
Woolfolk, Colonel 183
Worden, Mr. Frank 23, 25, 27
Wright, Colonel 18
Wyatt 53

Y

Young, Brigham 183
Young, Isaac 131

Z

Zimmerman, B. 80

About the Author and Researchers

The Author

Lee Hanchett thought he could retire from the professions of engineering and business, to relax and enjoy the golden years. Instead he, like many other retirees, has found more time consuming pursuits than he ever knew existed. Studying western history, along with his dealings in commercial real estate and, of course, getting to know his four grandsons consumes nearly all of his time. Still there are always moments to reflect on his wonderful wife who he was privileged to have been with for nearly fifty years of his life. Wendy, his biggest fan, passed away a few months before this book was finished. Knowing how much she enjoyed the West could only serve to spur him on to completion.

Lee has written and published six books on Territorial and Pre-territorial Arizona. These include *The Crooked Trail to Holbrook, Arizona's Graham-Tewksbury Feud, Black Mesa, Catch the Stage to Phoenix, Crossing Arizona* and *They Shot Billy Today*. Lee's next endeavor will be another book on Montana covering the road from Helena to Virginia City. Now that he has a summer home in Wolf Creek, he is determined to learn as much as he can about Montana's history.

The Researchers

Two young, dedicated employees of the Montana Historical Society gave up many Saturdays over the last two years to provide the research basis for this book. Without them there simply would have been no book. Clint Attebery, a graduate of Carroll College, took the first shift from September 2005 to August, 2006. Karen Bjork, a graduate of the University of Wollongong in Australia and the University of Wisconsin-Milwaukee where she completed a dual masters degree in History and Library and Information Studies, handled the second half from September 2006 through September 2007.